SPIRITUAL PERSONS, GIFTS, AND CHURCHES

A COMMENTARY ON
1 CORINTHIANS 12-14

by
George M. Flattery, Ed.D.

Network211
Springfield, Missouri

www.network211.com

Network211 Second Edition
Springfield, MO USA
www.network211.com

Library of Congress Cataloging-in-Publication Data

Published by Network211 in cooperation with Three Clicks Publishing with the permission of George M. Flattery.

ISBN: Network211 Paperback Second Edition: 978-0-9851788-4-0

Printed in the United States of America

03-112015 1

Three Clicks Publishing
" ..no place like home"

CONTENTS

Page

Introduction v

Chapter

1. Jesus Is Lord: 12:1-3 1
2. Spiritual Gifts, Ministries, and Workings: 12:4-6 17
3. Manifestation of the Spirit: 12:7-9 33
4. Distributing as He Wills: 12:10-11 49
5. The Body of Christ: 12: 12-27 64
6. God Has Placed Gifts: 12:28-31 82
7. The Most Excellent Way: 13:1-7 101
8. The Greatest Is Love: 13:8-13 115
9. Tongues, Interpretation, and Prophecy: 14:1-5 129
10. The Bugle Sound: 14:6-12 144
11. Praying and Singing: 14:13-19 159
12. Tongues and Prophecy as Signs: 14:20-25 173
13. Edifying Participation: 14:26-33 190
14. Women Speaking in the Church: 14:34-36 207
15. The Outcome: 14:37-40 226

Sources 233

Scripture Index 241

Greek Indexes 247

Textual Forms 247
Lexical Forms 255
Transliterated Textual Forms 262
Transliterated Lexical Forms 269

INTRODUCTION

When we look out on our world, we see millions of people who do not know Christ or who know about Him but have not believed in Him. Our task is to present Christ to them in the power of the Spirit and believe that the Spirit will draw them to Christ. Then, when people have accepted Christ, the Spirit will help us encourage them in their walk with God. Moreover, the Spirit will help all of us as believers to bond together into a united body of Christ functioning individually in diverse ways. Whatever we do, whatever our ministry is, we must exalt Christ. Along with those whom we help, we, too, are making the journey toward spiritual maturity.

Even though people are committed to Christ, sometimes problems arise. Apparently, the believers in the church at Corinth wanted to think of themselves as being spiritual, but this had both positive and negative consequences. On the positive side, the church was very open to the supernatural dimension of the Spirit's work through the believers. However, some of the believers suffered from attitudes of superiority, inferiority, and related feelings. These problems became an opportunity for Paul to teach. He dealt with their pride and envy. His teaching, however, was not just corrective; he taught many positive truths about spiritual matters. Their problems were his opportunity to benefit the church with his teaching.

No doubt Paul had all these things in mind when he wrote 1 Corinthians 12-14. He begins in 12:1 with the statement "Now concerning 'spirituals.'" The word "spirituals" is interpreted variously to mean "spiritual things," "spiritual matters," "spiritual gifts" or "spiritual persons." The term "spiritual matters" can be used to refer to all aspects of spirituality. Obviously, it includes "spiritual gifts" and "spiritual persons."

Paul often uses the term "spiritual" when talking about spiritual maturity. This is not overlooked in 1 Corinthians 12-14. Indeed, he devotes the entire thirteenth chapter to the subject of love. He applies his teaching about love to motivation for the use of spiritual gifts, but his teaching has a broader application also. Broadly speaking, his admonition about love applies to all of Christian life. While including his teaching on love, in these chapters Paul puts a special focus on the spiritual ministries of the believers and how they affect the church.

Major Spiritual Concerns

Therefore, several themes stand out as we read 1 Corinthians 12-14. His major spiritual concerns are that the believers will be truly spiritual people, that they will properly exercise spiritual gifts, and that the local churches will be spiritual. All of this should exalt Jesus Christ as Lord and be motivated by love for God and each other. Paul's comments on these themes are woven together throughout these chapters. When spiritual people exercise spiritual gifts in spiritual churches, their ministry tasks will be properly accomplished. The entire body of Christ will be blessed.

Spiritual People

In 1 Corinthians 12-14, Paul emphasizes that we must be truly spiritual in our devotion and service. Truly spiritual people, according to Paul, will obey the Lord's commandments and do things God's way. Therefore, Paul sets forth God's way of enabling us to work with Him to meet spiritual needs. Building on this premise, Paul deals with ministries and church services that are inspired by the Spirit. In the middle of his discussion, he tells us that love is the proper motive for service and worship.

Spiritual people act out of love for God and others. With the help of the Spirit, they can be persuasive in witnessing, effective in service, intense in love for Christ and others, and lifted up by the worship services. Everything they do will be for the growth and edification of the body of Christ. The body of Christ is made up of individuals who are united with Him and who do His will in His way.

Spiritual Gifts

Paul's teaching about spiritual matters includes spiritual gifts. His comments on spiritual gifts appear throughout 1 Corinthians 12-14. Clearly, he is concerned about the proper use of spiritual gifts and the underlying attitudes of the believers. Although other topics are treated, this is the dominant subject of these chapters.

Our Triune God enables us to work with Him. Using a threefold description, Paul says that He enables us through spiritual gifts, ministries, and workings (12:4-6). These are three ways of describing the same thing. Also, Paul calls this enablement, the manifestation of the Spirit. All of these terms can be used, but the term "spiritual gifts" is undoubtedly the most common. Under God's supervision, we do His work when we exercise the spiritual gifts.

There are many gifts, not just the nine listed in 1 Corinthians 12:8-10. Paul gives us several lists of gifts. As you read these lists, it becomes apparent that Paul makes no attempt to comprehensively include all gifts. As a matter of fact, he could not have foreseen all of the ways to minister that people now have in the church. Modern technology and life have opened the way for many more ministries to develop. The Spirit empowers us to work with God in many different ways.

As members of the body of Christ, we should eagerly desire the spiritual gifts because they enable us to serve. Our love for Christ and for others should motivate us to be involved in His work. Through our service, we can win people to Christ and build up the body of Christ. Moreover, as believers, we can serve with the confidence that the Holy Spirit will empower us. When we trust in Christ, the Spirit will enable us to reach His objectives.

Spiritual Gift Issues

At this point, we will consider several issues concerning spiritual gifts. Some of these issues are addressed by Paul, but others are not. With regard to issues Paul does not address, we can at times deduce the answer from the implications of the context. In any case, we must rely on the Spirit to lead us. He will lead us to work within the guidelines set down by Paul.

My comments represent conclusions reached through a study of the text. These conclusions could be stated at the end of this volume, but I will state them now, in concise form, in order to highlight some of the issues that will arise in my exposition of the text. Several additional issues will be considered in connection with Paul's threefold description of spiritual gifts in my second chapter. The issues identified here are:

First, when we talk about spiritual gifts, a major issue has to do with whether they are totally supernatural or build on natural talent. Some gifts obviously are more supernatural than others. Without the divine element, it is not a gift of the Spirit, but the Spirit uses our natural talents and efforts. It is important to know this because it will lead to our greater involvement in the work of God.

There are two extremes. One extreme is to minimize the supernatural aspect. Sometimes, this results in saying that some gifts, which appear to be totally supernatural, have ceased. The other extreme is to say that some of the gifts are totally supernatural without any element of natural talent. However, there are both divine and human aspects to the operation of all the gifts of the Spirit. Just how divine and how natural depends on the gift as well as how any given gift is exercised.

With regard to church services, when the Spirit manifests His presence, the worshipping congregation is abundantly blessed. Sometimes His presence is seen in the vocal gifts, gifts of healing, inspired teaching, or some other way. In any case, believing that God is present turns an ordinary event into a special moment of blessedness. At the same time, we need not deny the role of natural talents in the church services. Natural talent, too, is from God.

Second, the issue of motivation and purpose arises. Paul deals with this issue in very strong terms. Love should be the driving force in the operation of the gifts. Without love, the gifts profit us nothing. If we act through love, all pride and superiority will go away. Even a sense of inferiority which focuses on ourselves will go away. As Paul states in 13:13, "But now abide faith, hope, love, these three; but the greatest of these is love."

Third, Paul was not writing a systematic theology of the gifts of the Spirit with precise definitions and tightly organized themes. He used random lists with words often capable of multiple meanings to describe the church in action. The temptation is to overly organize Paul's presentation into categories. In contrast to this, Paul can mix seemingly ordinary gifts in with gifts that he recognizes as being very important. For example, in 12:28, he lists the gift of helps in the same verse with apostles, prophets, and teachers.

Fourth, the language that Paul uses predominantly makes the ministers the recipients of the gifts. However, there is a sense in which a gift exercised by a minister is also a gift to the individual who is blessed by the ministry. When a minister exercises a gift of healing, for example, the person who is healed is blessed by the gift. One could say that the gift is given to them as well as to the one who ministers.

Fifth, Paul's lists of gifts include persons, ministries, and actions. He includes apostles, prophets, and teachers. Whether or not he includes offices is much debated. Clearly, the Spirit enables ministries such as teaching, singing, praying, and prophesying. These gifts are expressed as events take place. Paul's use of terms with regard to spiritual gifts is wonderfully flexible.

Sixth, Paul is very concerned about both individuals and the body of Christ. The gifts, therefore, have both individual and corporate aspects. The individual acts, other individuals are helped, and the corporate body is blessed. All are involved. When in church, the individual ministers, and the people are blessed. Sometimes, through an activity such as unison praying, all the people participate at the same time. As long as this is done in an orderly way, it can be a great blessing to the entire congregation.

Seventh, the gifts are diverse, but the body of Christ should be united in using them. Paul clearly states this in 12:12-27 as he deals with the body of Christ. There should be no feeling of inferiority or superiority. Although some gifts attract more attention than others, all the gifts are needed. There is no room for pride, arrogance, and boasting in the exercise of the gifts. The Spirit manifests His presence in accordance with His will.

Eighth, many of the gifts can be exercised either outside the walls of the church or in the church services. Because of problems in the church at Corinth, Paul is especially concerned about how the gifts are exercised in the church services. This does not mean that they are only to be used in that context. For example, one might exercise a gift of healing while praying in a hospital room. Similarly, a prophetic word of exhortation, edification, and consolation could be uttered anywhere.

Spiritual Churches

Spiritual churches are simply churches that are filled with spiritual people. They are indwelt and empowered by the Spirit and are living and ministering in spiritual ways. Their spiritual lives include the exercise of spiritual gifts in ways that benefit the entire body of Christ. Therefore, Paul encourages all believers to be motivated by love and to be spiritual in all that they do.

With regard to the local church, pastors want their church members to be actively involved in the ministries of the church. The spiritual gifts are ways to become involved. As stated above, many of the gifts can be exercised either in the church services or outside the walls of the church. The church services, indeed, are very important. As shepherds of their congregations, pastors have the responsibility of leading the services. Pastors desire that their services be alive with the presence of the Spirit. In addition, they want their services to be conducted in an orderly way. These objectives raise the issues of how much and in what ways the believers should participate in the services.

Churches, to one degree or another, are open to supernatural dimensions of ministry. For example, they proclaim that the Spirit works supernaturally in salvation. However, some churches are much more open than others to some of the supernatural aspects of our ministries. Some churches are very concerned about the vocal gifts. Much discussion, for example, may focus on whether or not to exercise the vocal gifts of the Spirit in the public services.

The Corinthian Situation

The apostle Paul is addressing the people in Corinth. To understand his teaching, we will benefit by knowing the context. His comments apply to a very realistic and live situation. The problems he discusses develop out of actual life situations. The principles Paul lays down apply specifically to Corinth. However, they are not limited to Corinth. Other churches have similar problems. So, what he says applies to people and churches everywhere. As we discuss the situation at Corinth, we will include the city of Corinth, the local church at Corinth, and Paul's dialogue with Corinth.

The City of Corinth

Many commentaries discuss the history of the city of Corinth at some length. For my purpose, the main point is to recognize the Greek, Roman, and Jewish influences on the culture of the city. Scholars debate whether the dominant influence was Greek (Fee, 1987, 2) or Roman (Garland 2003, 3). Most agree that the Jewish input was less influential, but some emphasize it more than others. Taylor states:

> The history of ancient Corinth is the story of two cities, the old Greek city and the new Roman Corinth of Paul's time. The old Corinth dates back to pre-historic times that, by the eighth century BC, grew to be one of the wealthiest and most prominent cities in Greece and a rival to Athens located approximately fifty miles to the east. . . . The Roman Corinth of the New Testament era was a large cosmopolitan city boasting a population surpassed only by Rome and Alexandria. Julius Caesar colonized the city with freed slaves, soldiers, and urban laborers. Over time many different ethnic groups migrated to Corinth, including Jews, resulting in a society of cultural and religious pluralism (2014, 18-19).

Obviously, Corinth was cosmopolitan, and there was a mixture of cultures. Today, in large cities with people from many cultural backgrounds and nations, the people tend to depart from some of their cultural roots. The people become a cultural, religious, and social melting-pot with some cultural islands remaining. This, very likely, was the case in Corinth as well.

The Church in Corinth

As recorded in Acts 18:1-17, the church at Corinth was founded by the apostle Paul. He began by speaking in the synagogue every Sabbath where he tried to persuade the Jews and the Greeks. Luke says he tried to persuade the Jews that Jesus was the Christ. When he met opposition, he turned to the Gentiles, left the synagogue, and went to the house of a God-fearer named Titus Justus. The context suggests that the meetings of the church were in his house. Although some Jews attended, the membership became predominantly Gentile, including people of Greek, Roman, and other backgrounds.

The cultural, religious, and social background of the population in Corinth clearly had a strong impact on the way the people thought and lived. This was true of the population at large, but it also was true of the believers in the church.

As Garland avers, "Few Christians could have been unaffected by the dominant culture surrounding them, even if they assimilated its values only subliminally" (2003, 5). This background gave rise to many of the problems that Paul had to deal with in his letter.

Commentators on 1 Corinthians generally recognize that there were divisions in the church. However, they have different stances with regard to the divisions. Fee points out that many scholars hold that the church was split into parties with Paul siding with one group over another or sometimes admonishing both groups. Fee acknowledges the divisions, but he holds that the main conflict was between the church and its founder. Therefore, Paul's letter in its entirety was addressed to the whole church, not to one side then another (1987, 5-6). The difference between these views seems to be more a matter of emphasis than mutually exclusive positions.

Although Paul addresses his comments to the church in Corinth, his teaching is not limited to that one church. The word "church" can refer to the gathering of the members in a meeting, the local church, or the universal church. The truths that he taught are for all the contemporary churches and the churches of all ages. Given the flexibility of the term, one has to determine the specific meaning based on the context.

Paul's Dialogue with Corinth

First Corinthians was a part of an ongoing dialogue between Paul and the church at Corinth. This was not a dialogue between equals trying to reconcile their different views. Rather, Paul was rendering judgments and teaching the believers with apostolic authority. The dialogue involved both letters and oral reports.

After staying in Corinth for one year and six months (Acts 18:11), Paul made his way to Ephesus. His stay in Ephesus lasted between two and three years (Acts 19:8-22 and 20:31). Based on 1 Corinthians 16:8, it appears that Paul wrote to the Corinthians just before Pentecost, near the end of his stay in Ephesus. Many scholars believe the letter was written in either AD 54 or 55.

According to 1 Corinthians 5:9, Paul had written a letter to them before. This letter has become known as the "previous letter." In this letter, Paul exhorted them not to associate with immoral people. They thought he meant people of the world, so Paul explained that he meant immoral believers. This letter was not preserved for the church. However, we do know from 7:1 that the Corinthians wrote to Paul, apparently in response to his previous letter. Some of the issues raised in the 7:1 letter were probably discussed by Paul in his previous letter. No doubt the Corinthians raised new issues as well.

In 7:1, Paul writes, "Now concerning (*peri de*, περὶ δὲ) the things about which you wrote." With this statement he began his discussion of marriage. Although Paul does not again say "about which you wrote," he uses the phrase *peri de* in 7:25, 8:1 (*peri* in 8:4); 12:1; 16:1; and 16:12 to introduce his teachings on issues raised by the Corinthians. Respectively, he discusses the status of virgins, things sacrificed to idols, spiritual persons or gifts, the collection for the saints, and his encouraging words to Apollos.

Paul received information about Corinth not only from their letter, but also from oral reports. In 1:11, Paul said, "For I have been informed concerning you, my brethren, by Chloe's *people*, that there are quarrels among you." Then, in 11:18, he says, "I hear that there are divisions among you." Also, in 5:1, Paul mentions the reports about immorality among them. In 15:12, Paul asks how some of them say that there is no resurrection of the dead. Obviously, he had heard about this from others. With his teaching, Paul sought to unify and instruct the church.

Writing from Ephesus, Paul says, "I am rejoicing over the coming of Stephanus, Fortunatus, and Achaicus because they have supplied what was lacking on your part" (16:7). It may be that they delivered the letter mentioned in 7:1, but that is not certain. Obviously, they were able to speak personally with Paul as well. Paul was pleased that they came.

About This Book

Several background points about this book may be helpful to the reader. These points include comments about sources consulted, features of the book, related books, and acknowledgements.

Sources

My research for this volume included major commentaries as well as individual volumes and articles. The authors come from many different backgrounds, including evangelical, Pentecostal, and other branches of the church. In addition, over the years, I have talked with many scholars and ministers about these matters. Through interaction with these sources and people, most of the major issues have been examined and considered.

There is a surprising level of agreement on what happened in the church at Corinth. The disagreements that exist do not readily divide between those held by Pentecostal and non-Pentecostal or charismatic and non-charismatic thinkers. There is more disagreement over what should be happening now. The church at Corinth was alive with the manifestation of the Spirit and needed some boundaries. All too often, today, the manifestation is absent. What is needed is a strong encouragement to allow the Spirit to move among us.

Features

Each chapter in this book deals with a paragraph in 1 Corinthians 12-14. I have followed the paragraph divisions in the NIV. Some verses are transitional and could go with what precedes or what follows, but the NIV paragraph divisions are helpful in presenting the discussions.

In my comments, all Scripture references that do not name a book of the Bible refer to 1 Corinthians. For example, 12:1 refers to 1 Corinthians 12:1. All quotations of Scripture, unless otherwise noted, are from the New American Standard Bible[95] (NASB[95], 1995 Updated Edition), known also as the NAU. With regard to sources, the author cited, the publication date, and the page number or numbers are named in the text. The full data about each of the sources is given in the list of Sources.

Concerning the Greek words in this text, the first time they are used in a given section, they are cited with both the Greek letters and in the transliterated form. Otherwise, only the transliterated form is used. All the Greek words are defined in English, so it is not necessary for the reader to know the Greek words.

With regard to Greek words, we have included these four special indexes: (1) the Greek Index by Textual Form, (2) the Greek Index by Lexical Form, (3) the Transliterated Greek Index by Textual Form, and (4) the Transliterated Greek Index by Lexical Form. The Textual Form is the form used in this commentary both in the Scriptures cited and in my comments. Each entry in all the indexes includes the word in Greek letters and in transliterated form. In all cases, the page numbers are given where the words are used. Each of the indexes is appropriately alphabetized.

When giving the English translation of Greek words, I have used standard lexicons and other sources. One of these sources is *A Greek-English Lexicon of the New Testament and Other Early Christian Literature*. Originally, it was written by Walter Bauer. The first edition was translated by Arndt and Gingrich. When revisions were made, Danker assisted. Each time that I have cited this lexicon, I have given Bauer as the author. Many authors refer to the volume as BDAG.

Related Books

This book is a companion to the four-volume set entitled *A Biblical Theology of the Holy Spirit*. Respectively, the content covered by the four volumes is as follows: (1) Old Testament, (2) Luke-Acts, (3) John-Paul, and (4) Contemporary Issues in Pneumatology. It was my privilege to write volumes one through three. Each chapter of the fourth volume was written by a different author. In addition, I wrote another book which is a systematic summary of the content of the first three volumes in the above set. This book is entitled, *The Holy Spirit in Your Life: A Systematic Approach to a Vibrant Relationship*.

Acknowledgements

My sincerely felt thanks goes to Dr. James E. Richardson who was the General Editor of the four-volume set above and who edited the additional book that I wrote on *The Holy Spirit in Your*

Life. In addition, he kindly consented to edit this volume. His input is especially significant because of his expertise in biblical languages. He taught Greek at the Assemblies of God Theological Seminary for several years. In addition, he has written study guides for three graduate-level courses on the Greek and Hebrew languages for Global University. Dr. Richardson helpfully developed the Greek indexes which are a special feature of this book.

Our grandsons, Ethan and Luke Flattery, have helped me with the publishing of my writings about the Holy Spirit. I very much appreciate the assistance of Ethan who carefully did technical editing on this book. Also, I am grateful for Luke's help in publishing some of my works on the Internet.

Many thanks to our two sons for their interest in my studies about the Holy Spirit. George is the senior pastor of a thriving church who has a great heart for world missions. Mark is a missionary who directs a global Internet ministry of evangelism and discipleship. I have interacted with them about this subject many times.

Above all, I thank Esther, my beloved wife. We have worked together throughout our life-long missionary ministries. As many people say, she has been a blessing to untold numbers of people throughout the world. She supported me fully as I wrote this volume as well as those mentioned above. Her support has meant much to me.

George M. Flattery, Ed.D.

CHAPTER ONE

JESUS IS LORD

Introduction

People who follow Christ sometimes ask: "Who is truly spiritual?" In times of renewal, the question can become even more urgent. Our minds are focused on spiritual matters; we want to know what traits characterize a spiritual person. Broadly speaking, we are interested in all aspects of spirituality. Among those aspects is the subject of spiritual gifts. We desire to know what the gifts are and how they should be exercised.

The Corinthians had a special interest in spiritual gifts. In 1 Corinthians 12-14, Paul deals with this subject. In 12:1-3, he lays the groundwork for his discussion of spiritual gifts. He names his topic, contrasts the life of former unbelievers with the Christian life, and exalts Jesus Christ. One cannot truly claim to be a follower of Christ except by the Holy Spirit. Moreover, any activity claiming to be spiritual that diminishes Christ is not a true manifestation of the Spirit of God. Paul writes:

> [1]Now concerning spiritual *gifts*, brethren, I do not want you to be unaware. [2]You know that when you were pagans, *you were* led astray to the mute idols, however you were led. [3]Therefore I make known to you that no one speaking by the Spirit of God says, "Jesus is accursed"; and no one can say, "Jesus is Lord," except by the Holy Spirit. (NASB[95])

Christ is central to all of our doctrine and experience of the Spirit. Faith in Christ is the dividing line between being an unbeliever and a Christian. The work and presence of the Spirit make our salvation possible. When we come to faith, the Spirit enables us to exercise spiritual gifts. To be truly spiritual, the gifts must exalt Jesus. When supposed spiritual activity does not exalt Christ, it does not derive from the Holy Spirit. Lifting up Christ is the ultimate criterion of the validity of spiritual gifts.

Concerning Spiritual Matters (12:1)

In verse 1, Paul names his topic, addresses the believers in Corinth, and expresses a major concern. He writes: "Now concerning (*peri de,* περὶ δὲ) spiritual gifts (*pneumatikōn,* πνευματικῶν), brethren (*adelphoi,* ἀδελφοί), I do not want you to be unaware (*agnoein,* ἀγνοεῖν)." His topic is spiritual matters (persons, gifts, and things); his audience is the "brothers;" and his concern is that they not be ignorant about spiritual matters. He goes on to deal especially with spiritual gifts.

"Now Concerning"

Paul has heard from the Corinthians by letter and through oral reports. In 1 Corinthians, he replies to their concerns and deals with other topics of his choice. He introduces several topics with the Greek phrase *peri de* (περὶ δὲ) which means "now concerning." He responds in 7:1 to an issue raised in the letter by saying, "Now concerning the things about which you wrote." Paul does not explicitly mention this letter from the Corinthians again, but he does use the phrase *peri de* in our text (12:1) and in 7:25, 8:1; 16:1; and 16:12. Many believe that these passages refer to issues raised in the letter, but it may be that he was responding to oral reports as well. He mentions such reports in 1:11-12; 5:1; 6:1; 11:18; and probably 15:12. It is likely that some of the content of the letter and the oral reports dealt with the same topics.[1]

"Spiritual Matters"

Paul announces his topic with the adjective *pneumatikōn* (πνευματικῶν) which means "spiritual." There are two lines of thought with regard to this word. One view is that it was a favorite word of the Corinthians and that Paul used it to refer to their erroneous ideas. The opposite view is that this is Paul's word that he uses to teach about spiritual matters. In my view, Paul had in mind both the views of the Corinthians and his own teaching. We know

---

[1]Fee states: "When a problem is *reported* to him, Paul feels compelled to tell what he knows (cf. 1:11-12; 5:1; 6:1; 11:17-22); thus, we, too, have a better idea of what was going on. When responding to their letter, unless he quotes from it (7:1; 8:1, 4), he picks up right on that point, so we are not always informed as to the precise nature of the problem" (1987, 570).

that Paul corrects the Corinthian views while expressing his teaching in a very positive way. So Paul does not invalidate the term, but rather he uses it to teach the Corinthians.

What does Paul mean by the adjective "spiritual"? An answer to this question is twofold: we must consider (1) what noun should be supplied to go with the adjective and (2) what spiritual things or matters Paul includes in his teaching.

First, we might expect to see a plural noun that would be modified by the plural adjective *pneumatikōn*, but the Greek text does not include one. Thus, in Greek, the adjective functions as a noun. However, when the text is translated, a noun normally is supplied. Because this form of the Greek adjective can be either neuter or masculine, the supplied noun could be either "gifts" or "persons."

The commentators who favor "spiritual gifts" cite Paul's use of the neuter noun *charismata* (χαρίσματα, "gifts") in 12:31 and the neuter adjective *pneumatika* (πνευματικά) in 14:1. Those who support "spiritual persons" cite 14:37 where Paul uses the masculine form of the adjective *pneumatikos* (πνευματικός). In this case, Paul refers to a spiritual person. After discussing this debate, Barrett concludes, "It seems impossible to find objective ground for a decision between the two possibilities, and little difference in sense is involved—spiritual persons are those who have spiritual gifts" (1971, 278).

Another possible option, which includes spiritual gifts and spiritual persons, is to translate *pneumatikōn* as "things of the Spirit." Fee avoids deciding between spiritual gifts and spiritual persons by using the translation "things of the Spirit." This phrase, he writes, "would refer primarily to manifestations/gifts from the perspective of the *Spirit's* endowment; at the same time, the expression also points toward those who are so endowed" (1994, 153). Thus, in his view, "things of the Spirit" includes both "spiritual gifts" and "spiritual persons." Another way of saying "things of the Spirit" is to refer to "spiritual matters."

Second, what spiritual matters (*pneumatikōn*) does Paul have in mind? Paul uses this word twenty-three times in his epistles, with three of those times being in 1 Corinthians 12-14. Very often it has to do with matters related to spiritual maturity (e.g. Gal. 6:1). In chapters 12-14, the main emphasis is on the work of the Spirit in ministry; but even so, Paul encourages maturity in ministry. For example, chapter 13 deals with love. Thus, the fruit of the Spirit are never far from Paul's mind.

With regard to the Spirit in ministry, Paul's concerns are fully identified in chapters 12-14. For example, as 12:3 indicates, he sets forth the centrality of Christ. It is within the realm of faith in Christ that all true spiritual gifts operate. All three chapters deal with the distribution and exercise of spiritual gifts. They deal with both the people who claim to be spiritual and the gifts that the Spirit distributes among them. Given all this, we need not limit the meaning of the term. We can include all of the items discussed in the discourse.

"Brothers"

Paul addresses his comments to the *adelphoi* (ἀδελφοί) or the "brethren." He uses this term in 14:6, 20, 26, and 39. Usually, expositors take this term in all these cases as including both men and women. We know that women attended the church in Corinth. In 11:5, Paul writes about women who are praying and prophesying. Also, Paul says in 14:26, "When you assemble, each one has a psalm, has a teaching, has a revelation, has a tongue, has an interpretation." It is apparent to me that this includes women as well as men. It is interesting that, in all four of the cases mentioned above, the NIV translates *adelphoi* as "brothers and sisters." This point will be important as we discuss 14:34-35 in chapter fourteen of this book.

"I Do Not Want You to Be Unaware"

Paul says, "I do not want you to be unaware (*agnoein*, ἀγνοεῖν)." Here, in 12:1, Paul uses the present infinitive of the verb *agnoeō* (ἀγνοέω). As used in this verse, this verb is usually translated as "ignorant," "unaware," or "uninformed." The NASB[95] chooses "unaware," while the NIV says "uninformed." Lenski says that this clause "is equivalent to: 'I want you to know'" (1946, 490). With this statement, Paul introduces what he wants to talk about. This raises the question as to what it is that Paul wants them to be informed about. The answer has to be that he wants them to be informed about "spiritual matters."

In Paul's concluding remarks (14:37), he narrows the discussion to those who think they are spiritual. He warns them against disregarding his teaching. In 14:38, Paul uses the present indicative form (*agnoei,* ἀγνοεῖ) of the same Greek verb that he used in 12:1. In 14:38, the verb is interpreted to mean more than simply being uninformed; it has the connotation of not recognizing the commandment of the Lord as delivered by Paul.

The church at Corinth had problems with people posing as spiritual people. In addition, some of the believers exercised the gifts in the wrong way or with poor motivation. The apostle Paul wrote to correct these problems. Beyond this, he wanted to encourage the true exercise of spiritual gifts. To do so, he would have to enlighten them about spiritual matters, including persons and gifts. Obviously, a part of their problem was their lack of understanding about the gifts.

Many churches today do not have a problem with the undisciplined exercise of spiritual gifts, such as those listed in 1 Corinthians 12:8-10, because they are not in use. Paul was encouraging the proper exercise of such gifts, not prohibiting them. If the apostle Paul were to visit these churches, his mission probably would be entirely different. His instructions might be more similar to what he said to Timothy: "For this reason I remind you to kindle afresh the gift of God which is in you through the laying on of my hands" (2 Tim. 1:6 NASB[95]).

The Former Life of the Believers (12:2)

In verse 2, Paul writes, "You know that when you were pagans (*ethnē,* ἔθνη), *you were* led astray to the mute idols, however you were led" (NASB[95]). The NIV provides this translation, "You know that when you were pagans, somehow or other you were influenced and led astray to mute idols."

The apostle Paul was speaking to the people in the church at Corinth. He reminded them of their past life as pagans. When they had been pagans, they were led astray to mute idols. Paul was drawing a contrast between their former life and their life now. They had been deceived and led away to idols that could not speak. Whatever message they were accepting, it did not come from the idols. There were many influences in the environment to point them to idols.

"You Know That"

Paul does not begin verse 2 by teaching the believers what they need to know. Instead, he reminds them of their spiritual condition before they came to Christ. He simply says, "You know that." The Corinthians already knew what their past condition was. Thus, verse 2 does not present truths that will help the believers to become informed. It simply establishes the need for that kind of instruction.

Many expositors posit that the pagans were using inspired speech, even ecstatic speech, and this in some way might influence the church. We will deal with this below, but all that the verse actually says is that they had been pagans who were led away to dumb idols. They know this already.

"When You Were Pagans"

Paul addressed the people who attended the Corinthian church. The Greek word *ethnē* (ἔθνη) can refer to nations, peoples, pagans, or Gentiles. The KJV says "Gentiles," but this leads to the problem that Gentiles who accept Christ are still Gentiles.[2] The RSV, NASB[95], and NIV all use the word "pagans" as a translation. Kistemaker writes:

> The term Gentiles relates to the preconversion days of those church members who had left paganism. Paul refers to their former days as he now addresses them as Gentile Christians. He had directed his earlier discourses to both Jewish and Gentile believers, but here he speaks to those Christians who formerly were pagans and worshiped idols. (1993, 413)

Although Paul, in verse 2, addresses the believers who had been pagans, there were both Jews and Gentiles in the congregation. For example, as Luke records, "Crispus, the leader of the synagogue, believed in the Lord with all his household" (Acts 18:8). Apparently, most of the members were former pagans. According to Fee, "This sentence offers the clearest evidence in the

---

[2]With a different view, Barrett writes: "Paul's readers are *Gentiles* no longer; but neither are they Jews. He does not describe them as a 'new' or 'third race' (e.g. *Diognetus* I), but the thought is not far away" (1971, 279).

letter of the predominantly Gentile character of the church in Corinth (cf. [1 Cor.] 6:9-11 and 8:1-10:22)" (1994, 153).

"You Were Led Away"

Paul reminded the people in the congregation that they had been led away to mute idols.[3] Paul uses the imperfect verb

---

[3] Some scholars regard the sentence in verse 2 as a grammatical problem because it does not contain the verb *ēte* (ἦτε, "you were") twice as would be expected. As we study this verse, the following Greek-English interlinear display should be helpful:

Οἴδατε	ὅτι	ὅτε	ἔθνη	ἦτε	πρὸς	τὰ	εἴδωλα
Oidate	hoti	hote	ethnē	ēte	pros	ta	eidōla
You know	that	when	pagans	you were	to	the	idols

τὰ ἄφωνα	ὡς ἄν	ἤγεσθε	ἀπαγόμενοι
ta aphōna	hōs an	ēgesthe	apagomenoi
voiceless	however	you were led	being led away

To solve the problem of the verb appearing only once, we just have to supply the second *ēte* (ἦτε) with the present participle (*apagomenoi*, ἀπαγόμενοι) at the end of the sentence. According to Fee:

Either something dropped out in the transmission of the text, or else Paul himself intended his readers to supply a second "you were" at some point in the sentence. Literally it reads, "You know that when you were pagans, to mute idols whenever (or however) you would be led, being carried away." The best solution is to repeat the verb "you were" with the final participle "carried away," so that the sentence reads, "When you were pagans, you were carried away, as you were continually being led about to mute idols." (1987, 576-577)

The Greek words *hōs an* (ὡς ἄν) shed light on the meaning of the text. The NASB[95] and NIV put the emphasis on the indefiniteness of the way in which the pagans were led. The NASB[95] translation is "*however* you were led," while the NIV states, "*somehow or other* you were influenced and led astray to mute idols." Others emphasize the iterative force of *hōs an*. With a recognition of this meaning, Fee's translation is "continually being led" (1987, 577). Similarly, Robertson maintains that *hōs an* contains the idea of repetition (1931, 167; 1934, 974). His translation is: "as often as ye were led." Putting these translations together, the former pagans were somehow being led in an ongoing way to the mute idols.

8

(*ēgesthe*, ἤγεσθε, "you were led") and a present participle (*apagomenoi*, ἀπαγόμενοι, "being led away") to express his point. According to Lenski, both verbs in this sentence should be taken as passives (1946, 491).[4] The passive verbs suggest that they had experienced some loss, if not total loss, of self-control. Here, Paul does not name those who led them astray. One of the possibilities is that they were led by pagan friends.

These former pagans were led to, not by, mute idols. The idols were voiceless and could not interact with the people. The inability of the idols to speak stands in stark contrast to the Spirit of God who so powerfully speaks and enables the believers. Paul reminds the former pagans of their past experience in order to draw the contrast with being led by the Spirit of God.

According to a common view, the former pagans were led by demons to dumb idols. Supporters often cite 1 Corinthians 10:19-20. While not denying the influence of Satan, this may not be Paul's point here. Garland argues against this view and suggests that they could have been led by social pressure to participate in idol festivals (2003, 565). Actually, verse 2 does not say by whom or how they were led. Options have to be supported by evidence beyond the text.

People can be led away to "idols" in many different ways and by many different people. They can be led by friends, by associates at work, by students and teachers in college classrooms, through the popular entertainment media, and in many other ways. Apparently, Paul was not concerned in this verse with making a list; rather, he simply states the fact.

Inspired Speech and Ecstasy (12:2)

Verse 2 brings into focus two interrelated issues: (1) inspired speech and (2) ecstasy. This verse does not explicitly mention either issue. However, given what Paul says in verse 3 about

---

[4]Lenski avers that: "Both verbs are passive. The former is sometimes considered a middle: 'as you might allow yourselves to be led'; but then the second should also be a middle: 'you allowed yourselves to be led away,' for no difference is indicated between the two. The passives suit the thought exactly, the middles would add a complicating feature" (1946, 491-492).

speaking by the Spirit, commentators often raise these issues in connection with verse 2.

Inspired Speech

Many scholars believe that the former pagans experienced "inspired speech." Some draw this conclusion from sources that describe pagan worship of the times and believe Paul was referring to this. As indicated above, one view is that they spoke under the influence of demons. Moreover, they hold that Paul sought to contrast true Spirit-inspired speech with their pagan experience. This "inspired speech" was not the same as the speech expressed by Christians.

Others observe that verse 2 does not deal with "inspired speech." Garland represents this view with the following comment about Paul's intent, "He is not reminding them that inspired utterances ironically were part of the worship in some cults in spite of mute idols. . . . He simply intends to contrast their former pagan life (cf. 1 Cor. 8:7; Gal. 4:8-9; 1 Thess. 1:9) with their current life in the Spirit" (2003, 566).

Paul does have both spurious and true inspired speech in mind in verse 3. Because of this, some scholars hold that the former pagans were engaged in inspired and ecstatic speech. However, because verse 2 is silent on the issue, we cannot say with certainty that he had inspired speech and ecstasy in mind in verse 2.

Ecstasy

Quite a few scholars describe the pagan worshippers as being ecstatic. In making this judgment, they use an English word taken from the Greek word *ekstasis* (ἔκστασις). Although the Greek word does not limit what scholars mean by "ecstatic," it does provide an interesting background.

According to Bauer, *ekstasis* means (e.g. Mark 5:42) "being beside oneself" (2000, 309). The meanings include distraction, confusion, terror, and astonishment. Some scholars define ecstasy as a form of irrational and even mad behavior. This irrational behavior suggests a total loss of self-control. However, the word *ecstasy* does not necessarily mean all this. It can refer just to an emotional experience that may or may not include an influence from outside.

It may be that the pagans experienced ecstasy, but this was not Paul's point. His point was that they were led astray, no matter how this was done. In any case, a common approach is to assume that ecstatic behavior included "inspired utterances." This behavior was accompanied by a significant loss of self-control. Much of this goes beyond what Paul says and is based on other sources that deal with worship.

Some authors go further and hold that the Corinthian believers were in danger of being ecstatic. Dunn, for example, holds that verse 2 is an implied rebuke to the believers. They were ecstatic and were misusing speaking in tongues (1975, 234). This view posits wild ecstatic behavior on the part of the former pagans and similar behavior on the part of those who were converted. Along with this comes the position that Paul was rebuking the believers.

With regard to believers, our experience, when properly defined, can include ecstasy. Sometimes, more than the normal inspiration of a writer or speaker is involved. Both the reception and the delivery of the message are involved, but the believer is not ecstatic in the sense of loss of self-control. The apostle Paul declared, "The spirits of prophets are subject to prophets" (1 Cor. 14:32 NASB[95]).

Speaking by the Spirit (12:3)

In verse 3, Paul makes his points: "Therefore (*dio,* διὸ) I make known to you that no one speaking by the Spirit of God says, 'Jesus is accursed'; and no one can say, 'Jesus is Lord,' except by the Holy Spirit."

Paul begins verse 3 with the conjunction *dio*, meaning "therefore." With this conjunction, he draws an inference from what he has said. Many scholars connect verse 3 with verse 2, but verse 3 does not state an inference from what Paul said in verse 2 by itself. Rather, the conjunction *dio* connects with verse 1 or, as Carson says, with verses 1 and 2 together. As Carson explains:

In short, the flow runs like this: I do not want you to be ignorant of certain central truths (v. 1). You know of course that when you were pagans your ignorance on such matters was profound (v. 2). Now, since I do not want you to be ignorant in these matters, vv. 1-2), I am making them known to you (v. 3). (1987, 26)

The next question is: What are the central truths with regard to spiritual matters that Paul wants to teach? At the heart of our faith is the truth that Christ is central to all spiritual matters. Without Him, there is no salvation, no access to God the Father. It is by the Holy Spirit that we become sons of God. With this established, we can deal with the subject of whether or not people are speaking by the Holy Spirit. People who say "Jesus is accursed" are not doing so. People *are* enabled by the Spirit when they genuinely say "Jesus is Lord." We will examine these statements now.

"Jesus Is Accursed"

The NASB[95] translation of verse 3a says: "Therefore I make known to you that no one speaking by the Spirit of God says, 'Jesus is [indicative] accursed (*anathema,* ἀνάθεμα).'" By way of contrast, in the NIV, the translation of this pronouncement is: "Jesus be [imperative] cursed." The Greek words literally mean, "Jesus accursed," so the supplied verb can be in either the indicative or the imperative mood. Both are grammatically possible.

Because the Greek statement "Jesus accursed" does not have a verb, Winter, who supplies the verb "grant," contends that Christians were asking Jesus to curse their enemies. In other words, the translation would be "Jesus, grant a curse." Thus, because of their behavior, they were no better than their pagan counterparts. Therefore, Paul opposed them (2001, 175). Concerning this idea, Taylor writes:

> As intriguing as this proposal may be, the grammatical parallelism of the two confessions seems to argue against it. In other words, the parallel to "Jesus (is) cursed" is "Jesus (is) Lord." The Greek sentence structure is the same for both. (2014, 285)

Many attempts have been made to identify who might have said "Jesus is accursed." It is not my purpose to list them all and to argue for and against them. I will present, however, several major views. I do this, knowing that the main point is that anyone who makes such a statement is not speaking by the inspiration of the Holy Spirit. The content of this declaration unequivocally determines that it is not inspired by the Holy Spirit.

First, some scholars hold that "Jesus is accursed" was a hypothetical statement. However, it is difficult to think that Paul would have used this as a possibility if it had not occurred. "Moreover," as Fee says, "the clause 'Jesus is/be cursed' possesses all the earmarks of an actual curse formula" (1994, 156). This seems like more of a "way around" a difficulty rather than a real solution.

Second, many believe it was the pagans who were speaking this way. This would include unconverted pagans, both past and present. Also, it would include believers who were pagans when they spoke this way. Under this view, Paul contrasts the former life of the believers with their current life. One problem with this approach is that the Corinthians church consisted mainly of Gentile believers, and the word *anathema* is a Jewish term. However, this does not completely negate the view because Corinth was a cosmopolitan city. No doubt, many Gentiles were familiar with Jewish words.

Third, another position is that it was unbelieving Jews who were uttering this formula. Garland argues for this position. He reminds us that not all the Christians were former pagans. In support of this view, he writes:

> As a statement, "Jesus is accursed," it fits perfectly the assessment of Jesus found in Jewish circles (Acts 7:54-60). They could not declare "the Christ" accursed, as pagans could, since it is the Greek term for the Messiah. They could, however, declare Jesus accursed as one who was crucified (a stumbling block to the Jews; 1 Cor. 1:23) and one whom Christians impiously claimed to be the Messiah.[5] (2003, 571)

Another factor that bears on this issue is that the Jews believed that people, especially their prophets, were empowered by the Holy Spirit to speak. The pagans probably did not ascribe anything to the

---

[5]Garland gives this illustration: "Justin Martyr's dialogue with Rabbi Trypho specifically mentions Jews anathematizing Christ in their synagogues (see Dial. 47:4; 96:2; 137:2) and cursing Christians (16:4)" (2003, 571).

Holy Spirit. So, to my mind, this is in favor of the view that the unbelieving Jews were making the statement that "Jesus is accursed."

Fourth, Paul does not say where the people were when they made this pronouncement. Pagans very likely would have been at their place of idol worship, and unconverted Jews in their synagogues. The question is: Did anyone say this in the church? If anyone did, it would not have been a true believer.[6] Some who said "Jesus is accursed" may have claimed to be believers who were not. We know that unbelievers did attend the church (14:23-25). Also, we know that there was a lot of participation in the meeting. So it is possible that a pagan or unbelieving Jew spoke up and uttered these words.

We do not know with certainty who uttered the words, "Jesus is accursed." What we do know is that it was not the Spirit of God who inspired this statement. Paul made this very clear and unequivocal. Moreover, this would be true whether the words were spoken by pagans, by antagonistic Jews, or by people in the church who claimed to be believers but were not. Without further information, it will always be uncertain as to who was uttering this statement, but we can be very certain it did not originate with the Spirit of God.

Anyone today who would utter the words "Jesus is accursed" would clearly be known as an unbeliever. The gospel is Christ-centered, and this is very well known. It would be very rare to hear this statement in a church. However, there are many ways to deny Christ, and there are many ways to distort His gospel. So, all believers must be on guard at all times to stay close to Christ, to be truly led by the Spirit, and to stay solidly grounded in the Word of

---

[6]According to Kistemaker, "Other scholars have suggested that Paul is opposing Gnostic teachers who taught a dualism of the material and the spiritual. The physical body of Jesus belonging to the material world had to be cursed, only the spiritual Christ was confessed as the exalted Lord. This proposal assumes that Gnosticism was firmly rooted in the Christian Community of Corinth during the middle of the first century. But Paul's epistles to the Corinthians hardly support the suggestion that Gnosticism was rampant in Corinth. This assumption would gain credibility if it applied to events near the end of that century, not in Paul's day. Also, the Gnostics would ascribe lordship not to Jesus but only to Christ" (1993, 415).

God. We must be vigilant at all times to safeguard the message that has been entrusted to us.

"Jesus Is Lord"

In verse 3b, Paul says: "and no one can say, 'Jesus is Lord,' except by the Holy Spirit." There are two approaches to this sentence. One is that Paul had in mind the determination of what speech is inspired by the Holy Spirit and what is not. The other is that Paul was dealing more broadly with the presence and work of the Holy Spirit in salvation.

Carson brings this issue into focus when he says, "the purpose of 12:1-3 is *not* to provide a confessional test to enable Christians to distinguish true from false spirits, but to provide a sufficient test to establish who has the Holy Spirit at all" (1987, 27). My position is that Paul is doing both, but the entry point into the discussion is whether or not what is said is inspired by the Spirit. Being able to test whether or not a statement is empowered by the Spirit can only be done by those who have been blessed by the presence and saving work of the Spirit. The former purpose presupposes the latter.

First, when we put the emphasis on the event of speaking, the ultimate criterion of whether or not speech is inspired by the Holy Spirit is whether or not Jesus is exalted. The main point is to establish who is operating by the Spirit. Obviously, this results in discerning between true and false verbal statements. The ultimate test is the content of the speech.

The believers at Corinth were concerned about spiritual matters. Those spiritual matters clearly included the vocal gifts and their operation. Apparently, the vocal gifts were often in use. It was important to determine what speech was enabled by the Holy Spirit and what was not. Those who confessed that Jesus is Lord would stand in direct contrast to those who said "Jesus is accursed." This would be true no matter who uttered these words.

Second, another view is that Paul, in verse 3a, is dealing with the presence and work of the Spirit in salvation. Although Paul clearly highlights the enablement of the Spirit in connection with inspired speech, the presence and work of the Spirit clearly is assumed. Some commentators, such as Carson, believe that this is his main point. Either way, the role of the Spirit in salvation has to be recognized. Christ is central in our faith.

All matters spiritual, for the believing saints, center in Christ. When a person comes to faith, the Spirit does His objective saving work. As Riggs states, "At the very beginning of the salvation process, it is the Holy Spirit who takes the initiative and brings conviction to the sinning heart. 'No man can say that Jesus is the Lord, but by the Holy Ghost.' 1 Cor. 12:3" (1949, 42). Moreover, when the Spirit does His work, He indwells the believer. Therefore, in a basic sense, the term "spiritual" applies to all believers in Christ because they have experienced His work and have the indwelling Spirit. There are, of course, varying depths of experience with the Spirit.

In verse 3, the work of the Spirit in salvation is a deduction from the fact that no one can genuinely say "Jesus is Lord" except by the Spirit. The issue of spiritual gifts arose because of the need to determine whether speech was or was not inspired by the Holy Spirit. When we are considering the spiritual gifts and related matters, this is an important discussion to have.

Conclusion

Paul's message is direct and simple. He writes concerning spiritual matters, including gifts, persons, and things. He does not want them to be ignorant about these matters. As pagans, people were led astray to mute idols. The mute idols cannot speak and cannot enlighten. Also, many Jewish people were antagonistic to Christ. It may be that some of them were led away to dumb idols as well.

By God's design, Jesus is central to the story of salvation. Moreover, the presence and work of the Spirit in salvation is essential to our faith. We cannot be saved except by the work of the Holy Spirit. The Holy Spirit lifts up and exalts Jesus as our Savior. The Holy Spirit indwells people who believe in Christ, and they are, in a basic sense, spiritual people.

When Paul introduces the subject of spiritual gifts, he immediately establishes the ultimate criterion. All of the spiritual manifestations must exalt Christ as the Son of God, the Savior of the world. No other position is possible, given what Christ has done for us. The Lordship of Christ is the ultimate test of the validity of manifestations that purport to be inspired of the Spirit.

Those who say that "Jesus is accursed" do not speak by inspiration of the Holy Spirit; and one cannot say with allegiance that "Jesus is Lord," apart from the Holy Spirit. With all this understood, we are prepared to talk about spiritual persons and gifts. As we exalt Jesus, He will enable us to exercise the spiritual gifts properly.

CHAPTER TWO

GIFTS, MINISTRIES, AND WORKINGS

Introduction

In 1 Corinthians 12:4-6, Paul explains what he means by spiritual matters. He does this by giving us a threefold description, classifying spiritual matters as "gifts," "ministries," and "workings." Each of these very interrelated terms is connected respectively with one of the three members of the Triune Godhead. The Triune God is the source of the manifestation of the Spirit. Therefore, we see that both unity and diversity are evident in the nature of God himself.

The verses in 12:4-11 can be thought of as one paragraph. However, the NIV breaks this passage into two paragraphs: (1) verses 4-6 and (2) verses 7-11. Given two paragraphs, it would be possible to consider verse 7 as a part of either the first paragraph or the second. We will follow the NIV and put it with the second. Here is what Paul says in verses 4-6:

> [4]Now there are varieties of gifts, but the same Spirit. [5]And there are varieties of ministries, and the same Lord. [6]There are varieties of effects, but the same God who works all things in all *persons*.

As spiritual matters are discussed, many questions frequently arise. Very often, these questions are answered in connection with the term "spiritual gifts." However, we gain greater understanding of some issues by responding in terms of all three elements of the threefold description. The "spiritual ministries" and "spiritual workings" must be considered as well. We will discuss these issues after examining verses 4-6.

Diversity and Unity

Paul recognizes and encourages both diversity and unity within the body of Christ. These characteristics are grounded in God; that is, they are evident in His very nature, and He is the source of their existence in our lives and our exercise of them. The basis of all spiritual unity and diversity is God.

First, our text says "Now (*de,* δὲ)[7] there are "varieties" (*diaireseis,* διαιρέσεις) of gifts, ministries, and effects, but the same Spirit, the same Lord, and the same God. Beginning with the term *diaireseis,* there are two possible interpretations. On the one hand, this noun can mean "varieties," "different kinds of," or "diversities." On the other hand, it can mean "distributions," "allotments," or "apportionments." Either set of meanings is possible.

Those who favor "distributions" point out that, in 12:11, the cognate verb *diairoun* (διαιροῦν, present participle) clearly means "distributing." After acknowledging that "distributions" is one possible meaning, Fee states: "the meaning 'difference' or 'variety' is also well established; the context rules in favor of the latter here" (1987, 586). Given the context, Fee translates *diaireseis* as "different kinds of" (1987, 583). In addition, he employs the word "diversities."

Distribution and variety are complementary concepts. Some authors suggest that both meanings are possible. For example, Palma acknowledges the two approaches; then he states, "This may be a case of both-and, since Paul's extended treatment of spiritual gifts emphasizes both the variety among them and the Lord who distributes them sovereignly as He wills" (2001, 188). The "both-and" view has a lot of merit.[8] Throughout his discussion of spiritual gifts, Paul supports the variety of gifts. Also, he very strongly supports the point that it is the Triune God who distributes the gifts.

---

[7]Carson states that the connecting "(*de*) is probably adversative: I want you to know that all who truly confess Jesus as Lord do so by the Holy Spirit, and thus attest his presence in their lives; *but* that does not mean there are no distinctions to be made among them. Paul's concern now is not so much with unity as with diversity" (1987, 31-32).

[8]Taylor writes: "Paul's argument in 12:4-11 supports both ideas. In favor of 'varieties/different kinds' is the theme of unity and diversity that governs the passage. The different gifts proceed form the one and the same Spirit/ Lord/God. In favor of 'allotments/distributions' is the use of the cognate verb 'to apportion' in 12:11, meaning that the Spirit 'allots' or 'apportions' the gifts as he chooses" (2014, 286).

Second, Paul gives a threefold description of the gifts. I say threefold because he describes the same spiritual matters in three different ways. As Palma states, "Paul is not making a distinction between three different types of manifestation of the Spirit, nor is he providing a threefold categorization scheme for them. Rather, they present different aspects of spiritual gifts in general" (2001, 188-189). Thus, the three descriptions are not absolutely synonymous, but they deal with aspects of the manifestation of the Spirit. All three of the descriptions are grounded in God and are interrelated.

Third, we recognize that both diversity and unity are evident in the nature of God. Although Paul was not specifically teaching on the doctrine of the Trinity, the language he uses is in total harmony with that doctrine. The name God can refer to God the Father or to the Triune Godhead, but here God the Father fits the context. The three Persons of the Godhead exist in absolute unity, yet each one has His own characteristics. All three Persons are one, yet different. Given the nature of God, we can expect to find unity and diversity in all spiritual matters.

Fourth, the source of the unity and diversity of the spiritual matters is the Triune God. This is true of both the existence and the operation of the spiritual gifts, ministries, and effects. As Paul presents his descriptions, he attaches each one to a Person of the Godhead: gifts are attached to the Spirit, ministries to the Lord Jesus, and workings to God the Father. The respective attachments are not exclusive. For example, the gifts, ministries, and workings are all attributed to the Spirit in 12:7 and 11. However, the term "gifts" especially fits with the Spirit, "service" with the Lord, and "workings" with God the Father. Ultimately, all three Persons are involved in the existence and operation of the various spiritual gifts.

Varieties of Gifts: One Spirit

Now we turn to an examination of the first element in Paul's threefold description. In verse 4, he says, "There are varieties of gifts (*charismatōn*, χαρισμάτων), but the same Spirit." Because Paul relates the gifts to the Holy Spirit, the implication is that the gifts are given by the Spirit. This implication is made explicit in verses 7 and 11.

First, Bauer defines the words *charis* (χάρις), *charisma* (χάρισμα), and *charizomai* (χαρίζομαι) as follows: The noun *charis* means "grace" and "favor" (2000, 1079); the noun *charisma* means *"a gift (freely and graciously given)"* or *"a favor bestowed"* (2000, 1081); the verb *charizomai* means to *"give freely or graciously as a favor"* (2000, 1078). All three of these words have the same underlying emphasis on grace and favor freely given.

Second, Paul uses the word *charisma*, which occurs just seventeen times in the New Testament,[9] in a variety of ways. For example, he speaks about the gift of redemption. In Romans 6:23, he writes: "For the wages of sin is death, but the free gift (*charisma*) of God is eternal life in Christ Jesus our Lord." As another example, in 2 Corinthians 1:10-11, he writes about God rescuing him from peril as a gift (*charisma*). In addition, Paul uses this term in 1 Corinthians 12:4, 9, 28, 30, and 31 to designate spiritual gifts. It is best to think of a range of applications. According to Garland:

> Paul applies the word charisma to a wide range of phenomena. He uses it to refer to God's action in Christ to bring salvation to humans (Rom. 5:15-16; 6:23) and to his own miraculous deliverance from life-threatening danger (2 Cor. 1:11). He applies it to God's election and calling of Israel (Rom. 11:29). In this letter he uses it to characterize the absence of sexual passion that allows celibate devotion to God (7:7). The majority of uses, however, refer to the manifestations of God's working in the members of the Christian community, from which the whole community benefits (Rom. 1:11; 1 Cor. 1:4-7). (2003, 576)

Third, the majority usage mentioned by Garland includes the gifts of the Spirit. Here, my primary concern is with Paul's usage of *charisma* in connection with spiritual gifts.

---

[9]Schatzmann points out that the word "charisma" occurs only seventeen times in the New Testament. He says: "With the exception of 1 Pet 4:10, all the references are found in the Pauline corpus. Of the sixteen citations in Paul, six occur in Romans (1:11; 5:15, 16; 6:23; 11:29; 12:6) and seven in 1 Corinthians (1:7; 7:7; 12:4, 9, 28, 30, 31). The remaining three references are found in 2 Cor 1:11, 1 Tim 4:14, and 2 Tim 1:6" (1987, 4).

One, there are many spiritual gifts. Some people have thought of spiritual gifts (*charismata, χαρισμάτα*) as being mainly the nine gifts listed in 1 Corinthians 12:8-10. The number of gifts widens in 1 Corinthians 12:28-30 to include apostles, prophets, teachers, helps, and administrations. The list of *charismata* in Romans 12:6-8 includes some of the gifts in 1 Corinthians 12 plus exhorting, giving, leading, and showing mercy. In Ephesians 4:8, Paul calls the gifts *domata* (δόματα). The spiritual gifts include (Eph. 4:11) apostles, prophets, evangelists, pastors and teachers or pastors-teachers.

Two, Paul's lists of the *charismata* include ministers as well as ministries. Ministers such as apostles, prophets, and teachers are included. In such cases, the ministers are included because of their ministries. Both Garland (2003, 562) and Carson (1987, 22) hold that *charismata* never refers to persons, but persons are listed among the gifts (12:28-31; Rom. 12:6-8). Such persons are not the ministry, but they have the ministry. Because they have the ministry, they, too, can be called a gift.

Three, when Paul speaks about the *charismata* in 1 Corinthians 12-14, his main focus is on the ministers. He teaches them about the right motivation for spiritual gifts and their proper use. When he does this, he is referring primarily to the gifts given to the ministers for the benefit of others. Nevertheless, in a secondary sense, it is the people served who receive the gift. When a minister exercises a gift of healing given to him, someone is healed and the healed person receives the gift.

Four, scholars commonly recognize that the exercise of the spiritual gifts brings concrete results. Not as many go as far as Dunn who says that "only the actual deed or word is the charisma" (1975, 253-354).[10] To be sure, the *charisma* does include the actual word or deed, but the word is not limited to it. A minister, for example, a teacher has a gift of teaching whether or not he is teaching at the moment. In the case of Timothy, the gift was dormant (2 Tim. 1:6).

---

[10]Dunn maintains that *charisma* is a particular expression of *charis*. This means that *charisma* (1) "is always an event," (2) "is always a specific act of God, of God's Spirit through a man," (3) "is typically an experience," (4) "is not to be confused with human talent and natural ability" (1975, 253-254).

Fourth, we note the relationship between *pneumatikōn* (πνευματικῶν) and *charismata*. Paul opens 1 Corinthians 12-14 in 12:1 by naming *pneumatikōn* as his topic. The spiritual things that he calls *pneumatikōn* in 12:1 and *pneumatika* (πνευματικά) in 14:1, he calls *charismatōn* in 12:4 and *charismata* in 12:31. This brings up the issue of whether or not we can regard these two terms as synonymous.

As we noted in chapter one, it is widely held that the Corinthians raised the issue of spiritual matters. Moreover, some scholars hold that *pneumatikōn* was a word the Corinthians favored. This may be, but it does not, as some suggest, invalidate the word itself. Paul can correct their understanding without invalidating the word. Instead of discarding the word, Paul uses it to make his case.

Opinions on this issue range from the terms being synonymous to the view that there is no overlapping meaning at all.[11] The middle ground is that the terms sometimes, but not always, are interchangeable. It appears to me that both terms have a range of meaning from narrow to broad and that, at times, they can be used interchangeably and synonymously. However, this is not to say that they are totally the same.

Fifth, Paul says there are varieties of gifts, *but the same Spirit*. Here, he puts the emphasis on the Spirit as the giver of the gifts. This emphasis is evident throughout 1 Corinthians 12-14. The Spirit is Himself a gift to us, but here He is the giver of spiritual gifts. The same Spirit is the source of all of the gifts, so no person can take pride in having one gift versus another person having another gift. Moreover, these gifts are not given to us because of our own worthiness. Rather, they are given because of God's love for us and the people to whom we minister by means of the gifts.

Although Paul attributes the *charismata* to the Spirit, this does not exclude the involvement of the Father and the Son. In Pauline thinking, God (Rom. 12:3), Christ (Eph. 4:7, 11), and the Spirit (1

---

[11]Schatzmann says that three positions are generally maintained with regard to *pneumatika* and *charismata*: (1) the two words are synonymous, (2) they are synonymous in a qualified way, and (3) they are not synonymous (My Paraphrase). He states: "Qualified interchangeability best characterizes Paul's use of the terms" (1987, 7).

Cor. 12:11) are the direct givers of gifts. In 2 Timothy 1:6, Timothy's gift is specifically called the "gift of God" (cp. 1 Cor. 12:18, 24, and 28). Because we serve the Triune God, it should not be surprising that the bestowal of gifts is attributed to all three Persons of the Godhead. Furthermore, we should not try to draw too many distinctions based on who is the named giver. Although all three Persons are givers of gifts, the Holy Spirit is named throughout.

Varieties of Ministries: One Lord

Next, Paul says, "There are varieties (*diaireseis*, διαιρέσεις) of ministries (*diakoniōn*, διακονιῶν), and the same Lord" (verse 5). Here Paul uses the word *diakoniōn* to describe the spiritual matters and refers to the "Lord" (cp. verse 3: Jesus is Lord) as the distributor of the ministries.

First, the term *diakoniōn* can be translated "services" or "ministries." The minister is not the ministry, but he has the ministry. The purpose of the spiritual ministries, as we can call them, is to render service to others, to serve the body of Christ. Essentially, the spiritual things that Paul has in mind are ways to minister. When you consider all of the needs that people have, a great number and variety of ministries are necessary. The ministries in the body of Christ match the needs that people have.

Second, Jesus as Lord is the distributor of the ministries. This is explicitly said in Ephesians 4:7-11, where Paul writes in verse 7, "but to each one of us grace (*charis*, χάρις) was given (*dōreas*, δωρεᾶς) according to the measure of Christ's gift." Quoting from Psalm 68:18, verse 8 says, "And He [Christ] gave gifts (*domata*, δόματα) to men."

Then, in verse 11, Paul declares, "And He [Christ] gave (*edōken*, ἔδωκεν) some *as* apostles, and some *as* prophets, and some *as* evangelists, and some *as* pastors and teachers."

Although there are many ministries, there is but one Lord. One Lord distributes the ministries, and all three Persons of the Trinity are involved. As just stated, the ministries in Ephesians 4:7 are Christ's gifts. Then, the apostle Paul says in 1 Corinthians 12:28: "And God has appointed in the church, first apostles, second prophets, third teachers, then miracles, then gifts of healings, helps, administrations, *various* kinds of tongues."

Third, in a sense, we are the ones who serve; but in the final analysis, it is the Lord who serves through us. As we yield ourselves to Him, He can use us to render service to people who are in need. So that we may be used of the Holy Spirit, all of us should concentrate on sustaining an intimate personal relationship with Him. Jesus calls us, commands us to go, and promises to be with us.

Varieties of Workings: One God

Paul says, "There are varieties (*diaireseis*, διαιρέσεις) of effects (*energēmatōn*, ἐνεργημάτων), but the same God who works (*energōn*, ἐνεργῶν) all things in all persons" (verse 6). This verse continues the enrichment of our understanding of the nature of "spiritual things" that Paul has in mind.

First, the NASB[95] translates the noun *energēmatōn* as "effects" and the present participle *energōn* as "works." Respectively, the NIV says "different kinds of working" and "works;" and the NEB has "many forms of work" and "work." According to Robertson *energēmatōn* is "the effect of a thing wrought (from the verb *energeō*, ἐνεργέω), meaning "to operate, perform, energize" (1930, 168). One of the sources of the English verb "to energize" is the Greek word *energeō*. God is the source of these spiritual workings.[12]

Second, there are varieties of workings, but it is "the same God who works all things in all persons." God is the source of the gifts. The minister is not the "working," but he is the one through whom God works. When God acts, we as servants' are empowered for specific purposes. When God energizes and works through us, concrete results are obtained. Sometimes these results are visible to our eyes, but sometimes they are not. Whether or not we can see the results, it is God who is at work.

---

[12]Kistemaker notes the following: "The Greek word *energēmata*, which I translate 'activities,' occurs twice in the New Testament (vv. 6 and 10). In verse 6, the word is closely connected with the concept *gifts*, while in v. 10 it signifies miraculous powers. The word, which has derivatives in English (energy, energetic, and energize), means action as the result of God's energizing power" (1993, 419).

Third, the name "God" could refer to the Triune God, including the Father, the Son, and the Holy Spirit. However, given the references to the Spirit (verse 4) and the Lord (verse 5), it appears in this case to refer to God the Father. We see the same approach in Ephesians 4:4-6 where the reference to God the Father is explicit. There are varieties of effects, but it is the same Father God who works all things in all persons. This, of course, does not preclude the involvement of the Holy Spirit and the Son.

The Human Side

In 12:4-6, Paul clearly spells out the divine source and involvement in the exercise of the spiritual gifts. Our Triune God is the source of all gifts and the enabler of all that we do. Each member of the Trinity is involved in all three descriptions. Clearly, based on the character of God, Paul establishes that there must be both unity and diversity in the body of Christ.

In addition to what God does, there are responsibilities that He assigns to us. In other words, there is a human side to the operation of spiritual gifts. Man's part is to serve under the Lordship of Christ, to be empowered for the task, and to exercise the gift. We see the human side in all three chapters, but especially in chapter 14. Some of the responsibilities Paul names are as follows:

- *Motive*: Paul exhorts us to "earnestly desire" spiritual gifts (12:31; 14:1). We should desire especially to prophesy (14:1, 39). We have to want to be on the team!

- *Love*: Paul says to "pursue love." It is the highest motive for desiring spiritual gifts. We must allow God's love to flow through us.

- *Prayer*: Paul says that when a person speaks in tongues, he should "pray that he may interpret" (14:13). As believers, we have that responsibility.

- *Choice*: In 14:15, Paul says "I shall pray with the spirit," and "I shall pray with the mind also." In other words, he will choose to pray both with the spirit and with the mind.

- *Judgment*: In 14:29, Paul says that, when the prophets speak, "let the others pass judgment." As the Spirit leads, there is a human input both from the speaker and from those who evaluate the prophecies.

- *Control*: Paul says, "spirits of prophets are subject to prophets" (14:32). Being inspired by the Spirit does not mean a loss of self-control. Our duty is to maintain that control under the Spirit's leadership.
- *Obedience*: Paul exhorts (14:37-38) us to acknowledge and obey the Lord's commandment.
- *Forbid Not:* Paul exhorts the church "do not forbid to speak in tongues." This is an exhortation to man (14:39).

Working Together with God

In our text (12:4-6), Paul describes the gracious way that the Triune God empowers us to do His work. In another passage, Colossians 1:28-29, Paul makes comments that wonderfully inform our understanding of 1 Corinthians 12-14. When we exercise one of the spiritual gifts, we are workers together with God. With the spiritual gifts, we do His divine will. As Paul proclaims in 1 Corinthians 3:9: "For we are God's fellow workers (*sunergoi*, συνεργοί); you are God's field, God's building."[13]

In Colossians 1:28-29, Paul explains that God energizes us to do His work. He declares:

[28]We proclaim Him, admonishing every man and teaching every man with all wisdom, so that we may present every man complete in Christ. [29]For this purpose also I labor, striving according to His power, which mightily works (*energoumenēn*, ἐνεργουμένην) within me.

The body of Christ is engaged in many ministries which collectively affect every aspect of our lives. It would not be possible to list all the ministries in a single passage of Scripture. However, in Colossians 1:28, Paul does give us the central and overarching goal of our ministries: we are to proclaim Christ with the goal of presenting every person complete in Christ. The goal includes all ministries from evangelism to spiritual maturity in all

---

[13]Fee gives this translation, "'God's we are, being fellow workers; God's field, God's building, you are.'" He maintains that as believers we work together *under* God, not *with* God (1987, 134). However, the preposition "with" does not necessarily suggest peer level cooperation. Clearly, believers work "under" God, but properly understood, we work "with" God as well (cp. 2 Cor. 6:1).

its elements. This goal is accomplished through the gifts of admonition and teaching.

To accomplish this mission, in verse 29, Paul says, "I labor." Paul uses the Greek verb *kopiō* (κοπιῶ) which Bruce says is "a strong word, denoting toil to the point of weariness or exhaustion" (1984, 88). Fortunately, Paul does not labor alone; he is enabled by God's power. As Lenski translates the last clause, Paul says that he is straining or agonizing "according to the working (*energeian*, ἐνέργειαν) of him which is working in me in power" (1946, 80). In 1 Corinthians 12:6, Paul uses the same noun *energēmatōn* (ἐνεργημάτων, plural) to describe spiritual gifts. We take our English word "energy" from this Greek word. Paul labored as an instrument in the hands of the Spirit. The Holy Spirit energizes us, as He did Paul, to do God's work. Our goal as ministers is to help the people become like Christ. That is why we work together with God. There could be no higher privilege!

Flexibility of Terms

Broadly speaking, the threefold description applies to all the gifts that Paul mentions, but each gift has its own distinctiveness. Thus, no one formula exists for all the gifts. For example, everything that is said about "miracles" does not necessarily apply to "teaching." Each gift must be described in its own right. So there is diversity within the unity of all the gifts. This will readily appear as we discuss the gifts in our next chapter.

First, the variety and flexibility of Paul's terminology is evident in this entire passage (verses 4-6). He does not rigidly adhere to just one meaning of a term. Various terms are interrelated. The spiritual matters from one perspective are "gifts," from another perspective they are "ministries," and from still another perspective, they are "effects" or "workings." As Fee states:

> Given the flexibility of language . . . one should probably not overanalyze the different words used to describe the individual activities of the divine Persons: "gifts," "ministries" or "services," "workings." They are simply three different ways of looking at what in v. 7 Paul calls "manifestations" of the Spirit. (1994, 161)

Second, many of the terms that Paul uses in chapters 12-14 have both broad, narrow, and even overlapping meanings. The temptation is to turn a term with general meaning into a technical term that is very narrowly defined. Sometimes this can be done, but not always. Many times, words overlap in their meaning. This is true, to some extent, with regard to "gifts," "ministries," and "workings." The gifts involve ministries and workings; the ministries are gifts and workings; and the workings are ministries and gifts. As another example, the terms "word of wisdom" and "word of knowledge" have overlapping meanings. It is better in such instances to remain open and inclusive about the meanings. Without a specific reason to narrow the meaning, the broader meaning is best.

Special Issues

Whenever spiritual gifts are discussed, several issues tend to surface. The discussions often focus on the term *charismata* (χαρίσματα, gifts) without much, if any, emphasis on the other terms (*diakoniōn*, διακονιῶν and *energēmatōn*, ἐνεργημάτων) in Paul's threefold description. The issues can be better resolved when we have in focus all three descriptions of spiritual matters. Therefore, we need to answer the questions with the three descriptions in mind, not just the term *gifts*.

First, one issue is: Are all of the gifts, ministries, and workings for us today? In my judgment, all of them should be exercised today in the church with the exception of apostles in the narrow sense of the term. Narrowly speaking, the term "apostles" refers only to the apostles in the early church. When the term is used in a broad sense, it refers to anyone "sent on a mission." Similarly, the term "prophet" is often reserved in common usage for people who are being used of God in outstanding ways. However, in a broader way, the Spirit is poured out in Acts upon all mankind and all believers can prophesy (Acts 2:17-18; 1 Cor. 14:31). No one today, of course, has the ministry of composing Scriptures as did some of the apostles and prophets of the past.

Second, a question sometimes posed is: Are the spiritual gifts "special abilities" or "ministries"? The issue revolves around the meaning of the Greek word *charismata*. Scholars agree that *charismata* refers to gifts freely given. Many of them hold that this term, like the English word "gifts," refers to special abilities given to people to enable them to minister to others. Although the noun *charisma* means "gracious gift," the use of it in connection with the gifts of the Spirit suggests "special abilities."

Berding takes a different approach. He acknowledges the "conventional" view of *charismata* as abilities, but says that the word itself does not refer to special abilities. Instead, he holds that the *charismata* are all ministries. Even so, he says that the ministries may in some cases be both ministries and special abilities (2006, 33-34). He writes:

> All the items in Paul's lists, without exception, can be described as Spirit-given ministries or as persons in their ministries. Still, there's a category of these spiritual ministries that are both ministries and special enablements. These are the miraculous ministries such as healings, prophecy, tongues, and miracles, which can't be done without a special—not simply general—enablement from the Holy Spirit. (2006, 33)

It is helpful to answer this question with Paul's threefold description in mind. In verse 4, he describes spiritual things as "gifts." All would agree that they are freely given to us. He indicates in verse 5 that these gifts are "services" or "ministries." Then, in verse 6, Paul describes the gifts as "workings." The gifts are divinely empowered. The Spirit will empower us to whatever degree is needed to accomplish the ministry. Obviously, when a miracle occurs, the empowerment of the Spirit stands out in bold relief to all the witnesses. All three terms apply to one degree or another to all of the gifts.

Third, as indicated earlier, a major issue is: Are the spiritual gifts supernatural, natural, or natural talents that are divinely enhanced? Paul's threefold description does not make such distinctions.[14] In 12:4-6, Paul stresses the supernatural aspect with

---

[14]Carson declares that Paul's lists of gifts "as a whole contain an impressive mixture of what some might label 'natural' and 'supernatural' endowments, or 'spectacular' and 'more ordinary' gifts. . . . The intriguing thing is that Paul himself makes no such distinctions: it is the same God who works all things in all men. Paul's overarching doctrine of divine sovereignty is precisely what can prompt him to ask the Corinthians elsewhere: 'For who makes you different form anyone else? What do you have that you did not receive? And if you did receive it, why do you boast as though you did not?' (1 Cor. 4:7). This suggests in turn that Paul would not have been uncomfortable with spiritual

his threefold description by naming the three Persons of the Trinity as the source. Without supernatural empowerment, we cannot have spiritual gifts. However, natural elements may be involved to some degree. Moreover, the gifts of the Spirit vary somewhat with regard to whether they are natural, supernatural, or natural talents enhanced by the Spirit.

The gift of "helps" (*antilēmpseis*, ἀντιλήμψεὶς), for example, is listed (12:28) right along with miracles, gifts of healings, and various kinds of tongues. It is easy for us to think of "helps" as largely a manifestation of natural abilities. We must keep in mind that even natural abilities are gifts from God (James 1:17). Moreover, it sometimes takes a lot of God's grace to keep on helping when others do not. So God enhances our natural talent with His grace. In contrast, other gifts seem almost purely supernatural, such as miracles and gifts of healings.

Fourth, another issue is: Are the spiritual gifts momentary or permanent? Once again, it helps to consider that they are "ministries" and "workings" as well as gifts. This will lead us to a "both-and" conclusion. In one sense, they are temporary. While commenting on verse 6, as Rea points out, the workings signify the results produced by God who imparts the energy. Then, he states:

> In this sense the gifts are not regular, permanent abilities. Instead they are momentary powers to effect a miracle, to bring healing, to know something in a flash. And it is the same God who energizes or activates all these gifts, both in those who act as agents and in those on whom the effect is produced. (1998, 216)

However, in another sense, the spiritual gifts are permanent. Many who minister have been given a special understanding of the need. For example, some who have the gifts of healing have been made attuned by deep sickness on their part. Some people are often used of God to inspire faith for healing. Even though the gifts crystallize into action in momentary acts as when one prays for the sick, the empowerment of the minister continues. The same could be said for the gift of teaching.

---

gifts made up of some mix of so-called natural talent—what he would consider still to be God's gift—and of specific, Spirit-energized endowment" (1987, 37).

Application

As an example of the exercise of a spiritual gift, consider this. In a Sunday morning service, the pastor invites the people to come forward for prayer for healing. One of the prayer workers has been used of the Lord in praying for the sick. She prays for a lady who comes. A few days later, the lady reports that she was dramatically healed and is doing fine.

We can say that the Holy Spirit had distributed a gift of healing to the prayer worker, that she exercised the gift in the Sunday morning service, that a lady who was healed benefited from the gift (even that she received the gift). The prayer worker engaged in a ministry under the Lord's supervision and was energized by God the Father. While the prayer worker was used of the Lord, the healing was clearly a supernatural action.

Now, let us consider another example. As the same Sunday morning service was about to convene, a church parking attendant was guiding people as to where to park their cars. He had been doing this for years. One person was having a difficult time finding a place to park and was becoming upset. With considerable diplomacy, the parking attendant spoke calmly to the person and helped him find a place.

We can say that the Holy Spirit had distributed a gift of "helps" to the parking attendant, that he exercised the gift in a tense situation, and that the man parking his car benefited from this (even received the gift). The parking attendant, too, engaged in a ministry led by the Lord and was energized by God the Father. We readily recognize that natural talent was involved, but the parking attendant also was led by the Spirit to calmly assist. Clearly, the event was under the control of the Spirit. The body of Christ obviously needed this gifted attendant.

Conclusion

First Corinthians 12:4-6 is a strong passage that declares that God is the Triune source of spiritual gifts, ministries, and effects or energizing. Paul indicates that there are varieties of distributions of these spiritual matters, but respectively the same Spirit, the same Lord, and the same God. Both the variety and the unity are grounded in the very nature of God. There is great diversity in spiritual matters within the unity of God's operations. There are different kinds of gifts, but the same Spirit; there are different kinds of services, but the same Lord; and there are different kinds of effects, but the same God.

Many times, discussions of spiritual things raise interesting issues. These issues have to do with each of the three elements of Paul's threefold description of what he had in mind. Because of the interrelatedness of the three elements, a better picture emerges when all three are included for consideration. We have to see spiritual things through all three perspectives. Sometimes issues are resolved by taking a "both-and" position. For example, natural talents can be used by God in harmony with the spiritual gifts, but the element that has to be present is the manifestation of the Spirit.

CHAPTER THREE

MANIFESTATION OF THE SPIRIT

Introduction

In 12:1-3, Paul introduces his subject for 1 Corinthians 12-14. The subject is "spiritual matters" that are important to the Corinthians and to him. All spiritual things must exalt Christ. Next, in 12:4-6, he gives us a threefold description of spiritual matters. They are gifts, ministries, and workings, respectively of the Holy Spirit, the Lord Jesus, and God the Father.

Now, in 12:7-11, Paul puts all these spiritual things under the rubric of "the manifestation of the Spirit." This term is inclusive of the other three descriptions. The manifestations are commonly called spiritual gifts. In this chapter and the next, we will discuss each of these nine manifestations. The role of the Spirit is strongly emphasized throughout. Paul writes:

[7]But to each one is given the manifestation of the Spirit for the common good. [8]For to one is given the word of wisdom through the Spirit, and to another the word of knowledge according to the same Spirit; [9]to another faith by the same Spirit, and to another gifts of healing by the one Spirit, [10]and to another the effecting of miracles, and to another prophecy, and to another the distinguishing of spirits, to another *various* kinds of tongues, and to another the interpretation of tongues. [11]But one and the same Spirit works all these things, distributing to each one individually just as He wills.

Although Paul elaborates on some of these gifts, he does not say much about others. Much of what commentators say is drawn from other Biblical content or just represents ideas that they think fit Paul's overall theological framework.

As we study the gifts, it becomes apparent that they overlap in scope and that the terms are flexible. For example, it is difficult to distinguish between the *word of wisdom* and the *word of knowledge*. Also, the gifts of prophecy and teaching can share some common ground. Each of these gifts may include divine revelation or heightened insight. So it is not wise to define the gifts too narrowly or too exclusively. The overlap and flexibility of the terms is significant.

As we discuss each manifestation, we will revisit the relevant issues presented in our last chapter. Some answers to the issues may apply to all the gifts, but some may vary manifestation-by-manifestation. The temptation is to apply all of our answers equally to all of the manifestations. When it comes to the spiritual gifts, there are few "hard and fast" categories. A more flexible approach certainly encourages the exercise of the gifts.

To Each One (12:7)

Paul introduces his list of gifts in verse 7 and makes a concluding comment in verse 11. In verse 7, he declares: "But to each one (*hekastō*, ἑκάστῳ) is given (*didotai*, δίδοται) the manifestation (*phanerōsis*, φανέρωσις) of the Spirit for the common good (*sumpheron*, συμφέρον)." Several points stand out.

First, what does Paul mean when he says, "But to each one is given"? Fee holds that the main point of this clause is that the believers have diverse gifts, not that every single believer has a gift. Concerning the latter point, he says, "That may or may not be true, depending on how broadly or narrowly one defines the word χάρισμα (*charisma*, transliteration mine)" (1994, 163). His approach leaves open who is to be included in "each one."

Some expositors hold that Paul was referring to everyone within the special group of believers who have received gifts. In other words, all believers do not receive these special gifts.[15] Harold Horton would limit the group to "every man who is filled with the Spirit as these Corinthians were" (1962, 29). However, in his exposition of the body of Christ (12:12-27), Paul stresses the functional significance of every member.

Barrett expresses the most commonly held view when he says, "Each member of the church has a gift; none is excluded" (1971,

---

[15]For example, Grosheide states: "Since verse 8 is to enumerate the various workings of the Spirit, Paul's words '*to each one is given*' must mean: to everyone who has special gifts of the Spirit is given" (1953, 284).

284).[16] Thinking in terms of potential, Gee declares, "All may have a part" (1980, 27). Although this privilege may not have been realized by some individuals, every believer is eligible to receive at least one gift. My view is that this approach sustains the inclusiveness of the clause and opens the way for believers to have diverse gifts.

Second, let us consider the *phanerōsis* of the Spirit. According to Thayer, *phanerōsis* means "manifestation." To manifest something means to make it "apparent, manifest, evident, known" (1962, 648-649). The term "manifestation" is a singular noun. Concerning this, Arrington says:

> Nowhere does Paul speak of 'manifestations of the Spirit.' Using only the singular may be due to Paul's regarding the phrase 'manifestation of the Spirit' as a comprehensive term for the several ways that the Holy Spirit manifests Himself. Similarly he seems to use the singular 'fruit of the Spirit' and then gives a list of the nine. (Gal. 5:22, 23)

Although Paul does not speak of the "manifestations" of the Spirit, the plural is commonly used. There is only one Spirit manifested, but He works in many ways. Therefore, His works can be called "manifestations of the Spirit."

Third, the phrase "of the Spirit" can be interpreted in either a subjective or an objective sense.[17] In a subjective sense, the Spirit

---

[16]Palma maintains that: "The consensus of New Testament writers, especially Paul, is that every believer is given at least one gift (Rom. 12:6; 1 Cor. 1:7; 3:5; 12:7, 11, 18; 14:1, 26; Eph. 4:7, 11; 1 Pet. 4:10; see also Matt. 25:15)" (2001, 195). Stanley Horton, with a different view, writes: "In fact, the gifts are given with the divine intention that everyone will profit by them (12:7). This does not mean that everyone has a specific gift, but there are gifts (manifestations, disclosures, means by which the spirit makes himself known openly) being given (continuously for everyone to profit (use, invest, grow). 'Profit' has the idea of something useful, helpful, especially in building the Church, both spiritually and in numbers" (1976, 213).

[17]On the one hand, Kistemaker favors the objective approach. He writes, "Perhaps we should accept the objective interpretation of this phrase in view of the passive verb *is given*, which implies that God is the one who gives the various gifts" (1993, 420). On the other hand, Lenski supports the subjective approach with these comments: "When the question is properly put it practically answers itself. What is it that is given to each of us? Is the gift this

is the one who enables the gifts. The gifts are the manifestations of the Spirit. In 12:11, Paul writes, "But one and the same Spirit works all these things." In an objective sense, the phrase refers to that which manifests the Spirit. In other words, the gifts of the Spirit make known the Spirit's presence and power. For example, when the gift of prophecy is exercised, an unbeliever may be convicted in such a way that he will fall down and worship God (14:24-25).

Both approaches are true. Under either one, the presence of the Spirit is powerfully "seen and felt." On this point there is little difference between the two approaches. We do not have to choose between the objective sense and the subjective. Thus, we might agree with Dunn that "it is quite likely that Paul was being deliberately ambiguous, his thought being that *the Spirit reveals himself* in the charismata" (1975, 21). However, rather than "deliberately ambiguous," we might say "deliberately inclusive."

Fourth, with regard to the verb "is given" (*didotai*), Paul uses the present tense. The action of the present tense is either continuous or undefined. Here, the Spirit manifests Himself through the spiritual gifts. The manifestation of the Spirit is given to the believers as they exercise the gifts. When believers frequently manifest the Spirit in a given way, we describe them as "having" that gift in an ongoing way. Therefore, the manifestation has both a temporary and permanent quality.

Fifth, the manifestation of the Spirit is given to each one "for the common good" (*sumpheron,* present participle). Literally, the Greek present participle means "for the profiting." The question is, "Who benefits from the exercise of the gifts? Is it the individual who exercises the gift? Is it the persons who are blessed by the operation of the gift? Or, is it the community as a whole that is in focus here? Obviously, when the community is blessed, all members within the community are benefited as well. The "common good" includes everyone in the community.

[objective] that *we* make manifest *the Spirit* for the common good, or that [subjective] the Spirit manifests himself in us by his gift for the common good? Certainly the latter" (1946, 497).

Actually, all of the above, including the individual, can be blessed by the manifestation of the Spirit.[18] The main emphasis, however, that Paul makes in our text is on building up the community. At this point, Paul does not mention the body of Christ; but in verses 12-27, he deals extensively with this subject. The spiritual gifts are bestowed within the body; that is, they are given to members of the body. Moreover, the gifts are given for its common good. Through the gifts, we are enabled to enlarge, care for, and edify the body of Christ.

Building up the body of Christ through spiritual gifts does not exclude evangelism. On the contrary, the gifts can have a strong influence in drawing people to Christ. The gift of prophecy, for example, has an evangelistic impact (1 Cor. 14:24-25). When the healing gifts are exercised, many people are attracted to Christ, the healer. Many of these people become members of the body of Christ.

Word of Wisdom and Word of Knowledge (12:8)

In verse 8, Paul writes: "For (*gar*, γὰρ) to one (*hō*, ᾧ) is given (*didotai*, δίδοται) the word (*logos*, λόγος) of wisdom (*sophias*, σοφίας) through (*dia*, διὰ) the Spirit, and to another (*allō*, ἄλλῳ) the word of knowledge (*gnōseōs*, γνώσεως) according to (*kata*, κατὰ) the same Spirit." Both the *word of wisdom* and the *word of knowledge* are manifestations of the Spirit.

Before we study the word of wisdom and the word of knowledge, it will be helpful to briefly mention the relationship between wisdom and knowledge in general. A common distinction is that knowledge has to do with information and facts, whereas wisdom refers to the ability to apply knowledge. As Petts states, "Perhaps we could say that knowledge is the faculty whereby we are aware that something is true, whereas wisdom is the faculty whereby we know *what to do* in certain circumstances" (2002, 225).

Even so, it is difficult to draw a sharp line between knowledge and wisdom. It is true enough that the word *knowledge* emphasizes

---

[18]Carson points out that the "common good" "does not rule out all benefit for the individual . . . providing that the resulting matrix is for the common good" (1987, 35).

facts and information about a wide variety of topics, but the word of knowledge also can include information about wise courses of action. Similarly, the word of wisdom does often emphasize the application of knowledge, but those applications may be based on a body of knowledge that we call wisdom.

Wisdom and Knowledge

Before commenting separately on the word of wisdom and the word of knowledge, we will consider several points that have to do with both of these manifestations of the Spirit.

First, the conjunction "for" links what Paul has just said with what follows. He supports and illustrates the points that each person may have a spiritual gift and that the gifts are diverse. One person is given one gift, and another person is given a different gift. Each person has a gift for the benefit of others, and the gifts that they have are different.

Second, when Paul says "to one is given (*didotai*, δίδοται) the word of wisdom," he uses the same present tense verb that he used in verse 7. He does not repeat this verb in his list of the nine gifts, but it is understood that the verb should be supplied. Therefore, we understand that the Spirit gives each of the nine manifestations. This is confirmed in verse 11 when Paul says "But one and the same Spirit works all these things."

Third, the word *logos* (λόγος) is very flexible and has many meanings. According to Bauer, the exact translation of *logos* depends on the context. It can mean "speaking," "word," "the subject under discussion," "matter," "thing," and "speaking wisely" (2000, 599). In comparison, Thayer lists "a word," "what someone has said," "a kind or style of speaking," and "the act of speaking" (1962, 380). With regard to our text, Thayer says, *logos* refers to "the art of speaking to the purpose about things pertaining to wisdom and knowledge" (1962, 380). As we discuss the word of wisdom and the word of knowledge separately, we will discuss what Paul means in verse 8.

Fourth, in verses 7-10, Paul uses three prepositions to describe the role of the Spirit in the operation of the gifts. The word of wisdom is exercised *through* (*dia*, διὰ) the Spirit; the word of knowledge *according to* (*kata*, κατὰ) the Spirit; both faith and healing *by* (*en*, ἐν) the Spirit. In my view, the prepositions do not divide the gifts into categories; all three apply to each of the gifts. Each of the manifestations is "through," "according to," and "in" the Spirit. Although each preposition has its own special nuances, they sometimes overlap in meaning as well.[19] Here, the main thought is that the presence and activity of the Spirit is absolutely essential to the existence and operation of the gifts.

Without the Spirit, even though natural elements may be involved, there is no gift. The presence of the Spirit provides the supernatural character of the gift. As Gee declares, "There is only one way to consistently deal with the whole subject of these spiritual gifts, and that is to regard them as each and all involving some measure of a supernatural operation of the Holy Spirit" (1980, 34).

Fifth, although much is said in the New Testament about both wisdom and knowledge, the terms "word of wisdom" and "word of knowledge" appear only in this verse. However, Paul does use the word "knowledge" by itself to stand for the word of knowledge. Neither Paul nor anyone else specifically labels any events or happenings as a word of wisdom or a word of knowledge. Many times scholars draw examples from the Bible that fit their definitions.

Word of Wisdom

In verse 8 Paul declares: "For to one is given (*didotai*, δίδοται) the word (*logos*, λόγος) of wisdom (*sophias*, σοφίας) through (*dia*, διὰ) the Spirit." As with all the gifts, the purpose is to build up the body of Christ and to reach the world with the gospel.

First, as indicated above, the term *logos* may refer to speaking ability. The manifestation of the Spirit is evident in the gifted expression of wisdom. This would be true no matter what the content of the wisdom would be. Many commentators believe that the content of the word of wisdom is the gospel. However, others include a more wide ranging array of content.

---

[19]For example: according to Bauer, *dia* can mean "by," and it can refer to the originator of an action (2000, 223-226); the NIV translates *kata* " as "by means of" rather than "according to;" and the preposition *en* can mean either "by" or "in."

Both Schatzmann and Gee maintain that the wisdom expressed is the gospel. They base this in part on what Paul says about wisdom in 1 Corinthians 1:17-2:16. Given the wisdom of the gospel, they put the emphasis upon the expression of wisdom. Schatzmann says, "Thus the charisma consists not in wisdom as the content of the utterance but in the actual utterance of wisdom which becomes a shared experience because it results in the upbuilding of the body" (1987, 35-36).

Similarly, Gee regards the word of wisdom as the inspired preaching of the gospel. He states: "The use of 'word of wisdom' is here [1 Corinthians 2:1-4, 10; Luke 10:21] shown to be particularly the preaching of Christ and the Cross and those things that God has prepared for them that love Him" (1980, 35). In his understanding of the gift, Gee edges toward the gift being content when he says that the inspired preaching sometimes has an element of revelation in it.

Many expositors do not limit the ability to express wisdom to the wisdom of the gospel. For example, many leaders are called upon to speak wisely to those whom they lead. Using their ability to communicate, they wisely guide people in practical and productive ways. In such cases, it is very difficult to divide between the ability to express wisdom and the wisdom that is being expressed. They tend to go together. So, now we will consider the other view of the word of wisdom.

Second, the other view is that the "word of wisdom" refers to the content of what is expressed. As indicated above, many commentators uphold the view that Paul is speaking about the wisdom of the gospel. Such wisdom could be classified as knowledge, but Paul identifies the knowledge as a body of wisdom.

It is not necessary, however, to limit the content of wisdom to the gospel. Palma acknowledges that some scholars define "word of wisdom" in terms of insight into the plan of salvation. Then, he states:

It is possible, however, to look in a completely different direction for the meaning of this gift. It may be significant that the Greek word *logos* ("word") in this gift and in the following gift is unaccompanied by the Greek article *ho* ('the'). Therefore, this gift would validly be understood as 'a wise saying' or 'speaking wisely'." (2001, 222)

As an example, Palma (2001, 223) points to the promise of Jesus to his disciples that, when they are brought before the authorities, the Holy Spirit will teach them what to say (Luke 12:11-12; cp. Matt. 10:20). Peter experienced a fulfillment of this promise when he was brought before the authorities in Jerusalem (Acts 4:8-12). In such cases, the Holy Spirit reveals the wisdom to the disciples. The content is supernaturally revealed.[20]

Sometimes the Holy Spirit guides us while at the same time using our own experience and understanding. This is done in the spirit of Proverbs 16:9 which says, "The mind of man plans his way, but the Lord directs His steps." Without the inspiration and guidance of the Spirit, there would be no manifestation of the Spirit, but the Spirit often inspires and includes our own understandings. For example, at the Jerusalem Council, the apostles and the brethren made a decision and said, "it seemed good to the Holy Spirit and to us" (Acts 15:28).

Moreover, it is possible that the Holy Spirit may reveal wisdom to an individual without intending for it to be expressed to others. The main thrust of the word of wisdom is on wisdom expressed, but expression perhaps is not always required. Palma writes:

> Both with regard to this gift [word of wisdom] and the gift of a word of knowledge, it may be that the gift is not always meant to be vocalized. The Holy Spirit may give a word to a person for guidance or insight into a specific situation which faces him or her, but the Spirit may intend that the word not be expressed to others. (2001, 223)

In my view, the word of wisdom can refer to both the expression of wisdom and to what is expressed. The two approaches are interrelated: one, a person cannot wisely express a message without having content that is at least acceptable and

---

[20]Harold Horton holds that the word of wisdom is totally supernatural. He says: "Supernatural Wisdom is not natural wisdom developed, augmented or intensified" (1962, 65). He gives this definition: "The Word of Wisdom is therefore the supernatural revelation, by the Spirit, of Divine Purpose; the supernatural declaration of the Mind and Will of God; the supernatural unfolding of His Plans and Purposes concerning things, places, people: individuals, communities, nations" (1962, 67).

perhaps considered wise; two, a person who has wise content may not have to express it wisely, but it will help if he does. There is no reason to exclude either aspect of this spiritual gift. Under either approach, the Spirit may reveal wisdom to the gifted person. We can include wisdom revealed to an individual but not vocalized. Also, wisdom may deal with the application of truth in given situations.

Word of Knowledge

In verse 8, Paul continues with this comment: "and to another (*allō*, ἄλλῳ) the word (*logos*, λόγος) of knowledge (*gnōseōs*, γνώσεως) according (*kata*, κατὰ) to the same (*auto*, αὐτὸ) Spirit." The term *word of knowledge* does not occur elsewhere in Paul's writings, but he does speak about "knowledge" as a gift in 13:2, 8-12; and 14:6. As in the case of the word of wisdom, we can think of the word of knowledge in terms of either content, the expression of content, or both.

First, one view of the word of knowledge is that it refers to the expression of knowledge. Some exegetes call the word of knowledge "inspired teaching." When viewed in this way, there seems to be little difference between this gift and the gift of teaching or being a teacher (Rom. 12:7; 1 Cor. 12:28). Applying this to teaching the gospel, Lenski states:

> "Knowledge" deals with the explanation, the unfolding, and the correlation of gospel facts, or we may call them doctrines. The "expression" or *logos* of knowledge is the ability to impart this personal knowledge to others. This gift is of great value to teachers, to apologists, and to many others in the church. (1946, 501)

Although the gospel is included, the communication of other information can be inspired by the Spirit as well. Sometimes that information has to do with the application of knowledge to a given course of action. Under this view, the focus can be on many kinds of knowledge, but the gift is the expression of knowledge. Schatzmann contends that "whatever the particular nature of the *gnosis* may have been, it was the inspired utterance of knowledge for the common good which Paul considered a gift of the Spirit" (1987, 35).

Second, many exegetes maintain that the "word of knowledge" refers to content rather than the ability to express content. They differ with regard to how the content of a word of knowledge is acquired, learned, interpreted, and used. Two approaches stand out.

One approach is that knowledge is acquired through the accumulation and interpretation of data, through study, instruction, and other normal means.[21] This may include knowledge of the Bible and its revealed truth. The Bible is the ultimate depository of our spiritual knowledge. The question is, "What does this have to do with the manifestation of the Spirit?" As we pursue truth, the Spirit guides us, inspires us, and illuminates our minds. The essential element in the gift is the inspiration of the Spirit, but the Spirit uses our efforts as well.

Another way of thinking is that the "word of knowledge" refers to the content that the Spirit reveals to us that could not otherwise be known. In other words, there is little difference between the word of knowledge and revelation. According to Fee, the word of knowledge is most likely "a 'Spirit utterance' of some revelatory kind" (1994, 167). An often cited case is God revealing to Peter that Ananias had lied about keeping some of the proceeds from the sale of his property (Acts 5:1-5).

Once again, I prefer to maintain the flexibility of the terms. The word of knowledge can include various categories of content. Knowledge learned under the inspiration of the Spirit, Biblical knowledge, and specific knowledge freshly revealed are all included. Moreover, the word of knowledge can include the expression of knowledge, the manner in which it is conveyed. As with all the manifestations of the Spirit, the action of the Spirit is essential to the spiritual gift. Without it, there is no spiritual gift.

---

[21]Hobart Grazier said to me: "We must distinguish carefully between *gnosis*, knowledge, which is the accumulation and the interpretation of data, on the one hand, and revelation, which is the disclosure of a matter, on the other hand. . . . *Gnosis* is clearly the interpretative ability one has after accumulating certain data. It is true that, when a matter is disclosed by revelation, the thing is known; but the process of obtaining that knowledge is that of revelation and not the accumulation of data."

Faith and Gifts of Healings (12:9)

In verse 9, Paul declares: "to another (*heterō*, ἑτέρῳ) faith by (*en*, ἐν) the same Spirit, and to another (*allō*, ἄλλῳ) gifts of healing by (*en*, ἐν) the one Spirit." The gifts are diverse, but the Spirit is the same. So the theme of diversity within unity is again carried forward in this verse.

The Greek words translated "another" in verses 7-11 are *allō* and *heterō*. As many expositors point out, *allō* can mean "another of the same kind," while *heterō* can mean "another of a different kind."[22] However, the two words can be used interchangeably as well. According to Barrett, in this case, Paul uses these terms synonymously (1971, 285).

Faith

Paul continues his list of gifts by saying, "To another (*heterō*, ἑτέρῳ) faith." To one is given the word of knowledge; to another, the word of wisdom; and now, to another, faith. The Spirit chooses whom He wishes for each gift. Whatever the precise meaning of *heterō*, it is reasonable to assume that He assesses our personalities, talents, and aptitudes as He chooses, but the choice is entirely in His hands.

First, the word *faith* is used in many different contexts with a variety of meanings. For example, the scientist has natural faith when he believes the universe is orderly and that man's intelligence may be trusted. Some scientists acknowledge that their presuppositions are based on faith. Speaking in terms of theology, every believer in Christ is justified by saving faith. In addition, faith as a fruit of the Spirit is akin to faithfulness. All believers should be faithful in following Christ.

---

[22]In a recorded conversation with me, Hobart Grazier commented on the meaning of *heteros* in verses 9-10 as follows: "In my mind, the word *heteros* in verse 9 indicates that the kind of individual who would receive the *charisma* of faith is different from the individual who would receive wisdom and knowledge. This can be pointed out further when we consider the matter of tongues in verse 10. There, the word *heteros* occurs again, indicating that the individual who would be given the gift of tongues and interpretation is a different kind of individual than the one who had received the five preceding gifts."

Second, when Paul speaks about the manifestation of faith, he no doubt has in mind the faith that can move mountains (1 Cor. 13:2). Most writers agree that he is not speaking about the saving faith which all believers have, but rather faith that produces unusual results. The objective of this faith is different from saving faith. Such faith is not given to everyone. It is a manifestation that is distributed to individuals as the Spirit desires.

The movement of mountains can include unusual events in the rather normal course of life. Hobart Grazier said to me, "The *charisma* of faith is that gracious bestowment by the Holy Spirit on an individual, enabling that individual to trust God in a supernatural way in desperate circumstances to bring about God's will for the edifying of the church."

Some of the results can be described as miraculous. Other results may not be as clearly miraculous, depending in part on how "miracle" is defined. The term *miracle* can be broadly or narrowly defined. Either way, the results happen because of the Spirit's impartation of faith to the believer who exercises the gift. The believer trusts God in a supernatural way to do His will for the benefit of the body of Christ.

Third, it is important to consider how faith is related to other gifts. One view is that the gift of faith was given to "another," not to everyone, and that this distinguishes it from other gifts. My approach is that each gift has its own distinctiveness, but in some ways may overlap with other gifts. This is true of faith as well as other gifts. As Fee says:

> Although it is listed separately, as given 'to another,' there is a sense in which this and the following two items [gifts of healing and effecting of miracles] belong together—and indeed, they would at times seem not quite possible to differentiate. "Faith that moved a mountain" could also rightly be called the working of a miracle. (1994, 168)

Dunn recognizes the relationship between faith and the gifts of healing. Then he broadens the role of faith with this comment, "We should, however, note that in Rom. 12.3 Paul thinks of such faith in connection with charismata in general" (1975, 211). Assuming this view, faith is involved to some extent in the exercise of all the gifts.[23] With some events and actions, faith stands out as the gift being exercised.

In summary, the gift of faith is faith to "move mountains." Some of the results may be miraculous, but outstanding things may take place that are not called miracles. The Spirit is at work in many different ways. The gift of faith overlaps with other gifts. To some extent, faith supports all other gifts. However, in many instances, it is faith itself that stands out.

Gifts of Healings

Paul states, "and to another (*allō,* ἄλλῳ) gifts of healing (*charismata iamatōn,* χαρίσματα ἰαμάτων) by (*en,* ἐν) the one Spirit." The verb "is given" is understood and is to be supplied. In addition, we note in passing that Paul reverts from *heterō* to *allō.*

First, as many have noted, the two nouns *charismata* and *iamatōn* are both in the plural. This is true both here and in verses 28 and 30. Translators normally use the plural "gifts" to translate *charismata* but do not always use the plural healings for *iamatōn.* Paul does not say why he uses the plural nouns, but expositors often discuss their proposed significance.

As many exegetes agree, the plural noun *charismata* may indicate that every healing is a special gift. The Spirit distributes each gift of healing through a ministering believer. The believer may be used frequently to deliver healing to the sick, but the source of the healing is the Spirit. Each gift is realized in the healing of the sick person. Concerning *iamatōn* (healings), Palma states: "The second plural possibly calls attention to different types, or categories, of healings that would involve restoration of the entire person—body, soul, and spirit" (2001, 220).[24] While we

---

[23]Harold Horton distinguishes between the gift of faith and the faith by which other gifts operate. He calls the latter "general faith" (1962, 139-140). Petts holds a similar view. He cites Romans 12:6 as an illustration of the faith that is needed for the operation of other gifts (2002, 189-190).

[24]With regard to the use of the plurals, Carson states: "This strongly suggests that there were *different* gifts of healings: not everyone was getting healed by one person, and perhaps certain persons with *one* of these gifts of healing could by the Lord's grace heal certain diseases or heal a variety of diseases but only at certain times" (1987, 39). However, Palma responds to Carson by

cannot be dogmatic on this point, we do know that people are healed of many types of diseases.

Second, does all this mean that only those who exercise the gifts of healings can pray effectively for the sick? According to Gee, the special gifts of healings are given only to certain individuals, but this does not "preclude all believers in the Lord Jesus Christ from laying hands upon the sick for their recovery (Mark 16:18), or all elders in the church from anointing with oil for healing (James 5:14). Such ministries are not dependent upon possessing any spiritual gift of healing" (1980, 52). No doubt this is true; but when people are healed, it may be difficult to say that a gift of healing was not exercised. The person healed will just be grateful for the healing.

Third, what sorts of healing does Paul mean? Obviously, we look at the gospel records and the Book of Acts for examples. Clearly, physical healing is included. However, we see no need to limit the term. God is equally able to heal mental illness and brokenness in every arena of life. As Palma notes, the Gospels and the Book of Acts bear ample testimony to the wide diversity of healings effected by Jesus and his followers (2001, 220). Concerning Jesus, Mark says, "And He healed many who were ill with various diseases, and cast out many demons; and He was not permitting the demons to speak, because they knew who he was" (1:32-34).

Fourth, Fee states, "The use of charisma itself in this case suggests that the 'manifestation' is given not to the person who is healed, but to the person God uses for the healing of another" (1994, 168-169). Others hold that the gifts of healings are given to the people healed. Obviously, the person healed receives the benefit of being healed, a definite gift in one sense of the word. But in the sense of the *charismata* of the Spirit, the gifts of healings are given to the people whom God is using. As Palma says, "This is the whole tenor of the passage in 1 Corinthians 12:8-10, which focuses on the individual whom God uses in the exercise of the gift" (2001, 220).

---

saying "it goes beyond the evidence to maintain . . . that different persons each had a disease or group of diseases that they could cure" (2001, 220).

Fifth, the gifts of healings are manifestations of the Spirit. As such, they are definite actions in given situations. Each time God uses someone to bring healing to a person in need, the Spirit gives that gift. When a person is often used to bring healing to others, it is in order to say that the person has gifts of healings. They are characterized by the way God uses them. A gifted person, however, can only exercise these gifts at the prompting of the Spirit. The actual healings occur when the Spirit acts through us. It is God, not man, who does the healing.

In summary, the Spirit gives gifts of healings to believers in the body of Christ. Each healing is a gift distributed through the ministering believer. Healing is available for a wide range of needs. Indeed, we do not need to exclude prayer for any need. When a believer is often used to bring healing to those in need, they become known for having the "gifts of healings." The "gifts of healings" are temporary in the sense of healing power being manifested at the time of healing, but permanent in that people are often used to bring healing.

Conclusion

In 1 Corinthians 12:7-11, Paul strongly emphasizes the role of the Holy Spirit, calling the gifts, ministries, and workings of the Spirit by the name of "manifestation." The emphasis is on actualized instances of the spiritual gifts being exercised. However, a person who frequently exercises a gift can be described as having a gift. The spiritual gifts of the Spirit make the Spirit known to us. When He is present, we are all edified.

When spiritual gifts are exercised, both the Spirit and man are involved. Unless the Spirit acts, there is no spiritual gift exercised. It is when the Spirit is manifested that people are awed by the presence of God. When He is powerfully known, our spirits are lifted. All this, however, does not preclude the Spirit using man and his talents in any way He chooses. He uses us as instruments in His hands to deliver well-being to the body of Christ. It is our high and holy honor to make ourselves available and to serve.

CHAPTER FOUR

DISTRIBUTING AS HE WILLS

Introduction

In this chapter, we will continue our study of the manifestation of the Spirit. As discussed in chapter three, the Holy Spirit manifests Himself through all the spiritual gifts. Because of this, the spiritual gifts can be called manifestations of the Spirit. Chapter three focused on 1 Corinthians 12:7-9 and the four listed manifestations. This chapter will deal with 12:10-11 and the five manifestations that are named. These five manifestations are the working of miracles, prophecy, distinguishing of spirits, various kinds of tongues, and interpretation of tongues. Paul's paragraph follows:

> [7]But to each one is given the manifestation of the Spirit for the common good. [8]For to one is given the word of wisdom through the Spirit, and to another the word of knowledge according to the same Spirit; [9]to another faith by the same Spirit, and to another gifts of healing by the one Spirit, [10]and to another the effecting of miracles, and to another prophecy, and to another the distinguishing of spirits, to another *various* kinds of tongues, and to another the interpretation of tongues. [11]But one and the same Spirit works all these things, distributing to each one individually just as He wills.

The more we study the gifts, the more we realize that each gift stands on its own and is interrelated with others. There is both uniqueness and similarity between the gifts. The unifying force underlying all the gifts is the Holy Spirit who is the source of the gifts and the One who distributes them to the believers as He wills. The Spirit powerfully manifests Himself as He distributes the gifts.

Five Spiritual Gifts (12:10)

In verse 10, Paul names five gifts. He writes: "and to another (*allō*, ἄλλῳ) the effecting of miracles, and to another (*allō*, ἄλλῳ) prophecy, and to another (*allō*, ἄλλῳ) the distinguishing of spirits, to another (*heterō*, ἑτέρῳ) *various* kinds of tongues, and to another (*allō*, ἄλλῳ) the interpretation of tongues."

As we study verse 10, three grammatical comments will be helpful: (1) the present tense verb "is given" from 12:8 should be supplied with each spiritual gift; (2) as with gifts of healings, Paul uses plural nouns with workings of miracleṡ, distinguishings of spirits, and kinds of tongues; (3) interpretation is a singular noun used with the plural tongues, and (4) Paul uses *allō* four times and *heterō* once.[25]

Workings of Miracles

The first manifestation of the Spirit listed in verse 10 is "workings of miracles." Using two plural nouns, Paul writes: "and to another the effecting or workings (*energēmata*, ἐνεργήματα) of miracles (*dunameōn*, δυνάμεων)."

We use the English word "miracle" with a variety of meanings. With its most "miraculous" connotation, it refers to a divine intervention into human history and affairs. God is seen to be the cause of the intervention. In addition, a "miracle" can be an outstanding event or accomplishment that might seem to be at least partially human. Sometimes the word is used of just an amazing product or achievement without reference to a divine source. While recognizing these general usages, our interest in this chapter is on the meaning of "miracle" as a working of the Spirit. We now will turn to that discussion.

First, let us take a look at the key words in "workings of miracles." The term "workings" is a translation of the Greek word *energēmata*. This word can be translated "workings," "effects," or "energizings." All these translations are ways of describing God at work. The emphasis is on the result, but the process can be included as well.

In 12:6, Paul uses the same plural noun to describe all the spiritual gifts. He says: "There are different kinds of working

---

[25]The Greek words translated "another" in verses 7-11 are *allō* and *heterō*. As many expositors point out, *allō* can mean "another of the same kind," while *heterō* can mean "another of a different kind." However, the two words can be used interchangeably as well. According to Barrett, in this case, Paul uses these terms synonymously (1971, 285).

(*energēmatōn,* ἐνεργηψάτων), but in all of them and in everyone it is the same God at work (*energōn,* ἐνεργῶν) (NIV). With the present participle *energōn,* the NASB[95] translation says that God is working "all things in all *persons.*" This definitely broadens the meaning of *energōn* to include all manner of God's workings.

Here, in verse 10, Paul applies the term *energēmata* to miracles. This term specifically applies to what Paul calls "workings of miracles." The Greek word *dunameōn* is a plural form of *dunamis,* (δυνάμις). According to Thayer, *dunamis* means *"strength, ability, power"* and *"the power of performing miracles"* (1962, 159).[26] In 12:28-29, the word "miracles" in the plural occurs by itself, but the meaning is unchanged. Paul's reference is to the gift of miracles.

The use of two plural nouns brings up some of the same discussions as "gifts of healings." The plural noun "workings" may signal that each miracle is a special "working" of the Spirit. Even so, it is possible for a gifted person to be characterized as one whom God uses to work miracles. The plural "miracles" could indicate that there are many types of miracles that could occur in the life of the church. The miracles may occur in many aspects of life.[27]

Second, what does "workings of miracles" include? Harold Horton presents a view that is representative of many. He recognizes the general usage of the term, but holds that the gift of miracles is very narrow. His definition is: "A miracle, therefore, is a supernatural intervention in the ordinary course of nature; a temporary suspension of the accustomed order; an interruption of the system of nature as we know it" (1934, 125). Similarly, Petts

---

[26]Bauer defines *dunamis* as follows: "1. *Power, might, strength, force* . . . 2. a*bility, capability* . . . 5. *deed of power, miracle, wonder* . . . 6. *power* as a personal supernatural spirit or angel." He lists 1 Corinthians 12:10, 28 under category 5 and Matthew 25:15 under category 2 (2000, 262-263). According to Fee, "The word translated 'miracles' is the ordinary one for 'power, and . . . it is especially associated in Jewish antiquity with the Spirit of God" (1994, 369).

[27]Arrington states: "Again we have two plural nouns—'the workings of miracles' (*energēmata dunameōn,* 1 Corinthians 12:10, 29). The plural forms emphasize variety in the manifestations of this spiritual gift" (2003, 330).

says, "Usually we use the word 'miracle' to refer to something that is beyond our understanding and which cannot be explained naturally. It is *super*-natural, *above* and *beyond* the natural" (2002, 170). In summary, the workings of miracles have to do with striking supernatural happenings.

Assuming this view, what can be included as miracles? Possible miracles include healings, the mighty works of Jesus, and wondrous signs and wonders of all kinds. Depending on the definition of a miracle, some of the other gifts might be considered miraculous.

Although some hold that physical healings are not included because they are separate "gifts of healings," another approach includes them along with other miracles. MacGorman writes:

> Besides healings, the mighty works of Jesus included exorcisms (Mark 5:1-10), resuscitations (Luke 7:11-17; 8:40-42, 49-56), and nature miracles, e.g., the stilling of the storm on the lake (Mark 4:35-41) and the feeding of the five thousand (Mark 6:34-44). (1974, 39)

With regard to healing, it appears to me that healings can be called miracles. This is just another way the gifts overlap. In addition Paul makes the connection between miracles and signs and wonders, He tells the Romans that his ministry was accomplished "in the power (*dunamei*, δυνάμει) of signs and wonders, in the power (*dunamei*) of the Spirit; so that from Jerusalem and round about as far as Illyricum I have fully preached the gospel of Christ" (Rom. 15:19).

Third, another view does not limit miracles to results that are as strikingly supernatural. For example, Gee comments as follows: "Possibly all the manifestations of the gift of the working of miracles were not of such outstanding character [as the miracles by Peter and Paul], but it seems pretty clear that in some form or other this gift was quite commonly distributed among the churches" (1980, 54).

One form of this gift may be to lead with great ability and wisdom. Many outstanding administrators exercise this gift. Jesus used the term *dunamis* (δυνάμις) in the sense of ability in Matthew 25:15. He told a parable about a man who gave his servants talents "each according to his own ability [*dunamin*, δύναμιν]." In an interview with me, Hobart Grazier made this point:

> The Greek noun *dunamis* and the verb *dunamai* cannot be limited to the spectacular. The word means simply ability. When a man's native ability is augmented by the Holy Spirit, enabling him to do beyond his natural abilities, the gift of miracles is in operation.

As an illustration, Grazier referred to the development of his college under the leadership of its president. We commonly talk about events of this kind being miraculous. Granted that this broadens the definition, it also keeps open the door for the infusion of the Spirit's power into the otherwise somewhat ordinary courses of events.

In summary, "workings of miracles" are manifestations of the Spirit. The Spirit works through us to produce supernatural results. Each working is a spiritual gift, but people who are used in this way become known by the gift. Thus, there are both temporary and permanent aspects to "workings of miracles." The miracles may include strikingly supernatural effects, such as signs and wonders, but also results that may be unusual but not as spectacular. Fortunately, we do not have to distinguish between the supernatural and the natural aspects of an event or happening.[28] It is much better just to give glory to God for all that He does.

Prophecy

The next manifestation of the Spirit that Paul mentions is prophecy. He declares: "and to another (*allō*, ἄλλῳ) prophecy (*prophēteia*, προφητεία)." Like the other spiritual gifts, prophecy is given to individuals to minister to others. Prophecy is a wonderful gift with many benefits for the body of Christ.

First, the term *prophecy* (*prophēteia*) is widely used in both the Old Testament and New Testament with a broad scope of meaning. The question before us is what Paul meant by the gift of prophecy. Paul uses prophecy and its cognate terms frequently in 1 Corinthians 12-14 and in Romans 12:6 and Ephesians 4:11. As we

---

[28]Keener posits that "Natural and supernatural factors (to use today's common language) can coexist" (2011, Vol. 1, 3).

review the chapters in 1 Corinthians we will consider each instance in context.

Paul uses the noun *prophecy* in 12:10; 13:2, 8; 14:6, 22. The verbs *prophesy* is used in 13:9; 14:1, 5; 24, 31, 39 and *prophesies* in 14:3, 4, 5. Finally, the noun *prophet* appears in 14:37, and *prophets* in 12:28, 29; and 14:32. Elsewhere, in Ephesians 4:11, he writes about prophets; and in Romans 12:6, about prophecy. Given the coverage, it is easy to see that this was a major emphasis in Paul's view of Spirit-inspired and empowered ministry.

Second, when you consider prophecy throughout the Bible, you find that a Spirit-inspired person may speak praise to God or inspired messages from God to man. The inspired messages to man may include prediction, but not always.

Paul does indicate at least some of what he had in mind. In 14:3, he gives some detail: "But one who prophesies speaks to men for edification and exhortation and consolation." However, the label *prophecy* should not be withheld from any Spirit-inspired content. The essential element in the gift of prophecy is the inspiration of the Spirit.

Third, the gift of prophecy, like other gifts, is interrelated with the other gifts. The word of wisdom and the word knowledge, in some cases, are similar to prophecy. We can say the same about inspired preaching. A common element that sometimes occurs in all these gifts is revelation. Although new revelation is not always required it may be an element in the prophecy. Also, old revelation can be pronounced in a prophetic way with special emphasis on application to a current situation. Moreover, when the gift of prophecy is exercised, all may learn and be exhorted (14:31).

Fourth, the question arises concerning who may have the spiritual gift of prophecy. Paul indicates that God has set prophets in the church (14:28), that not all are prophets (14:29), but he wishes that all could prophesy (14:5). Although he wishes that all could prophesy, not everyone does. His wish signals the high priority he put on intelligible messages through the gift of prophecy.

Fifth, when the Spirit inspires a prophetic utterance, it is a supernatural manifestation. However, human elements can enter in. As human beings, we are imperfect vessels; and sometimes our own feelings and understandings cloud the message. This is why

Paul provides for others (14:29) to judge prophetic utterances. Also, when the Spirit moves on us to prophesy, let us do it wholeheartedly. Each of us should speak, as Paul says in Romans 12:6, "according to the proportion of his faith."

To summarize, Paul highly values prophecy. Prophetic messages include edification, exhortation, and consolation. Although Paul mentions these three types of prophetic utterances, the gift is not limited to those. Prophetic messages can include praises and predictions as well. The essential element, as with all the gifts, is the enabling of the Holy Spirit. The Spirit gives this gift as He wills. It is our privilege to deliver the messages and praises inspired by the Spirit.

Distinguishings of Spirits

At this point, Paul writes: "to another (*allō*, ἄλλῳ) the distinguishing (*diakriseis*, διακρίσεις) of spirits (*pneumatōn*, πνευμάτων)." The verb "is given" from verse 8 should be supplied. This spiritual gift is very helpful to the body of Christ in working with other gifts such as prophecy, the word of wisdom, and the word of knowledge. The body of Christ is enabled the expressions of other gifts.

As with gifts of healings and workings of miracles, Paul uses two plural nouns for "distinguishings of spirits;" these nouns are *diakriseis* and *pneumatōn*. When determining what Paul means by these two words, 12:10 and 14:29 are often considered together. Some scholars hold that these two words impact each other, while others hold that the messages are different.[29]

First, Paul uses the noun *diakriseis* in 12:10. Bauer defines this noun as "*distinguishing, differentiation* of good and evil;" with regard to 12:10, he writes "*ability to distinguish between spirits*" (edits mine, 2000, 231). In 14:29, Paul uses the cognate verb *diakrinō* (διακρίνω) in its present imperative form (*diakrinetōsan*, διακρινέτωσαν). Here, Bauer defines the verb *diakrinō* as "*pass*

---

[29]Kistemaker writes, "Paul is saying that some believers have received the gift to distinguish spirits. In another passage (14:29), he asserts that prophetic utterances should be examined and evaluated. But these two passages do not convey the same message and should not be used to explain each other" (1993, 425). However, the key words do overlap to some degree.

56

judgment on" (2000, 231). The NASB[95] translation in 14:29 is "let the others pass judgment." Thayer includes both ideas in his definition of *diakrisis* (διάκρισις) as "*a distinguishing, discerning, judging*" (1962, 139).

Second, many scholars hold that *pneumatōn*, as used in this verse, refers to the many spirits.[30] The demonic spirits that influence false prophets and others are often posited. People may be influenced by human spirits as well. The influence of these spirits includes but is not limited to purported prophetic utterances. Any kind of speech may be involved. When a person exercises the gift of "distinguishing of spirits," he determines whether the source of inspiration is good or evil. This view harmonizes with 1 John 4:1 which says, "test the spirits to see whether they are from God."

Third, another view is that Paul's admonition in 14:29 guides us as to the nature of the gift in 12:10. Paul says, "Let two or three prophets speak, and let the others pass judgment." Similarly, in 1 Thessalonians 5:20-21, Paul says: "Do not despise prophetic utterances. But examine everything *carefully*; hold fast to that which is good." Using this guideline, the term "spirits" of prophets in 14:32 could be a reference to spiritual gifts, such as prophecy, that are to be judged. Advocates of this view point to 14:12 where Paul says that the Corinthians are "zealous of" *pneumatōn*, meaning spiritual gifts.

Dunn maintains that those who pass judgment in 14:29 act under the inspiration of the Spirit. Moreover, they evaluate both the source and the significance of the prophetic utterances (1975, 236). Evaluating the source brings back in the distinguishing of spirits in the sense of distinguishing between the Spirit of God and the human spirit. Those who have this gift will pass judgment on the significance and meaning of the messages. It is their role to weigh carefully what is said.

---

[30]With regard to "spirits" in verse 10, Arrington says: "Notice the plural *spirits*, which must have a broad meaning and likely includes three possible sources: the Holy Spirit (Romans 8:32), the human spirit (1 Thessalonians 5:23) and evil spirits (Mark 5:2-16). The gift of discernment is the God-given power to distinguish what comes from the Spirit of truth and what comes from other possible sources" (2003, 339-340).

Fourth, the above views often stress the connection between prophecy and distinguishing of spirits or passing judgment. When someone prophesies, others determine the source of the prophecy and evaluate its message. Palma believes the latter is the primary function of "distinguishing of spirits," but he expands the meaning of "spirits" with this comment:

> The close connection of this gift with the gift of prophecy, however, does not exhaust its meaning. It would apply where there is a need to discern in a given situation whether the influence is the Holy Spirit, a demonic spirit, or the human spirit. Biblical illustrations might include the accounts of Ananias and Sapphira (Acts 5:1-9), Elymas the sorcerer (13:6-12), and the demon-possessed slave girl (16:16-18). The functioning of this gift is particularly applicable in cases of physical or mental illness, to enable a believer to know whether or not the illness is demonically based—and whether to pray for the person's healing or to engage in a 'power encounter' with spiritual forces (2001, 232-233).

In summary, the primary emphasis of 12:10 is on distinguishing between spirits, while the main emphasis of 14:29 is passing judgment on prophecies. However, each verse cannot be limited; the former can include the latter, and the latter can include the former. When the spirits are distinguished, the content of what is said as well as the source is judged. When the prophecies are judged, the source is distinguished as well.

Perhaps this gift more than any other shows both human and divine elements in its operation. Without the presence and action of the Spirit, there would be no gift of distinguishing of spirits or of passing judgment on prophecies. However, God has chosen to work through His servants. Inspired by the Spirit, the ones who exercise this gift must make their judgments. They are making judgments, in some cases, on the utterances of others who exercise gifts. It is a divine-human process.

Various Kinds of Tongues

Next, Paul states: "to another (*heterō*, ἑτέρῳ) *various* kinds (*gene*, γένη) of tongues (*glōssōn*, γλωσσῶν)" Paul frequently uses the plural "tongues," but he also uses the singular "tongue."[31] For example, on the one hand he says "I thank God, I speak in tongues (plural) more than you all" (14:18). On the other hand he says, "Therefore let one who speaks in a tongue (singular) pray that he may interpret (14:13). The difference may simply be due to rhetorical variety, in which case the singular and the plural would say the same thing. It would be possible, of course, for a person to speak in not only one but more than one unknown tongue.

First, the most controversial of all the gifts is speaking in tongues, but we must remember that "God has appointed in the church . . . various kinds of tongues" (1 Cor. 12:28). In addition, according to 12:7 and 12:11, the Spirit is the giver of this gift. Here, in verse 10, the verb "is given" should be supplied. Therefore, we can expect that speaking in tongues will have a proper role and value in the church. In 1 Corinthians 12-14, Paul explains how that value should be realized. Then, in 14:39, Paul says, "do not forbid to speak in tongues."

Second, speaking in tongues is an exercise that involves both the Holy Spirit and man. The Holy Spirit inspires the tongues, and people express them in various forms that they have not learned and do not understand. The forms used may be human languages, the language of angels, or special purpose tongues or languages. By "special purpose," I mean expressions that are not humanly intelligible. Some might call this gibberish, but what the Spirit has inspired is not gibberish. Whatever is uttered, God understands, and it is intelligible to Him.

Third, the purpose of speaking in tongues in 1 Corinthians 12-14 is for the believer to communicate with God (14:2). Also, speaking in tongues serves as a prelude to interpretation of tongues. When a person speaks in tongues, he is edified (14:4). Thus, speaking in tongues is very suitable for private prayer. In the public service, the speaker may be edified, but someone has to interpret the tongues for the church to be edified. Assuming

---

[31]Paul uses the singular "tongue" in 14:2, 4, 13, 14, 19, 26, and 27. In all these cases, an individual speaks in a single tongue. He uses the plural with more than one potential speaker in 12:10 (twice), 28, 30; 13:8; 14:5, 22, 23, 39. He uses the plural with one speaker in 14:5, 6, and 18. In 13:1, he speaks about tongues of men and angels.

someone else does not interpret the tongues, the speaker is exhorted to pray that he may interpret (14:13).

Fourth, using two plural nouns, Paul writes about different "kinds of tongues." Here, he does not say what the "kinds of tongues" are but we can gather some information from the context of chapters 12-14. Paul includes speaking, praying, singing, and blessing in tongues (1 Cor. 14:13-16).

For example, Paul mentions "spiritual songs" both in Ephesians 5:18–19 and Colossians 3:16. No doubt, "spiritual songs" includes spontaneous songs in one's own language and previously prepared songs. However, singing in tongues should be included as well.

In 1 Corinthians 13:1, Paul declares, "If I speak with the tongues of men and of angels, but do not have love, I have become a noisy gong or a clanging cymbal." Some scholars hold that this phrase refers to two kinds of speaking in tongues: (1) speaking in a human tongue unknown to the speaker and (2) speaking in a heavenly language. Both kinds are inspired by the Holy Spirit. Alternatively, tongues of men are said to be inspired speech in human languages known to the speakers. As I understand the passage, tongues of men can include inspired speech both in languages understood and not understood by the speaker. The tongues of angels are heavenly languages not understood by the speaker.

God has appointed speaking in tongues in the church. Although this gift is sometimes controversial, this does not diminish its role in the church. Paul is simply giving guidelines, especially in 1 Corinthians 14, for the proper use of the gift. Speaking in tongues is both a divine and a human activity. It is a spiritual gift because of the inspiration of the Holy Spirit. The purpose of tongues is to communicate with God and to prepare the way in the church for the gift of interpretation. There are various kinds of tongues, all of which are marked by the fact that the speaker speaks in a language He does understand. When the tongues are interpreted, the entire body of Christ is blessed.

Interpretation of Tongues

The companion gift to speaking in tongues is the "interpretation of tongues." Paul declares: "and to another the interpretation (hermēneia, ἑρμηνεία) of tongues." As with the other gifts, the verb "is given" should be supplied. The Holy Spirit distributes this manifestation to the church. Paul speaks about "an interpretation" in 14:26; an "interpreter" in 14:28; and some form of the cognate verb in 12:30; 14:5; 14:13; and 14:27. We will study these verses as we come to them in this series. Our attention now will be focused what is said in 12:10.

First, what does "interpretation mean?" In some cases, the interpretation may be a translation. No doubt it was on the Day of Pentecost. The Greek word *hermēneia* is often used to mean "translation." However, this word also can mean "interpretation." Concerning speaking in tongues, the right English word in some cases might be "translation;" but in other cases, it would be "interpretation."

Even translation often involves interpretation. Interpretation admits a much more flexible rendition of what was said originally. Experientially, this is the most likely approach to giving meaning to tongues. Even the word "explanation" may well be appropriate in some cases.

Second, is the interpretation addressed to God or to the people? The tongues are addressed to God, because he alone understands (14:2). The content may be for God or, when interpreted, for the people. Even if the tongues are addressed to God because of content, the interpretation is for the people. God does not need an interpretation. In any case, the interpretation can be praise to God or a message to man. In any case, the interpretation is for the people.

Third, assuming an interpretation is a message to man, how is this gift related to other spiritual gifts? The interpretation does not need another name; it is, for sure, an interpretation or translation. However, what Paul says in 14:6 suggests other possibilities. Paul says, "But now, brethren, if I come to you speaking in tongues, what will I profit you unless I speak to you either by way of revelation or of knowledge or of prophecy or of teaching?"

The other possibilities show a relationship of interpretation of tongues to other spiritual gifts. Both knowledge and prophecy are listed in 12:8-10. Revelation is not, but revelation is very much a part of several gifts, such as the word of knowledge, the word of wisdom, and prophecy. Teachers are mentioned as gifts in 14:29, Romans 12:7, and Ephesians 4:11.

As an alternative to the conjunction "unless," we could supply "instead of" or "in addition to" speaking in tongues. If we supply "instead of," speaking in tongues is eliminated and provides no profit. If we supply "in addition to," the tongues are still unintelligible and therefore are unprofitable to the body of Christ. The most likely meaning is "unless by way of interpretation, I speak revelation, knowledge, prophecy, or teaching." This gives meaning to the tongues and conveys a message through related manifestations of the Spirit.

Fourth, many times we hear people speak in tongues and an interpretation is given. Because both the speaker in tongues and the interpreter are inspired by the Spirit, we might ask, "Why the two stage approach?" Christenson says:

> In a public meeting, the gift of tongues is designed to operate with the sister gift of interpretation. The pattern is exactly the same as with the other gifts which we have mentioned. A person receives an utterance, and manifests it for the good of the body. The tongue plus the interpretation will be edifying for the church, just as a well-chosen prayer in English edifies the whole congregation. And it has added power. It lends a distinct note of the supernatural to the meeting. (1968, 122)

When the sister gifts of speaking in tongues and interpretation of tongues are exercised in the church, both of these gifts bless the people. The person whom the Spirit inspires to speak in tongues is himself edified (14:4). While he communicates with God in this manner, the audience is being prepared for an interpretation that the people will understand. A sense of the divine presence is felt by all who worship God. The members of the congregation can rejoice that the speaker in tongues has been edified and then share in the edification because they understand the interpretation.

Just As He Wills (12:11)

Paul begins the paragraph in verses 7-11 with these comments: "But to each one is given the manifestation of the Spirit for the common good." Then, in verse 11, he ends the paragraph with similar thoughts: "But one and the same Spirit works (*energei*, ἐνεργεῖ) all these things, distributing (*diairoun*, διαιροῦν) to each one individually (*idia*, ἰδίᾳ) just as He wills."

First, in 12:6, Paul names God (the Father) as the source of the workings. Here Paul reiterates that the Spirit works all these things. We do not need to draw fine distinctions between the roles of the members of the Trinity. In 12:6, Paul calls the spiritual things by the name "workings," using the same verb as in verse 11. The Spirit manifests Himself (verse 7) through all the gifts; and all the gifts are manifestations of the Spirit. There would be no spiritual gifts without the Spirit. There are many, diverse gifts, but the source is one, the Spirit of God.

Second, the Spirit distributes the gifts, but there is a human side to this as well. The Spirit works all these things while "distributing" (διαιροῦν, present participle) the gifts to each one individually (*idia*), just as He wills. The word "individually" is a translation of the Greek word *idia*. According to Thayer, *idia* refers to things "pertaining to one's self" and to "what is one's own as opposed to belonging to another" (1962, 296-297).[32] Our overall development is under the guidance of the Lord who uses us where we best fit.

Conclusion

In 1 Corinthians 12:7-11, Paul deals with the manifestation of the Spirit. He manifests himself through the gifts of the Spirit. As illustrations, he lists nine spiritual gifts that are given to believers. The Spirit distributes each of these gifts personally to everyone as He wills. Because the gifts are manifestations of the Spirit, the inspiration, enabling, and presence of the Spirit is absolutely essential.

Any church where these gifts are practiced will be alive with the presence and power of God. When good things are happening, when needs are being met, and when the presence of God is

---

[32]Based on the meaning of *idia*, Hobart Grazier recorded these comments:

"The Holy Spirit is said to give to each individual that charisma which is peculiarly adapted to the individual. I personally believe that the Holy Spirit gives these gifts of the Spirit to individuals on the basis of two considerations: first, that of the temperament and character of the individual receiving a gift, and second, on the basis of the need that exists in the church. We might mention a third consideration, and that is the ministry of the individual. It is much more likely that a man who is in a position of leading or superintending large sections of the church would be apt to receive the gift of wisdom as an enablement."

strongly felt, people are eager to attend church. Much depends, of course, upon hearts being prepared to acknowledge and receive the manifestations of the Spirit. When we are ready, He will make Himself known to us.

In our previous chapter, we discussed the word of wisdom, the word of knowledge, faith, and gifts of healings. Our topics in this chapter have been effecting of miracles, prophecy, distinguishings of spirits, various kinds of tongues, and interpretation of tongues. With all of these spiritual gifts, we readily recognize the absolutely essential role of the Spirit. With the Spirit's presence, we are an empowered body of believers that can do anything under His guidance. Without Him, we are powerless and fruitless.

The Spirit, however, takes into account our human aptitudes, abilities, and commitments. He uses what He chooses to use. Thus, there is a human factor as well in the operation of the spiritual gifts. The human factors are involved by God's design. It is a part of His plan. We must remember that even our human abilities and talents have been given to us and must be used in harmony with God's will. Ultimately, it is the divine element, the sense of God's presence that inspires and blesses the members of the body of Christ.

CHAPTER FIVE

THE BODY OF CHRIST

Introduction

After listing nine spiritual gifts that manifest the Spirit, Paul draws on an analogy to illustrate the desired unity and diversity among those who believe in Christ. In 1 Corinthians 12:12-27, Paul compares the body of Christ to a physical body which is one, yet has many parts. In verse 13, he presents the role of the Spirit who unites us with Christ and engenders both our functional unity and diversity. In verses 12-13, Paul writes:

> [12]For even as the body is one and *yet* has many members, and all the members of the body, though they are many, are one body, so also is Christ. [13]For by one Spirit we were all baptized into one body, whether Jews or Greeks, whether slaves or free, and we were all made to drink of one Spirit.

Verse 13 is subject to many interpretations. Just what does Paul mean? Does he refer to becoming a member of the body of Christ or to the body's functional unity and diversity? Does he mean baptized "in" or "by" the Spirit? Does he intend to say "into" or "unto" the body? Is he referring to conversion, enablement, or both? What does he mean by "made to drink of one Spirit"? Are there ongoing dimensions to "were all baptized" and "made to drink?" We must study this verse in the context of the entire chapter, with special emphasis on verses 12-27.

1 Corinthians 12:1-31

Paul was writing about spirituality and spiritual gifts. He was concerned that the members of the church would exercise their diverse gifts in unity. Their attitudes toward each other were extremely important. The source of both unity and diversity is the Holy Spirit. Verse 13 explains the basis for diversity and unity. That explanation brings into focus how believers become members of the body of Christ.

First, in verses 1-3, Paul introduces "spiritual things" as his subject. He reminds the believers that, in their former lives, they were led away to dumb idols. Then he declares that no one speaking by the Spirit of God says, "Jesus is accursed." Moreover, no one says, "Jesus is Lord," except by the Holy Spirit. This is not primarily a passage showing how conversion takes place, but faith in Christ is presupposed. Unless a person has experienced conversion, he cannot deliver speech inspired by the Holy Spirit. The exaltation of Jesus is the ultimate criterion of the validity of inspired speech. Christ is central to all that we do.

Second, Paul makes the point in verses 4-6 that there are differences of gifts, differences of ministries, and differences of workings; but respectively, there is one Spirit, one Lord, and one God. The three Persons of the Trinity are all involved in the giving and operating of the spiritual gifts. Each of the gifts, ministries, and workings can be attributed to all three Persons. For example, in verse 7, all of them are attributed to the Spirit. We do not need to distinguish sharply between the roles of the Persons of the Trinity.

Third, in verses 7-11, Paul stresses that the Holy Spirit manifests Himself through the spiritual gifts. The gifts, in turn, may be called manifestations of the Spirit. The Holy Spirit distributes the gifts of the Spirit "to each one individually just as He wills." No doubt the Spirit takes into account the personalities, aptitudes, and commitments of the people involved, but it is He who distributes the gifts. Paul has listed nine diverse gifts as illustrations. The work of the Spirit is the basis for both diversity and unity.

Fourth, in verses 12-27, Paul uses the human body as an analogy to teach truths about the body of Christ. His concern in this passage is that the diverse members of the one body of Christ function together in unity. These verses stress membership in the body of Christ and the functional unity and diversity of the members. When Paul speaks about the members of the body, he has in mind the fact that the Spirit has given gifts to them.

Paul's comments have much to do with attitudes and values. He calls upon the believers to place the right value on the gifts and to fully honor each other. In a way, Paul is saying that the gifts of the Spirit should operate within the framework of the fruit of the Spirit. Moreover, the principles that Paul lays down apply not only to the gifts but also broadly to all aspects of our lives and our journey with Christ.[33] We must exist and function as diverse members of the one body of Christ.

One, verses 12-13 constitute the first paragraph. Paul states his thesis in verse 12 with two complementary statements: (1) "the body is one, yet has many members;" and (2) "all the members of the body, though they are many, are one body." Both these statements include the unity and diversity of the body; but the first one stresses diversity, while the second emphasizes unity. These assertions, respectively, introduce Paul's comments on diversity in verses 14-19 and on unity in verses 20-26. Verse 27 recalls verse 12 and summarizes what he has said. Verses 12-27 provide the context for verse 13 which I will discuss below.

With the statement "so also is Christ," Paul compares the body of Christ to a physical body. We could have expected "so also is the body of Christ," but Paul simply says "Christ."[34] The title "Christ" stands by metonymy for "the body of Christ." When we are united with Christ, we become a member of His body. The nature of the body of Christ is much discussed by theologians, but it appears that the main point is that every believer is a member and should function as one.[35]

Two, verses 14-19 are devoted to the diversity of the members of the body. In verse 14, Paul says, "For the body is not one member, but many." The emphasis of this statement is upon the

---

[33]Fee advises that "This is one section of the letter that is ready-made for present-day application. The caution that must be raised, however, is that one not neglect altogether Paul's own concerns in favor of those kinds of easy, independent ones that are so quickly available from such rich metaphors" (1987, 616). True enough, but the principles can be broadly applied.

[34]As Taylor observes: "It is commonly noted that 'Christ' in 12:12 is short-hand for the church as the body of Christ in light of the parallelism with 12:27, 'You are the body of Christ.' Since this is the case, Christ may be said to be a body with many members. Already Paul has argued in 6:15 that believers are 'members of Christ'" (2014, 296).

[35]According to Palma: "Volumes have been written on the meaning and significance of the Church being the body of Christ, but it may be best to understand the phrase in a metaphorical, rather than a mystical, sense. More than anything else, it illustrates how the many members of the Church should relate to one another, and ultimately to the Lord" (2001, 190-191).

many. The members of the body are many and are diverse. Paul
states:

> [14]For the body is not one member, but many. [15]If the foot says,
> "Because I am not a hand, I am not *a part* of the body," it is not
> for this reason any the less *a part* of the body. [16]And if the ear
> says, "Because I am not an eye, I am not *a part* of the body," it
> is not for this reason any the less *a part* of the body. [17]If the
> whole body were an eye, where would the hearing be? If the
> whole were hearing, where would the sense of smell be? [18]But
> now God has placed the members, each one of them, in the
> body, just as He desired. [19]If they were all one member, where
> would the body be?

With several illustrations (verses 15-17), Paul shows the
importance of each of the many parts of the body. All of the body
parts belong to the body. Just because the foot is not a hand, or the
ear is not an eye, this does not mean they do not belong (verses 15-
16). The foot and the ear may feel inferior, but they still belong.[36]
Moreover, if the body were only one part, it could not function
properly (verse 17).

All this applies to the members of the body of Christ. All the
members, with their spiritual gifts and other qualities, belong to the
body. With regard to the gifts, both the member with a gift of
prophecy and one with the gift of teaching belong to the body of
Christ.[37] Apart from the gifts, both the Jews and the Gentiles who
have faith in Christ belong to the body. God has placed (verse 18)
each member in the body to function "just as he desired." Without
diverse members (verse 19), there would be no body.

---

[36]Carson posits that "In verses 14-19, he [Paul] tells the outsiders [people who
feel they do not belong to the body] that, precisely because of the diversity of
gifts God has distributed in the church, the member that seems inferior cannot
reasonably say it does not belong, or threaten to leave" (1987, 48).

[37]Kistemaker submits this comment: "Paul's implied application for the
Corinthians is to eradicate all envy with respect to a particular spiritual gift
that a member has not received. This one church member ought not to feel
inadequate because of a lack of some spiritual gift. And no one should
separate himself from the body of believers out of envy or spite" (1993, 432).

Three, verses 20-26 stress the unity of the members of the body. In verse 20, Paul says, "But now there are many members, but one body." Because of its unity, no part of the body should say (verse 21) to another part, "I have no need of you." Some members may feel superior, but they have no right to exclude anyone.[38] All of the members of the body belong to the body. Paul writes:

> [20]But now there are many members, but one body. [21]And the eye cannot say to the hand, "I have no need of you"; or again the head to the feet, "I have no need of you." [22]On the contrary, it is much truer that the members of the body which seem to be weaker are necessary; [23]and those *members* of the body which we deem less honorable, on these we bestow more abundant honor, and our less presentable members become much more presentable, [24]whereas our more presentable members have no need *of it*. But God has *so* composed the body, giving more abundant honor to that *member* which lacked, [25]so that there may be no division in the body, but *that* the members may have the same care for one another. [26]And if one member suffers, all the members suffer with it; if *one* member is honored, all the members rejoice with it.

Now Paul underscores the unity of the body. He applies his point in several ways. Even the weaker parts (verse 22) are necessary; we should bestow honor (verse 23-24) on the less presentable parts (*aschēmona*, ἀσχήμονα); and the parts that are more presentable (*euschēmona*, εὐσχήμονα) have no need of the honor.[39] God has composed the body to give abundant honor to those who lacked so that there would be no division in the body. Members should care for one another, suffer as one, and be

---

[38]Carson states: "Paul now turns to the elitists, themselves (vv. 20-26). No longer in this extended metaphor do the members speak to themselves from a position of inferiority, as in the preceding verses; here the members speak to those they judge inferior, in wretched, condescending tones. Few barbs hurt more than a blistering 'I don't need you!'" (1987, 48).

[39]With regard to 12:23-24, Bauer defines *aschēmona* (plural) as "*the unpresentable, i.e. private, parts*" (2000, 147) and *euschēmona* as "*the presentable parts*" (2000, 414). Garland says, "Paul refers euphemistically to the genitalia" (2003, 596).

honored and rejoice as one. The members are interdependent; all belong to the same body, and they should care for each other.

Paul does not say which spiritual gifts or people are less presentable, but the principle applies in many ways. Someone with the gift of "faith" should not say to someone with the gift of "helps," "I don't need you." Beyond the gifts of the Spirit, many are the examples that deal with social status. As an example, the wealthy member cannot say to the poor member, "I don't need you." Or, the highly educated member cannot say to one less educated, "I don't need you." God has placed us all in the body of Christ, and we are all needed.

Feelings of superiority can invade all of our lives. It might be useful just to review all the gifts that Paul lists and ask whether or not we appropriately value them. We may have a tendency to say we don't need some of the gifts, but we should not diminish any gift. Rather, we should give greater honor to those that seem unimportant to us. All the gifts that the Spirit distributes are needed. The people who have these gifts belong to the body of Christ.

Four, in verse 27, Paul summarizes the unity and diversity of the body in these words, "Now you are Christ's body, and individually members of it." All the members of the body are reassured that they belong. This verse recalls verse 12 which says, "For even as the body is one and *yet* has many members, and all the members of the body, though they are many, are one body, so also is Christ." Verse 27 takes us back to verse 12 and summarizes what Paul has just said, but it is also transitional and introduces his next paragraph.

Fifth, in verses 28-31, Paul applies the body analogy to the church. He declares (verse 28) that God has appointed the spiritual gifts in the church. The role of the Spirit in distributing the gifts among the members stands out in verses 7-11. All the gifts are attributed to the One Triune God. In verses 29-30, the diversity of the spiritual gifts is emphasized. Everyone does not have the same ministry. Then, in verse 31, Paul urges the Corinthians to "earnestly desire the greater gifts."

1 Corinthians 12:13

The controversial verse 13 is set in the context of 12:12-27. Paul compares the body of Christ to a physical body. His subject is how the diverse members function in unity, but to explain this, he has to deal also with how believers become members of the one body of Christ.[40] Therefore, Paul refers to both the beginning of our relationship with the Spirit as well His ongoing impact. Paul writes:

[13]For by (*en,* ἐν) one Spirit we were all baptized (*ebaptisthēmen,* ἐβαπτίσθημεν) into (*eis,* εἰς) one body, whether Jews or Greeks, whether slaves or free, and we were all made to drink (*epotisthēmen,* ἐποτίσθημεν) of one Spirit.

As I understand verse 13, Paul maintains that the role of the Spirit is absolutely essential both in becoming members of the body of Christ and in its effective functioning. Paul is eager for the diverse members of the body to work together in unity. He wants them to function as one body with many members. To help the believers reach this goal, he recalls that the presence and work of the Spirit was essential in their becoming members. That presence and work is just as essential in their ongoing diverse and united activity. Verse 13, therefore, has to do with both membership in the body of Christ and its ongoing functioning.

Verse 13 fits very well with the larger context of Paul's theology of the Spirit. Two points of that theology provide a strong connection with this verse.

---

[40]Fee maintains that: "Paul's concern in this sentence, therefore, is not to delineate how an individual becomes a believer (the question most people come to the text with), but to explain how the many of them, diverse as they are, are in fact one body. The answer: The Spirit, whom all alike have received" (1996, 196). As I understand his view, when he says "are in fact one body," he means one body functioning in unity. With this functionally united body in mind, he makes this assertion: "Here the Spirit is either the element into which they have all been baptized (as I think), or the agent by which they have been baptized to become one body" (1996, 197). Nevertheless, with regard to the metaphors in 13a (baptized) and 13c (made to drink), Fee writes "Most likely, therefore, Paul is referring to their common experience of conversion, and he does so in terms of its most crucial ingredient, the receiving of the Spirit" (1996, 197-198).

One, in Paul's thinking, there is a twofold gift to faith in salvation. The Spirit unites the believer with Christ, and the believer receives the Spirit. These two aspects of salvation occur at the same time. At the beginning, one does not occur before the other. The original twofold gift to faith establishes the position of the believer as a son of God.

Two, the believer's experience of Christ and the Spirit immediately begins to take place and continues throughout life. The Spirit enables us to function in both unity and diversity. Such enablement presupposes the presence and work of the Spirit in our becoming sons of God. What we have received, we can receive again and also continuously receive. Our experience is not only in the past tense, but also in the present and the future tenses. Also, our relationship with the Spirit includes special events as well as continual interaction.

As I discuss 12:13, I will refer to the clause in verse 13a, "For by one Spirit we were all baptized into one body," to the parenthetic phrase in verse 13b, "whether Jews or Greeks, whether slaves or free;" and to the clause in verse 13c, "and we were all made to drink of one Spirit." I will discuss them in the order that Paul presents them.

Verse 13a

Most, but not all, of the controversy arises over the 13a clause. Some of the language in this clause is ambiguous. Paul did not fully clarify the ambiguous aspects, so it may be that the lack of precision was intentional. There are many interpretations, and very often they each have different versions. Because many views are possible, many expositors rely to some extent on their view of the larger context of Paul's theology of conversion and service.

One issue has to do with baptism in water. Some expositors tie the clause "we were all baptized" to baptism in water. Through baptism in water and "in" or "by" the Spirit, people are united with Christ and indwelt by the Spirit.[41] In my view, this passage does

---

[41]This is a very large subject with a long list of scholars on each side. On the one hand, Beasley-Murray argues that Paul refers to baptism in water. But he says that "There is nothing automatic about this association of baptism and the Spirit" (1962, 169-170). Fee, on the other hand, posits that "In any case, one is

not refer to water baptism, but this does not minimize the importance of the presence of the Spirit at water baptism. As people are baptized in water, they should expect the Spirit to be powerfully present. While my approach is not sacramental, I do hold that the Spirit should be powerfully present at water baptism.

Another issue is the meaning of two Greek prepositions: *en* (ἐν) and *eis* (εἰς). Wallace calls *en* "the workhorse of prepositions in the NT" and lists several translations, including *in, by, with, within, with reference to*, and others (1996, 372). The two translations most often used with verse 13a are "in" and "by."[42] As a result, we have the translation "by one Spirit we were all baptized" with *en* being used in an instrumental sense, indicating the means or agent by which the action occurs. Another result is to use *en* in a locative sense, indicating the location or element in which the action occurs. This usage yields the translation "in one Spirit we were all baptized."

Similarly, as Wallace points out, the preposition *eis* can be translated in various ways (1996, 369). Among others, he lists *into, for, in order to, so that*, and *with reference to*. As with the preposition *en*, there are two main English prepositions used with verse 13a: "into" and "unto." The translations that result are respectively "into one body" and "unto one body." The preposition "into" is regarded as locative, while "unto" suggests purpose.

Some scholars feel constrained to choose between English prepositions, but others do not.[43] In my view, we should maintain the flexibility of the Greek prepositions. Given their flexibility,

---

hard pressed to find an equation between baptism and the reception of the Spirit in Paul's letters" (1987, 604).

[42]With regard to England and the European continent, Beasley-Murray says that English translation and exposition tends to say "by one Spirit" while Continental tradition seems to favor "in one Spirit" (1962, 167). The preposition *with* is often used as well. According to Palma, the preposition "'in' is preferable to 'with' because it properly conveys the imagery of baptism. The Greek verb *baptizō* means to immerse or to dip" (2001, 101).

[43]Kistemaker and Beasley-Murray do not feel that it is necessary to choose. Kistemaker says: "Believers are immersed by/in one Spirit into one body (12:13)" (1993, 295). Beasley-Murray explains: "Basically, the meaning is not greatly affected, since on the one interpretation the Spirit is viewed as the agent of baptism to membership in the Body and on the other He is the element in which one is baptized so as to be in the Body" (1962, 167).

several English prepositions can be used. For example, the two clauses (13a and 13c) can be related as "in/into," "in/unto," "by/into" and "by/unto." Based on these prepositions, several views of verse 13 are grammatically possible.

Membership in the Body

Many scholars hold that verse 13a refers to our becoming members of the body of Christ through the presence and work of the Spirit. As stated earlier, we become members of the body when we are united with Christ and indwelt by the Spirit. The question is: What does verse 13a say about the role of the Holy Spirit in our becoming members of the body of Christ? To answer this question, we will consider the role of the Spirit as an agent and as an element.

First, with the above prepositions in mind, let's think of the Spirit as an agent. We can read verse 13a as "*By* one Spirit we were all baptized *into* one body." Some would say "unto" with the purpose of being in a united body in mind. With this reading, the Spirit is the agent who baptizes all of us into Christ or the body of Christ. As I stated elsewhere:

> One approach to this verse supplies Christ as the element, yielding the meaning that we were baptized into Christ so as to become one body. Without supplying Christ, the body becomes the element. We were baptized into the body, but the body of Christ does not exist without Christ. Either way, we are united with Christ and become members of the body. (2009, 309-310)

In 1 Corinthians 12:3 and 9, with regard to the Holy Spirit, the preposition "by" is normally used to translate *en*. Many expositors refer to these verses in support of the preposition *en* being instrumental in 12:13. Also, the preposition "by" harmonizes very well with 1 Corinthians 6:11, "And such were some of you; but you were washed, but you were sanctified, but you were justified in the name of the Lord Jesus Christ, and in (*en*, ἐν) the Spirit of our God." (NASB[95]) Although the NASB[95] says "in," the NIV recognizes the strong instrumental sense with the use of "by" in its translation.[44]

---

[44]Another relevant verse is 1 Corinthians 10:2. Here, a construction similar to the clause in 13a is used by Paul who says, "and all were baptized into *(eis)*

74

Second, again with the prepositions in view, we can consider the Holy Spirit to be the element in which we are baptized. Under this option, we can read verse 13a as "For *in* one Spirit we were all baptized *into* one body." In other words, we are baptized in one Spirit into one united body for service. Also, we could say "*unto* one body." Using "unto," we are baptized "so as to become one body." The end result is about the same. Supporters of "in one Spirit" point that the other six references to baptism *en* the Spirit often use "in" as the translation.[45]

Using "in" as the translation, the Spirit is the element into which we are baptized, and Jesus is normally supplied as the baptizer. With this translation, the *work* of the Spirit as the agent of entry into the body of Christ is not explicitly mentioned. Because of this, we have to base what He does on other Scriptures. To say this another way, just as Jesus is supplied as the baptizer, the Spirit is supplied as the agent of entry into the body of Christ.

Functional Unity and Diversity

Another group of interpreters believes that Paul, in verse 13a, is referring to the functional unity and diversity of the body of Christ. That functional unity leads to working together effectively and powerfully. In support of this view, they note that all of 1 Corinthians 12 has to do primarily with the gifts and functions of the body of Christ. People with diverse gifts should work together effectively and in unity.

First, with regard to the functional unity and diversity of the body, as with membership in the body, we might think of the Holy Spirit as an agent or an element. If we were to view the Spirit as an agent, then we would read verse 13a as: "For *by* one Spirit we were

---

Moses in *(en)* the cloud and in *(en)* the sea." Concerning this Scripture, I wrote elsewhere:

When the Israelites cross the Red Sea, they became a part of the Moses movement. One could say that they were baptized either by or in the cloud and the sea respectively into Moses or unto Moses. The end result is about the same, but by the cloud and the sea is probably preferable (2012, 95-96).

[45]The references in the Gospels and Acts are: Matthew 3:11; Mark 1:8; Luke 3:16; Acts 1:5; and Acts 11:16. The NASB[95] translation in all these cases uses the preposition "with." Many translations use "in."

all baptized *into* or *unto* one body" for the *purpose* of helping us serve in unity with diverse members. It is just as feasible to say this as it is to say that He baptizes us into the body for membership.

Second, others aver that verse 13a refers to baptism *in* the Spirit, with the Spirit being the element into which the believer is baptized. According to them, the verse says, "For *in* one Spirit we were all baptized *unto* or *into* one body." Under this view, the clause says that all of the believers were baptized by Jesus in the Spirit for the purpose of enabling them to become diverse and harmonious servants in the body of Christ.

Third, whether the Spirit is viewed as an agent or an element, some authors contend that "were baptized" refers to the functioning of the body of Christ but not to membership in it, while others maintain that both membership and functioning are included.[46] In the view of the former authors, believers have become members of the body of Christ already, and membership is presupposed. The latter group says that the primary application is to functional unity and diversity, but that the Spirit's role in uniting people with Christ and His body is prerequisite to the harmony of diverse gifts and members.

In summary, the message of verse 13a is that the presence and work of the Spirit is essential in believers becoming members of the body of Christ and in the united functioning of the diverse members. With regard to both purposes, the Spirit can, at the same time, both be present and do His work. In other words, He can simultaneously be an agent and an element. As a result of the Spirit's presence and work, these purposes are achieved.

The Greek prepositions are very flexible and accommodate both the presence and work of the Spirit without further definition. When translated into English, the preposition *en* (ἐν) can mean

---

[46]The comments of Horton and Baker will illustrate this difference. See Fee in note 40 for a view that includes both unity of function and conversion as a basis for it. Against this approach, Baker writes: "The verse, therefore, means that baptism in the one Holy Spirit is for the one body of Christ; it has the one body in view, and it is for those who are already members of Christ to enable them to function effectively, and enrich and benefit the fellowship and life of His body, the Church (*cf.* Luke 11:13, Gal. 4:6)" (1967, 24). Compare Harold Horton (1962, 40).

either "by" or "in" and *eis* (εἰς) can mean either "into" or "unto." In English, various combinations of the prepositions are grammatically possible. Thus, we must rely even more on the context for the meaning of the clause.

As I prefer, for example, we can take the following approach: When the Spirit is viewed as an agent, those who come to faith are baptized *by* the Spirit "into" the body of Christ and "into" the functional unity of that body. When the Spirit is viewed as an element, the believers are baptized "in" the Spirit "unto" one body so as to achieve the same purposes. Thus, whether the Spirit is viewed as an agent or an element, the believers become members of the body and work together in unity.

Verse 13b

The parenthetic phrase in 13b says, "whether Jews or Greeks, whether slaves or free." This phrase is bracketed by the word "all" in the two clauses. Paul says, "we were *all* baptized into one body" and "we were *all* made to drink of one Spirit." Some scholars maintain that Paul refers not to every believer, but to all who have been baptized in the Spirit as a subsequent experience. In contrast, most scholars, including Pentecostals and non-Pentecostals, contend that Paul has all believers in mind.

In my opinion, the adjective "all" refers to everyone who has believed in Christ as Savior. It simply means that everyone, regardless of background, who believes in Christ, is a member of the body of Christ. During the early days of the church, however, it was controversial to include the Gentiles. Also, there were differences in social status between slaves and free men and between men and women. With regard to membership in the body of Christ, Paul proclaims that all are equal.

Paul deals with this inclusiveness in other passages. In Galatians 3:28, he says, "There is neither Jew nor Greek, there is neither slave nor free man, there is neither male nor female; for you are all one in Christ Jesus." In Romans 10:12, he writes: "For there is no distinction between Jew and Greek; for the same *Lord* is Lord of all, abounding in riches for all who call on Him." Clearly, in Christ, all men and women are on common ground.

Verse 13c

Paul's second clause (verse 13c) says, "and we were all made to drink (*epotisthēmen*, ἐποτίσθημεν) of one Spirit." Or, as the NIV translates it, "we were all given the One Spirit to drink." Either translation is possible, but the NIV translation is more appropriate. It harmonizes much better with Paul's usual emphasis on the Spirit's being given to us.

Paul employs the verb *epotisthēmen*, which is the aorist indicative passive form of (*potizō*, ποτίζω). With regard to verse 13c, Bauer says this verb means "made to drink." Also, he says that with persons, it can also mean "give to drink" (2000, 857). Either way, the truth implied is that the believer receives the Spirit. Paul does not identify the giver of the Spirit, but we can safely assume that it is Jesus.

Some scholars maintain that the verb *potizō* means that the Spirit is abundantly outpoured. For example, Dunn posits that this verb "has two common meanings: to give to drink, and to water or irrigate. Paul knows both meanings (1 Cor. 3.2, 6-8), and here he uses it in the second sense" (1970, 131). The metaphor of irrigation, according to Dunn, suggests that the Spirit was poured out upon them like "a rainstorm on a parched ground" (1970, 131).

Considerable theological discussion arises over whether this clause and the first clause in verse 13a say the same thing in two different ways or say two different but harmonious things. Much depends, of course, on what each of the clauses independently means. As I understand the clauses, they have the same purpose. They both present the role of the Spirit in believers becoming members of the body of Christ and functioning within it in unity, but they do express this in different ways.

Membership in the Body

In the second clause Paul does not state the purpose of the gift of the Spirit. This leads us to believe that the purpose was the same as in the first clause. The Spirit is given to us so that we might be united with Christ and to unite us functionally in service. Although function is the primary emphasis in this second clause, we cannot overlook union with Christ.

With regard to this union, we ask: What does the Spirit being given to us have to do with membership in the body of Christ? In Romans 8:9, Paul says, "But if anyone does not have the Spirit of Christ, he does not belong to him." The verb "does not have" is in the present tense, so Paul is speaking about a present reality in our lives. However, if this be true of the present, it is also true of the beginning of Christian life.

In this way, being given the Spirit to drink relates to our being united with Christ. As I understand Paul's theology of the Spirit, when we come to faith, we receive a twofold objective gift; we are united with Christ and we receive the Spirit. This twofold gift is given to us in order that we may be saved. Then, we immediately begin experiencing life in Christ and developing our relationship with the Spirit. We receive the Spirit continuously, repeatedly, and fully.

Functional Unity and Diversity

Becoming members of the body does not exhaust the work of the Spirit in and through us. The Spirit, Who is given to us, now gives spiritual gifts to us. In verses 4-11, we have already been told that we have been given spiritual gifts by the Spirit. Paul is eager for these diverse gifts to be manifested in unity. The Spirit, as the giver of the gifts, will help us to function in unity. Ultimately, the gifts are the workings of the Triune God. We should pray that we will be abundantly empowered by the Spirit.

Some of those who relate baptism "in/by" the Spirit to water baptism tie this clause (13c) to the Lord's Supper. In other words, when people participate in the Lord's Supper, they experience the ongoing presence of the Spirit as a gift to their spiritual lives. As I perceive the clause, it does not have to do with the Lord's Supper. However, I would acknowledge that the Spirit is very often present in a powerful way during communion services.

Ongoing Appropriation

The metaphors of baptism (13a) and drinking (13c) stress the work of the Spirit both in uniting us with Christ and in the ongoing life of the believers. The Spirit helps believers in an ongoing way to function harmoniously in the body. Perhaps the baptismal metaphor has more emphasis on the beginning, while the drinking metaphor highlights ongoing activity. However, the baptism metaphor does not exclude an ongoing relationship; neither does the drinking metaphor exclude the beginning.

First, the two verbs that Paul uses in 12:13 are aorist indicative passive verbs: *ebaptisthēmen* (ἐβαπτίσθημεν, were baptized) and *epotisthēmen* (ἐποτίσθημεν, were given to drink). They draw us back to the beginning of our Christian life. However, the verbs themselves do not limit us to one point in past time. Depending on the context, the aorist tense may be interpreted in several different ways. Wallace states:

> The aorist normally views the action *as a whole*, taking no interest in the internal workings of the action. It describes the action in summary fashion, without focusing on the beginning or the end of the actions specifically. This is by far the most common use of the aorist, especially with the indicative mood. (1996, 557)

The different usages of the aorist tense include the *ingressive* and the *constative* aorists. According to Wallace, "the ingressive aorist stresses the beginning of an action or the entrance into a state. Whether or not the action continues is left unstated" (1996, 558). With regard to the constative aorist, Wallace points out that it "covers a multitude of actions. The event might be iterative in nature, or durative, or momentary, but the aorist says none of this. It places the stress on the fact of the occurrence, not its nature" (1996, 557).

Second, beyond these two verbs, we must keep in mind the entire witness of the Scriptures. Our ongoing relationship, in all of its aspects, is strongly emphasized. We must keep on appropriating the Spirit. God continues to give His Spirit to us (1 Thess. 4:8; Phil. 1:19). Let us keep on receiving His Spirit. As we keep on receiving, we should be "diligent to preserve the unity of the Spirit in the bond of peace" (Eph. 4:3). With all our diverse gifts, we can be united in the work of the Lord.

Baptism in the Spirit

All this leaves the door open for a crisis-type experience such as the disciples enjoyed at Pentecost (Acts 2:4). In Acts 1:5 and 11:16, the disciples who had this experience were said to be "baptized in the Spirit." Although Luke did not use the term "baptized" concerning the Ephesus event, Paul led the disciples there to be "filled" with the Spirit (Acts 19:1-7). After Paul questions the Ephesian disciples about their experience of the Spirit, he prayed for them and they began speaking with tongues and prophesying. Given Paul's experience at Ephesus, we are certainly in order to include this in the scope of his theology.

Because Pentecostals believe in the baptism in the Spirit according to Acts 2:4, many of them want to know if this baptism is a gateway to the exercise of the gifts of the Spirit. Many ask, if baptism in the Spirit is not such a gateway, then what impact does the experience have with regard to the gifts? This issue arises because baptism in the Spirit is considered as an experience that is subsequent to salvation.

For many evangelicals, baptism in the Spirit is a salvation event. All believers are said to be baptized in the Spirit. Therefore, the gateway issue does not arise. Obviously, the baptism in the Spirit, as they see it, is a gateway to all spiritual experience. Pentecostals believe equally strongly in the presence and work of the Spirit in salvation. They may or may not use the term *baptism* in the Spirit concerning this aspect of the Spirit's work.

Our question, however, has to do with the baptism in the Spirit as experienced in Acts 2:4. Some have held that this experience must take place before the spiritual gifts can be exercised. Many who hold this view especially have in focus the nine gifts in 12:8-10. However, most Pentecostals maintain that the gifts can be exercised without the baptism in the Spirit, but that the exercise of these gifts is enhanced by this empowering experience.

Thus, among Pentecostals, when someone genuinely speaks in tongues, the question of the baptism in the Spirit being a gateway does not arise. The reason is that Pentecostals consider that he or she is baptized in the Spirit. The gateway question comes up with regard to the other gifts.

To explain further, Pentecostals maintain that speaking in tongues in Acts 2:4 and in 1 Corinthians 12-14 are the same in essence but different in purpose and use. In Acts 2:4, the tongues are an evidence of the Spirit's presence, but in 1 Corinthians, Paul is speaking about the exercise of a spiritual gift in the worship service. Despite the difference in purpose, there is no difference in the nature of the tongues.

Conclusion

In 1 Corinthians 12:12-27, Paul presents a physical body as an analogy to the body of Christ. He teaches the Corinthians about the unity and diversity of the body and admonishes them to work in unity. As they work, they should avoid both feelings of inferiority and superiority. This is Paul's main concern: Every member is important, gifted, and useful, and every member belongs.

In 12:13, Paul concentrates on the role of the Spirit. Through the Spirit, we all become members of the body of Christ; and, with all our diversity, function in unity. In verse 13a, Paul emphasizes the work of the Spirit in uniting us with the body of Christ. He does this because this work of the Spirit is prerequisite to the unified functioning of the body. In verse 13c, Paul stresses the reception of the Spirit and His impact on our experience. However, we can deduce that the Spirit is received in an objective way as we are united with the body. Although the two clauses have different emphases, they both deal with membership in the body and functional unity.

However we read the clauses in 12:13, we are still eligible for the baptism in the Spirit as it is described in Acts. The experience described in Acts will enhance our effectiveness in the body. Let us pray in faith that the Spirit will have complete control of us. The Lord will respond to our faith. We pray that the Holy Spirit will help us yield our lives fully to Him, to seek the best interests of the body of Christ, and to use us as members of the body for the benefit of all. We need His presence and work today.

CHAPTER SIX

GOD HAS PLACED GIFTS

In 1 Corinthians 12:1-27, Paul makes clear that the Triune God is the source and enabler of the spiritual gifts and that the body of Christ is both united and diverse. Both the unity and the diversity of the body of Christ flow from Him. The members of the body, united in Christ and equipped with diverse gifts, can minister effectively to one another. Moreover, through the spiritual gifts, God and the believers work together for the common good. The role of the believers varies in scope, but the manifest presence of the Spirit is essential. Without this, there are no spiritual gifts. Paul varies his approach but continues these themes in verses 28-31 where he says:

[28]And God has appointed in the church, first apostles, second prophets, third teachers, then miracles, then gifts of healings, helps, administrations, *various* kinds of tongues. [29]All are not apostles, are they? All are not prophets, are they? All are not teachers, are they? All are not *workers of* miracles, are they? [30]All do not have gifts of healings, do they? All do not speak with tongues, do they? All do not interpret, do they? [31]But earnestly desire the greater gifts. And I show you a still more excellent way.

Gift Lists

Before we discuss verses 28-31, it will be helpful to present all the gifts in four of Paul's lists. These lists are found in 1 Corinthians 12:8-10, 28-31, Romans 12:6-8, and Ephesians 4:11. Table 1 below presents all the gifts named in the four major lists and will serve to put verses 28-31 in the larger context. Other passages could be added, but these are the major lists. Several points are germane to our study.

First, the Greek terms *charismata* ($\chi\alpha\rho\acute{\iota}\sigma\mu\alpha\tau\alpha$) and *domata* ($\delta\acute{o}\mu\alpha\tau\alpha$) are among those that Paul uses to describe spiritual gifts. Paul speaks about the *charismata* in 12:31 and Romans 12:6. However, in Ephesians 4:8, Paul says that Christ "gave gifts (*domata*) to men." The fact that Paul uses *domata* in Ephesians 4:8

instead of *charismata* does not suggest two exclusive categories. In support of this point, we notice the overlap in the gift lists. For example, apostles, prophets, and teachers are named in 1 Corinthians 12:28-30 and in Ephesians 4:11. In addition, prophets are in the former list, and prophecy is listed in Romans 12:6.

Moreover, it is through grace that we receive both the *charismata* and the *domata*. In Ephesians 4:7, Paul states: "But to each of us grace (*charis*, χάρις) was given according to the measure of Christ's gift (*dōreas*, δωρεᾶς)." Similarly, in Romans 12:6, Paul declares, "we have gifts (*charismata*) that differ according to the grace (*charin*, χάριν) given to us." Given this evidence, there does not appear to be much difference between the term *charismata* and *domata*. They both refer to the spiritual gifts.

1 Corinthians 12:8-10	Romans 12:6-8	Ephesians 4:11
Word of Wisdom	Prophecy–According to	Apostles
Word of Knowledge	Faith	Prophets
Faith	Service–Serving	Evangelists
Gifts of Healing	He Who Teaches–	Pastors
Effecting of Miracles	Teaching	Teachers
Prophecy	He Who Exhorts–	
Distinguishing of Spirits	Exhortation	
Kinds of Tongues	He Who Gives–With	
Interpretation of Tongues	Liberality	
1 Corinthians 12:28–30	He Who Leads–With	
Apostles	Diligence	
Prophets	He Who Shows Mercy–	
Teachers	With Cheerfulness	
Miracles		
Gifts of Healings		
Helps		
Administrations		
Speak with Tongues		

Table 1

Second, the lists of gifts include persons and ministries.[47] Persons are known for their ministries; for example, a teacher is

---

[47] Carson (1987, 22) and Garland (2003, 562) hold that the term *charismata* never refers to persons. However, as I see it, this word in 12:31 includes all

known for his teaching. A prophet is known for his prophesying. Many of the gifts are mentioned without mentioning the person who exercises the gift. Also, the gifts are given to those who exercise them, but those who are blessed by the gifts might be said, in a sense, to receive the gifts as well.

Third, many attempts have been made to categorize the gifts. When teaching about the gifts, these attempts can be helpful, but we must remember that the lists are not highly structured. Much of the order seems random. As Keener states:

> A comparison of Paul's various gift lists (Rom. 12:4-8; 1 Cor. 12:28; 29-30; 13:1-2, 8-9; 14:26; Eph. 4:11; see also 1 Peter 4:10-11) demonstrates that his lists are ad hoc—that is, he is making them up "on the spot"—and vary considerably. He could have listed other gifts than those he listed, and even his first readers may not have known exactly what each of his examples meant. (2001, 114)

There are many gifts, but not all of them are named by Paul. His lists of gifts are illustrative, but not exhaustive. The Holy Spirit is entirely free to use us in any way fitting to Him. Each of the ways we minister, when empowered by the Spirit, could be called a spiritual gift. Moreover, as I have noted, those who exercise spiritual gifts are called gifts as well. For example, Christ gave apostles to the church (Eph. 4:8). Thus, the spiritual gifts include both the ministers and the ministries.

God's Placement

Paul makes this strong declaration, "And God has appointed (*etheto*, ἔθετο) in the church, first apostles, second prophets, third teachers, then miracles, then gifts of healings, helps, administrations, *various* kinds of tongues" (12:28). The Greek verb

---

the persons and ministries in 12:28-30. Paul leads the list with persons, including apostles, prophets, and teachers. These persons are included in Ephesians 4:8-11. Here, Paul uses the noun *domata* rather than *charismata*, but the lists of gifts overlap. In Romans 12:6-8, Paul says the believers have been given *charismata*. The listed *charismata* include both persons and the ministries. For example, Paul gives this exhortation: "he who teaches (*ho didaskōn,* ὁ διδάσκων), in his teaching." The phrase *ho didaskōn* (present participle) means "the [one] teaching."

etheto is the aorist form of *tithēmi* (τίθημι) which means "to appoint" or "to place." The NIV says, "And God has placed in the church."

The NASB[95] and NIV begin 12:28 simply with "And God." The Greek text, however, includes the words *hous men* (οὓς μὲν). The word *hous* can mean "those whom" (Fee, 1987, 618), "some" (Lenski, 1946, 537), or "that" (Strong's); the particle *men* can be translated as "surely" or "indeed" (Thayer, 1962, 397). The translation by Young's Literal Translation is "and some, indeed." Without translating *hous men*, the NASB[95] and NIV simply declare what God has done.

According to Bauer, the particle *men* can be used correlatively with the conjunction *de* (δὲ); and this sometimes, but not always, introduces a contrasting clause (2000, 629). When Paul writes *men*, we might expect to see *de*, but Paul does not include *de* in this verse; instead he begins an ordinal enumeration of gifts. After listing apostles, prophets, and teachers, he introduces the rest of the gifts with the word "then." We do not encounter the word *de* until verse 31. So, we will examine the particle *men* again when we consider verse 31. With this as background, we turn to other points about verse 28.

First, it is the Triune God who has placed the gifts. According to Paul in 12:6, it is "the same God [the Father] who works all things [the gifts] in all *persons*." Similarly, in Romans 12:3, Paul says, "God has allotted to each a measure of faith." The purpose of the faith is to exercise the gifts He has given. In Ephesians 4:11, Paul declares "And He [Christ] gave some" as ministers. The gifts are identified by Paul in 12:7 as "the manifestation of the Spirit." Then, in 12:11, Paul says that "the same Spirit works all these things." Clearly, it is the Triune God who places the gifts.

Second, the statement that God has placed the gifts enriches all the other vocabulary that Paul uses to describe spiritual matters. Paul describes spiritual things as gifts, ministries, workings, manifestation of the Spirit, and the distributions of the Spirit. Each description has its own shades of meaning, but all of them refer to the spiritual gifts. Each term highlights an aspect of the spiritual gifts. In 12:18, Paul adds that God has placed the gifts in the body (compare 12:24-25).

Third, Paul maintains that God has placed the gifts "in the church" (12:28). Whether Paul refers to the local or universal church is debated.[48] Many assume a *both-and* position. For example, Garland says: "'In the church' could refer to the church universal, but since apostles are the founders of local communities of faith, it could also refer to a local community" (2003, 598). Lenski contends that God's act of setting gifts in the church "extends far beyond the Corinthians who are only one congregation among many, and to whom, as a congregation, many members are yet to be added. Hence Paul writes: God did set 'in the church' and takes in the entire church of all places and all ages" (1946, 537). As I see it, both the local church and the universal church are included.

Status Issues

Verses 28-31 raise the issues of the status of the gifts, including both the people who exercise the gifts and the gifts themselves. This is an issue in the church that seems to never go away. Even when people are seeking to serve, it sometimes becomes an issue as to who is serving best. Paul recognizes the status issues and shows us a balanced way to serve.

Altogether in verses 28-31, Paul lists nine gifts. He begins this passage by enumerating three gifts: "first apostles, second prophets, third teachers." After this, he uses the adverb "then" (*epeita*, ἔπειτα) twice to present each of two gifts: miracles and gifts of healing. Next, without the adverb "then," Paul lists helps and administrations. It may be that Paul intended for the reader to supply the adverb. Finally, he lists various kinds of tongues. The first five gifts as well as the last are repeated in verses 29-30, and in verse 30, Paul adds interpretation of tongues. Then, in verse 31 he mentions the "greater gifts."

---

[48] Fee states: "Since this sentence is coordinate with v. 27, with its emphatic 'you are,' meaning the church in Corinth, there can be little question that by this phrase Paul also primarily intends the local assembly in Corinth. . . . But its use in this kind of context seems also to prepare the way for its broader use in the Prison Epistles to refer to the church universal—especially so since the first item 'God has placed in the church' are 'apostles' (plural)" (1987, 618).

First, Paul's enumeration of apostles, prophets, and teachers raises the issue of rank. All three of these ministries are gifts to the church. Robertson states, "Paul unhesitatingly ranks some spiritual gifts above others" (1931, 174). The question is: What does the ranking mean? Some scholars maintain that Paul ranks them in the order in which these persons become involved in the planting and development of a local church; the apostles appear first, the prophets next, and then the teachers. However, such an order was not absolute in the early church, nor is it now. Churches start in many different ways. Just which ministry is needed most at any given time is very situational.

Many hold that Paul was ranking apostles, prophets, and teachers in an order of importance. Without a doubt, these gifts were important in the church. However, Paul does not enumerate the other gifts. There are gifts, in addition to the first three, that are more prominent in the body of Christ. In 12:23-24, Paul speaks about the members that "we deem less honorable" and those that are our more "seemly members." He stresses, however, that we give honor to the less honorable and that all members are essential. There should be no feelings of superiority or inferiority. All of the gifts, Paul declares, are put in place by God.

Any ranking, however, is not hard and fast. For example, miracles and gifts of healings in this passage are in reverse order to their listing in 1 Corinthians 12:9-10. Moreover, when a person needs healing, it matters little whether the person praying for them is a teacher or a helper with faith. So we must not overstress the enumeration of the gifts.[49] For example, the fact that tongues and interpretation are listed last does not make them of least importance.

Second, does Paul have in mind not only ministries but also, to some degree, offices in the church? Commentators who maintain that offices or positions are among the gifts will include ministers such as apostles, prophets, and teachers. In other words, these ministers are viewed as office holders as well.

---

[49] While discussing the issue of rank, Taylor says, "Perhaps it is best to hold the idea of rank and interdependence in healthy tension since we find the same principles at work in Paul's argument regarding headship in in 11:2-16 (cf. esp. 11:3, 7-12)" (2014, 301).

The question is: To what extent did Paul recognize the offices or positions?[50] There is considerable debate over this question. People who regularly exercise certain gifts become known for those gifts. The minister becomes known for having a given ministry. The minister, as well as the ministry, can be called a gift. It is possible that this same line of thought extends to an office. The minister's gift can lead to an office for his ministry. The office holder can be classified as a gift because he exercises the gift. Therefore, conceivably, an office could be called a gift.

It is possible to hold an office without having the ministry gifts for the office. Also, many people have spiritual gifts without holding an office. Paul is emphasizing the gifts of the Spirit, not offices. When people with spiritual gifts hold offices, they can become effective in those offices. Many have ministries exercising gifts without holding offices. This appears to be the major emphasis of Paul.

Third, another consideration is: What is the relationship between the *charismata* ($\chi\alpha\rho\acute{\iota}\sigma\mu\alpha\tau\alpha$) and authority in the church? As Schatzmann points out, there are several approaches to this subject. One approach is that the charismata are an expression of authority in the church. Another approach is that charisma and authority are based upon bearers of offices. In other words, those who hold the offices have the authority. A third approach minimizes authority in connection with the charismata. Schatzmann concludes that charismata are not expressive of authority, but that charismata and authority belong together in the church (1987, 95-97).

---

[50]Palma writes: "It is undeniable, however that there were officebearers in the churches of Paul's time and in the church-at-large. How else can terms like apostle, prophet, and teacher be understood (1 Cor. 12:28; see Eph. 4:11, which mentions also evangelists and pastors)? . . . But even when office bearers are mentioned, the emphasis is not so much on their ecclesiastical office as it is on the variety of functions, activities, and ministries in the church" (2001, 204). In addition, he states: "In summary, Paul stresses function, even though the concept of office is in his letters. According to the general teaching of the New Testament, the sovereign working of the Spirit through any believer and the divine appointment of some to positions of leadership are not mutually exclusive, nor should these two concepts be at odds when the New Testament guidelines are observed" (2001, 205).

Clearly, there are leadership roles in the church. Leadership roles, such as administrations in verse 28, are gifts to the church. Very often, leadership involves the exercise of authority. It is possible to have authority without leadership gifts, but the church is much better served when the leaders are gifted to lead. Moreover, the motive for leadership should be service, not power. Jesus explained this clearly to the disciples (Matt. 20:25-27). The Gentiles stressed power, but greatness for the follower of Christ lies in service.

Description of Gifts: Verses 28-30

In 12:28-30, nine individual gifts are mentioned. In verse 28, eight of the nine are listed: apostles, prophets, teachers, miracles, gifts of healings, helps, administrations, and various kinds of tongues. Six of the eight are repeated in verses 29-30, but helps and administrations are not. The ninth gift, interpretation of tongues, is added in verse 30. Four of the nine gifts are repeated from 12:8-10; in addition, verse 28 lists prophets in the place of prophecy.

With respect to the gifts, God is the source of both unity and diversity in the body. With regard to diversity, Paul says, "But now God has placed (*etheto*, ἔθετο) the members, each one of them, in the body, just as He desired" (12:18). Concerning unity, he states: "But God so composed (*sunekerasen*, συνεκέρασεν) the body, giving more abundant honor to that *member* which lacked, so that there may be no division in the body, but *that* the members may have the same care for one another" (12:24-25). These passages provide the context for what Paul says in verses 29-30 where the diversity of the gifts stands out. Given the context, we recognize God as the source of the diversity.

Because we discussed "gifts of healings" in chapter three and "effecting of miracles," "various kinds of tongues," and "interpretation of tongues" in chapter four, we will not include them here. We will discuss apostles, prophets, teachers, helps, and administrations.

Apostles

One of the spiritual gifts listed in 12:28-30 is *apostles*. Our English word *apostle* is a translation of the Greek word *apostolos*, (ἀπόστολος). Literally translated, the Greek word means "the sent one." In the church, an apostle is one sent on a special mission. Here, a person with the Spirit-inspired ministry of a "sent one" is considered a gift of the Spirit. In some cases, we might say that the gifted person holds the office of apostle as well. The essential point is that the apostle is empowered by the Spirit for his or her mission.

First, the word *apostolos* is used in the New Testament with a range of meaning from narrow to broad. Beginning with Christ and expanding to individuals that Paul sent to Corinth, the term is used with various meanings. In the narrowest sense, Jesus is identified in Hebrews 3:1 as "the Apostle." In Matthew 10:2-4, Jesus names the twelve apostles, thereby widening the use of the term. After the ascension of Jesus, Matthias replaced Judas (Acts 1:24-25) as an apostle. Later, Luke names Paul and Barnabas as apostles (Acts 14:14). To them, we can add "James, the Lord's brother" (Gal. 1:19), Andronicus and Junias (Rom. 16:7), and probably Silvanus and Timothy (1 Thess. 2:6).

Many scholars recognize both the more restricted and broader usages of the word *apostolos*. In the most restricted sense, the term refers to Christ. The term applies to Him in a unique way. With regard to the more inclusive meaning, Arrington writes:

> In a broad sense, *apostle* referred to messengers or delegates sent out by churches. The congregation in Philippi had sent Epaphroditus as their apostle, or 'messenger' (Philippians 2:25). Paul designated individuals that he sent to Corinth as 'messengers [literally, apostles] of the churches' (2 Corinthians 8:23). These people had been personally appointed by the churches as delegates to assist Paul in carrying the offering to the poor Christians in Jerusalem. So the general meaning of apostles in the New Testament included people who had been commissioned and sent by local churches as missionaries, or sent with other special responsibilities (Acts 14:4, 14; Romans 16:7). (2003, 286)

Second, a review of what the apostles did reveals some similarities and numerous differences. Keener points out, for example, that apostles typically broke new ground, but what they did varied somewhat. He says that the Twelve apostles planted the church in Jerusalem; while Paul planted small Bible study groups across the Mediterranean (2001, 128). According to Petts, the apostles normally could be recognized by such ministry features as preaching accompanied by miraculous signs, planting churches, laying a foundation for local churches, having authority over those churches, and training others for works of service. He further concludes that "This does not mean that a person who fulfils any one of these is an apostle, nor does it mean that an apostle will fulfil all of these functions" (2002, 38).

Third, whether or not there are apostles today is an issue. Much depends on what is meant by the word "apostle." Some of the early church apostles wrote Scripture, but no one does that today. However, in the broader sense of one sent on a mission, there are many who could be called apostles. Some spiritual needs can be met today through apostles just as they were in the early church. As Keener says, "Given the need for bringing Christ's body to maturity (Eph. 4:12-13), Paul would presumably assume that this gift, like the others he mentions, would continue to function until Christ's return" (2001, 128).

Prophets

Both prophets (*prophētai*, προφήται) and prophecy are listed as gifts of the Spirit. We discussed the gift of prophecy in chapter four; here we will consider the gift of prophets. The subject of prophets in both Testaments is huge. Here, however, our main concern is with prophets as a gift of the Spirit.

Paul uses some form of *prophet* in 12:28, 29; 14:32, 37.[51] He includes prophets in his list of gifts in Ephesians 4:11. As in 12:10, Paul refers to prophecy (*prophēteian*, προφητείαν) in Romans 12:6. In both Ephesians 4:11 and 1 Corinthians 12:28, apostles and prophets are listed together and are closely linked.

First, were the prophets a special group in the church or simply those who occasionally or regularly prophesied? The term *prophet* is quite flexible and can be used with varied meanings. Generally, scholars recognize that the term *prophet* can refer broadly to any

---

[51] *Prophētas* (προφητας, masculine accusative plural) in 12:28; *prophētai* (προφηται, masculine nominative plural) in 12:29; *prophētōn* (προφητων, masculine genitive plural) and *prophētais* (προφηταις, masculine dative plural) in 14:32; and *prophētēs* (προφητης, masculine nominative singular) in 14:37.

92

believer who is moved upon by the Spirit to prophecy and more narrowly to a special group of people called prophets. Apparently, Luke refers to such groups in Acts 11:27 and 13:1. No doubt, many became known as prophets because they regularly prophesied. According to Arrington:

> Like the word *apostle* the term *prophētēs* is used in both a broad and a narrow sense. When used broadly, it refers to any believer whom the Spirit has moved to prophesy. . . . On the other hand, in the narrow meaning the term *prophet* refers to a distinct group in the church. For the most part this is the way Paul appears to use it. (2003, 290)

Second, both Luke and Paul touch on the issue of who can be a prophet. In Luke's approach, speaking in tongues was a form of prophecy (Acts 2:4; 2:17-18) and a sign of the baptism in the Holy Spirit. Paul spoke of prophecy as a ministry gift of the Spirit rather than as an evidence of the baptism in the Spirit as experienced in Acts 2:4. He wishes that all would prophesy (14:5) and indicates that potentially all can prophesy (14:31). They potentially are prophets in the sense that they could prophesy. However, he also acknowledges that all are not prophets (12:29). Given the context, this indicates that not all believers prophesy.

Third, as we discussed in chapter four, prophets both speak for God and exalt Him with praises. Sometimes prediction is involved. Very often, what they say is based on the information the Spirit has revealed to them. However, revelation is not always involved. The functions that Paul focuses on in 1 Corinthians 14:3 are edification, exhortation, and consolation. In 14:24-25, he says that prophecy has an evangelistic impact. Some scholars do not think that prophecy includes preaching, but preaching can be inspired by the Spirit, including planned and spontaneous content.

Fourth, can we have prophets in the church today? The answer depends, of course, on what is meant by "prophets." Some of the early church prophets ministered in ways that are not open to prophets today. As Petts points out, the New Testament prophets had a part in laying the foundation for the church universal (Eph. 2:19-20; 3:5). Today, he says, prophets may help start local churches, but the foundation for the universal church has been laid.

He concludes that the church today needs to make greater room for the ministry of prophets (2002, 53-56).

Teachers

The third enumerated gift that God has placed in the church is *teachers* (12:28-29). Teachers are named in both 1 Corinthians 12:28-29 and Ephesians 4:11, right after apostles and prophets. Paul uses the noun "teaching" is 14:6, 26 and in Romans 12:7. Also, in Romans 12:7, Paul speaks about "he who teaches." Clearly, the teachers and teaching had an important role in the early church.

Teachers are very essential to the progress of the church. In Ephesians 4:11, pastors and teachers are mentioned together. Some expositors hold that pastors and teachers are separate gifts, while others maintain that Paul means something like "teaching pastors." Whether or not pastors and teachers should be one or two gifts, it is clear that there is overlapping in gifts. Most teachers have functioned on occasion as shepherds, and shepherds or pastors regularly teach.

First, no doubt, there were many people in the early church who had teaching aptitudes, skills, and training. We might call these elements natural abilities. Even so, we must remember that all good things, including natural skills, come from God. As James declares, "Every good thing given and every perfect gift is from above, coming down from the Father of lights, with whom there is no variation of shifting shadow" (James 1:17). The gift of teaching includes, but goes beyond, natural abilities. Many teachers have experienced the inspiration of the Holy Spirit as they have taught. The Spirit often enlightens the minds of the teachers and enables them to communicate with the audience.

Second, people became known as teachers because of their teaching ministry. Their ministry includes both natural and supernatural qualities.[52] Like apostles and prophets, some teachers were a part of groups known as teachers (Acts 13:1). Their ongoing ministry of teaching made them a part of those groups known as "teachers." Teachers are a part of the core ministries of every local church.

---

[52]See page 29, footnote 14, for Carson's comments on this point.

Helps

With regard to the gifts in 14:28, Palma says, "The triad [apostles, prophets, teachers] is presented in terms of persons, whereas the remaining gifts [miracles, gifts of healings, helps, administrations, various kinds of tongues] are given in impersonal terms" (2001, 206). Therefore, both persons and actions are identified as gifts of the Spirit.

Paul includes the gift of *helps* in this list. It is the only mention made of this gift. The Greek word is *antilēmpseis* (ἀντιλήμψεις), and Bauer translates it as "helpful deeds" (2000, 89). According to Palma, this word "conveys the basic idea of assistance or support" (2001, 215). Many people are called upon to be helpers in the church. When they help others, they exercise the gift of helps.

Someone might ask, "Why is 'helps' called a spiritual gift?" The church has a need for helpers in all aspects of its ministry. Helpers can minister to both the physical and spiritual needs of the community. The help might be needed in aspects of ministry that are deeply spiritual or in realms that are quite natural. The need for the enabling of the Spirit in spiritual ministry is clear, but not as obvious in some natural areas of assistance. However, even with apparently natural aspects of the ministry, we should take a closer look.

People who exercise the gift of helps often do things that seem very ordinary. By ordinary, I mean that it would seem that almost anyone could accomplish what they do. However, they may do these things with special insight and spirit. They recognize when help is needed and are quick to respond to the need. They just naturally react to the situation and reach out to be a blessing to those around them. Very often, their action is motivated by the Spirit. This motivation is a supernatural aspect of the gift.

Administrations

Paul lists administrations (*kubernēseis*, κυβερνήσεις) as one of the gifts. Paul does not use this Greek term in his other lists. However, in Romans 12:8 he gives this exhortation: "he who leads, with diligence." He uses the present participle *proistamenos* (προϊστάμενος) The two words, *kubernēseis* and *proistamenos* are closely related and overlap in meaning.[53]

First, the Greek word *kubernēseis* can be translated as "administrations" or "acts of guidance." Because of Acts 27:11 and Revelation 18:17, the translation "acts of guidance" stands out. In Acts 27:11, Luke mentions the pilot or steersman of the ship Paul was sailing on. The word translated "pilot" is (*kubernētē*, κυβερνήτη). In Revelation 18:17, *kubernētēs* (κυβερνήτης) is translated as "shipmaster." Although "acts of guidance" stands out, all of the words are very flexible. They can encompass a variety of activities. All of these words describe some aspect of the spiritual gift that Paul mentions.

Second, in today's parlance, we might refer to the gift of "leadership." In a broad sense, leadership includes administration, management, guidance, and counseling. A major task of the leader, under God, is to guide or steer the organization toward given goals. Leaders have vision and inspire people to follow and work together. Acting under the leadership of Christ, leaders mobilize people in worthy causes. Throughout history, leaders are very much needed in the church. Today, most people recognize that this is a need.

Diversity of the Body

In 12:29-30, Paul asks a series of rhetorical questions about seven of the gifts. The obvious answer to each of the questions is "No." Because of the diversity of the body, each member has its own function. The members should not get in the way of each other. Each member is duly honored. All the members are essential to the proper functioning of the body. Although Paul does not repeat the gift of helps and administrations from verse 28, there is probably no particular significance to this. The gift of helps, however, is readily open to all who would serve.

In 12:30, Paul asks, "All do not speak with tongues, do they?" Here, he is referring to speaking in tongues as a ministry gift in the

---

[53]Bauer defines *proistēmi* as "be at the head (of), rule, direct" and "manage, conduct. He lists Romans 12:8 under "manage, conduct" (2000, 870). He defines *kubernēsis* as "*administration*; the pl. indicates proofs of ability to hold a leading position in the church 1 Cor. 12:28" (2000, 573).

church. The subject is not the evidence for the baptism in the Holy Spirit as experienced in Acts 2:4. This rhetorical question, therefore, does not teach against the view that all can speak in tongues as an evidence of the baptism in the Holy Spirit. As a gift for ministry in the church, not all speak in tongues.

Working with God

In 1 Corinthians 12:31, Paul concludes chapter 12 and introduces the next chapter. Paul writes: "But earnestly desire the greater gifts. And I show you a still more excellent way" (NASB[95]). The NIV translation is: "Now eagerly desire the greater gifts. And yet I will show you the most excellent way." Lenski translates the verb as "strive zealously" (1946, 542). All three translations emphasize the intensity of the desire.

As we interpret this verse, we need to consider whether or not the word *men* (μὲν) in verse 28 should be connected with the conjunction *de* (δὲ) in verse 31. Keep in mind that the *de* does not appear in verse 28. If Paul intends to connect these two verses with *men . . . de*, is he making contrasting statements or making a connection with a focus on cooperation?

As I reported when discussing 12:28, Bauer tells us that *men . . . de* can be connected correlatively and can indicate a contrast. Sometimes, this is expressed by the phrases "on the one hand" and "on the other hand." Another way to indicate a contrast is by translating *de* with the conjunction "but." However, *men . . . de* can be used simply to separate one clause from another without indicating a contrast (2000, 629).

We can connect verse 31 with verse 28. In verse 28, Paul tells us what God is doing, while in verse 31, he tells us what we ought to do. One might, in a sense, regard this as a contrast; but in another way, Paul simply describes two very complementary functions. In any case, the cooperation of God and man is achieved. Thus, a strong picture emerges of God and man working together to serve the body of Christ. God places gifts in the church; our role is to eagerly desire the greater gifts.

Earnestly Desire

My view is that we can connect verse 31 with verse 28, but verse 31 can be interpreted with or without that connection.

Without making this connection, the NASB[95] and NIV present two possibilities for the interpretation of the first clause of 12:31. Translating the Greek word *de*, the NASB[95] begins this clause with the word 'but," while the NIV begins with "now." The word "but" suggests a contrast, but the word "now" just indicates a current situation. Both the NASB[95] and NIV translations are acceptable approaches.

First, many scholars attempt to minimize the force of Paul's exhortation to eagerly desire greater gifts. Several approaches are taken: (1) some writers hold that Paul was citing the Corinthians and then correcting them; (2) others believe that Paul did not want them to seek the "greater gifts," but encouraged them to seek simply "spiritual gifts;" still others maintain that the desire for "greater gifts" should be avoided but love should be pursued.[54]

Obviously, the believers should avoid serving with wrong motives. However, that is not the point of the first clause of 12:31; 13:1-3 does make this point. When we consider 13:1-3, we find that seeking to exercise the gifts without love does not profit us, but that does not mean we should avoid eagerly desiring the gifts. Love is the supreme way to desire spiritual gifts.

Second, the verb *zēloute* (ζηλοῦτε, earnestly desire) can be interpreted in the indicative or in the imperative mood. If it is taken in the indicative mood, then Paul is saying "You earnestly desire the greater gifts." Advocates of this approach cite 14:12 where Paul says that the Corinthians were zealous for spiritual gifts (*pneumatōn*, πνευμάτων). In the imperative mood, Paul would be urging the Corinthians to "earnestly desire the greater gifts." The same form of the verb is used in 14:1 and 14:39. Paul exhorted the Corinthians to desire earnestly the spiritual gifts (14:1) and to prophesy (14:39). Clearly, Paul sustains both points.

---

[54] A colleague of mine, Dr. George Stotts, connects verses 28 and 31 but in a different way. He interprets the word *men* in 12:28 to mean "on the one hand." Paul then gives a list of persons and gifts that God has placed in the church. Following that he asks a series of rhetorical question with the intent of showing that everyone does not exercise every gift. Then, verse 31, Paul uses the particle *de* that was anticipated in verse 28. In verse 31, *de* means "but on the other hand." At this point Paul uses irony and says something like, "But you earnestly contend about which are the higher gifts so that you may continue to dazzle others with their importance."

Nevertheless, for me, the imperative sense of 12:31 is the better approach. As the next clause will indicate, love demands that we want to serve. Moreover, for believers to fulfill their role in working with God, they need to eagerly desire the greater gifts. God has placed the gifts in the church; we as believers are to earnestly desire the greater gifts. With regard to what gifts we receive, however, we understand that we are subject to the will of God. We can trust God to use us in the way that most benefits the body of Christ.

The Greater Gifts

Using the imperative mood, Paul exhorts the Corinthians to earnestly desire the "greater (*meizona*, μείζονα) gifts (*charismata*, χαρίσματα)." Despite his emphasis on the variety and importance of all gifts, Paul does indicate that some gifts are greater than others. As an example, in 1 Corinthians 14:5, he says, "greater (*meizōn*, μείζων) is one who prophesies than one who speaks in tongues, unless he interprets, so that the church may receive edifying." However, Paul does not give us a list of gifts that are greater. Within the overall context of what Paul says, we can surmise some thoughts that seem fitting.

First, some gifts, because they are most frequently needed to edify the body, can be said to be of greater value overall. We learn from chapter 14 that prophecy fits in this category. If we had to pick one gift which has the greatest value in the worship service, it probably would be prophecy.

Second, the principle of edifying the church easily fits with the thought that, in a different context, another gift might be the greater. For example, when confronted with people who are in need of healing, the gifts of healing take on great importance. We could make similar statements about other gifts in specific situations. It may be that the intelligible gifts in the overall picture do the most good for the body of Christ, but this does not diminish the importance of other gifts when they are specifically needed.

Third, it is applied according to the individual. The greater one for each individual might be different. Paul has made it clear that the Spirit distributes a variety of gifts to individuals who manifest them. As far as any individual is concerned, the best way he or she can edify the body is through the gift received. Thus, this becomes, for that individual, the greatest gift.

The Most Excellent Way

With regard to the second clause of 12:31, there are two issues that especially affect our interpretation. One has to do with whether the word "excellent" (*huperbolēn*, ὑπερβολὴν) should be treated in a comparative or a superlative sense. The other issue has to with what Paul means by an excellent "way."

Concerning the first issue, The NASB[95] translation, "And I show you a still more excellent way," treats the word "excellent" in a comparative sense. In contrast, the NIV opts for the superlative approach, yielding this translation: "And yet I show you the most excellent way." According to Bauer, one meaning of *huperbolēn* is "beyond measure," but with regard to 12:31, his translation is "a far better way" (2000, 1032). In the judgment of Robertson, Paul is not using a comparative term, but rather a superlative (1931, 174). The superlative approach, I believe, harmonizes best with Paul's treatment of love.

With regard to the second issue, what does Paul mean by a "way." Broadly speaking, he is referring to all that we do and all that we are. Our faith in Christ totally transforms every aspect of our lives. Specifically, in this context, Paul is speaking about the most excellent way to "eagerly desire the greater gifts." If we truly love people and want to help them, then we will sense the need for spiritual gifts. The spiritual gifts are demanded as ways to minister to the people in need. The broad meaning includes the narrower meaning.

The meaning is not that love—this most excellent way—is to be sought in place of the gifts. Love is not a substitute for the gifts. Rather, love is the proper motive in seeking and exercising spiritual gifts. Thus, we should seek to have both love and gifts. As Paul says in 1 Corinthians 14:1, "Pursue love, yet desire earnestly spiritual gifts, but especially that you may prophesy." When we love others, we will need the spiritual gifts in order to minister to them.

Conclusion

First Corinthians 12:28-31 is a passage packed with information about spiritual gifts. Paul declares that God places the gifts in the church, and these gifts include persons and functions. The persons listed exercise the gifts distributed to them. The gifts are ways to minister to the body of Christ. The lists of gifts are not highly structured. Instead, they seem to list gifts in somewhat random order. Paul does not expand on the meaning of many of the gifts. Unless he narrows the meaning of the terms, it is best to be open to the broader meanings.

The issue of the status of the gifts arises. This issue is always with us in the church. Paul presents a ranking of the apostles, prophets, and teachers, but does not explicitly say what the ranking means. Obviously, in Paul's thinking, the usefulness of the gifts is paramount. Whether or not the gifts include offices is debated. When a person regularly exercises a given gift, it can put that person in a leadership position.

The body of Christ is both unified and diverse; the diversity is stressed in the latter verses of this passage. Paul ends the passage by encouraging believers to earnestly desire spiritual gifts and explains that their desire should be derived from love for those in need. This latter exhortation leads into Paul's great chapter on love. The motivation of love affects every aspect of our lives. With love as the motive for what we do, many of the problems of relating to one another go away. Love is, indeed, the most excellent way.

CHAPTER SEVEN

THE MOST EXCELLENT WAY

In 1 Corinthians 13:1-13, Paul writes his amazing comments about love. The subject of love is huge and has many aspects to be considered. Volumes have been written concerning the nature of love. My purpose here is not to deal exhaustively with the subject, but to discuss what Paul says to the believers at Corinth. What he says to them applies to the church at all times and places. I will discuss 13:1-7 in this chapter and 13:8-13 in chapter eight.

In the Greek language, there are several words for love, but the word that Paul uses in 1 Corinthians 13 is *agapē* (ἀγάπη). The term *agapē* has a long history and has been used with a variety of meanings.[55] Discussions about *agapē* include many factors such as God's love for us, our love for God, and our love for each other. Love involves our feelings, actions, and thoughts. As Paul uses the term, love is the highest motivation in life.[56]

Rather than saying what love is, Paul tells us what love does and what it does not do. In this way, he develops a rather full description of what he means by love in action. The picture of what love is emerges. Love should have an impact on all aspects of our lives. This includes our relationships with God and people, the ethical aspects of our lives, the ways that we serve, and who we are and what we do.

When we think about *agapē* as Paul used the term, we encounter a paradox. As 13:1-3 points out, spiritual gifts and noble action without love profit us nothing. There is no return to us. The

---

[55] The only word used for love in 1 Corinthians 13 is *agapē*. According to Rea, "This was a more or less neutral word in classical Greek into which the Spirit poured the meaning of the unique quality of God's love" (1998, 230). As Blomberg indicates, "It is not the word itself that conveys the sense of divine love but the context" (1994, 261). The word itself is used in a variety of ways.

[56] Drummond asks: "What is the *summum bonum*—the supreme good? You have life before you. Once only you can live it. What is the noblest object of desire, the supreme gift to covet?" (No Date, 19) Paul's answer, Drummond says, is that love is the greatest thing in the world.

implication is that, when we act in love, without personal interests in mind, God paradoxically will reward us. As with any paradox, there is always some tension between these propositions. Most human actions spring from somewhat mixed motivation. However, with the help of God, we can avoid motivations that are selfish without due consideration of others.

Paul deals extensively with the relationship between love and the spiritual gifts. He makes two points about this relationship. On the one hand, as just noted, the exercise of spiritual gifts without love profits us nothing. This does not diminish the value of the gifts; it just says that we should be motivated by love. On the other hand, love without spiritual gifts also falls short of the ideal. Our love for others is expressed, in large measure, through the spiritual gifts. Love is the most excellent way to seek and exercise the gifts.

Thus, love and spiritual gifts go together. As Taylor says, chapter 13 "certainly possesses a 'stand-alone' quality and one can profit much from it apart from chaps. 12 and 14. But in order to fully and correctly appreciate its content, Paul's words must be read in light of the full argument of the letter" (2014, 302).

The content of 13:1-13 is bracketed by 12:31 and 14:1. In 12:31, Paul says, "Now eagerly desire the greater gifts. And yet I will show you the most excellent way" (NIV). After writing about love, Paul states: "Pursue love, yet desire earnestly spiritual *gifts*, but especially that you may prophesy" (14:1). As we seek to minister to others through the gifts, being motivated by love is paramount.

As Galatians 5:22 tells us, love is a fruit of the Spirit. Also, Romans 5:5 says, "the love of God has been poured out within our hearts through the Holy Spirit who was given to us." So, like the spiritual gifts, the Spirit is the source of true love. Unlike any given spiritual gift, the fruit of love is for every believer. In 13:13, Paul says that love is the greatest of spiritual characteristics. It is the motive that drives all of our service to others.

Gifts without Love

In 13:1-3, Paul focuses on service without the motivation of love. The results of serving without love are stark. Without love as the motivation for our actions, we are nothing. There is clearly a sharp contrast between love and improper motives for desiring spiritual gifts. The way to desire the gifts is through love. Paul goes beyond spiritual gifts and includes actions of personal sacrifice as well. We will comment on each verse below. He states:

[1]If I speak with the tongues of men and of angels, but do not have love, I have become a noisy gong or a clanging cymbal.[2]If I have *the gift of* prophecy, and know all mysteries and all knowledge; and if I have all faith, so as to remove mountains, but do not have love, I am nothing. [3]And if I give all my possessions to feed *the poor*, and if I surrender my body to be burned, but do not have love, it profits me nothing.

Paul says "if I" rather than "if you." He does not say why he uses the first person, but it may have simply been his way of being tactful.[57] By using the first person, Paul applies the results specifically to himself. However, the implication is that they apply to others as well. It is an effective way to present his very strong message.

First, the topics in verse 1 include speaking with the tongues of men and of angels, speaking without having love, and the dire result that this has for the speaker. These three topics highlight key points in Paul's view.

One, there are many views with regard to the phrase "tongues of men and of angels."[58] Some expositors hold that this phrase means to "speak eloquently." Others believe that "tongues of men" refers to eloquence, while "tongues of angels" has to do with

---

[57]Fee suggests that "Paul uses himself as the hypothetical person precisely because many of the Corinthians were like this in reality. Bringing them into the argument in this most indirect way is its own form of powerful argumentation" (1987, 630). Because Fee believes the majority of the Corinthian community called his authority and spirituality in question (1987, 8), he adds another reason. He says, "At the same time, as in 14:6, this use of the first person could reflect an undercurrent of their disapproval of him for not being known to speak in tongues, hence of his not being truly πνευματικός (*pneumatikos*); cf. on 2:15" (1987, 630, Transliteration Mine).

[58]Although they hold to a given point of view, some authors also call attention to Paul's main emphasis. According to Taylor, "The point of Paul's statement is not to establish different kinds of tongues but rather to emphasize that the gift, if exercised apart from love, is meaningless noise" (2014, 306). Similarly, Montague maintains that "Paul simply wants to be as inclusive as possible" (1976, 164).

ecstatic speech. Still others hold that "tongues of men" refers to the gift of tongues, and that, by hyperbole, the rhetorical impact of the phrase "tongues of angels" is escalated.

Another view is that both the "tongues of men" and the "tongues of angels" are inspired by the Spirit and are not understood by the speaker. Among those who hold this view are those who hold that Paul refers to two forms of speaking in tongues. Others among them believe that "tongues of men" refers to inspired speech in languages understood by the speaker while "tongues of angels" refers to speaking in tongues. For example, Dunn states:

> Since he [Paul] is presumably thinking throughout 13:1-3 of different types of charismata as such, 'tongues of men' will denote not simply 'ordinary human speech', but inspired speech of different kinds in the vernacular . . . while 'tongues of angels' will be Paul's and/or the Corinthians' description of glossolalia. (1975, 244)

In my view, the tongues of men could include prophecy, understood by the speaker, and human tongues not understood by the speaker. With regard to tongues of angels, many hold that Paul was speaking in hyperbole and that no one actually speaks in the language of angels. Others go further and question whether or not there actually are tongues of angels. We do know that angels communicate. The tongues of angels are real, and the Spirit could inspire someone to speak in such tongues.

Two, Paul continues with this comment, "but do not have love." The ideal for our service is to have unconditional love for others, but the term *agapē* does not require unconditional love. Paul does not speak about degrees of love or mixed motivations. No doubt, the believers in Paul's time sometimes had mixed motivations and, at other times, behaved in ways that came close to the ideal of unconditional love. Just how and when God will reward expressions of love are entirely in His hands. When others act, we cannot know the depths of their heart. God does.

Three, now Paul deals with what happens to us when we do not act in love. He says, "I have become a noisy gong (*chalkos*, χαλκὸς) or a clanging cymbal (*kumbalon*, κύμβαλον)." According to Bauer, *chalkos* means "copper, brass, bronze," and in 13:1 it means "a noisy (brass) gong" (2000, 1076). Scholars discuss whether or not the gong was used as an instrument, as a name for a piece of armor, or some other purpose, but it definitely signifies empty and unpleasant sound.[59]

The cymbal was an instrument used in worship. Bauer describes the cymbal (*kumbalon*) as a "metal basin." He says that when two such basins were struck against each other, a shrill sound resulted. He holds that in 13:1 the meaning is "a clashing cymbal" (2000, 575). As Lim points out, the cymbal was a loud percussion instrument used in Jewish temple worship and in pagan worship as well (1991, 115).

Paul does not deny that the people may benefit when we speak "in the tongues of men and of angels." When tongues are interpreted, they do benefit. However, when love is absent, there is no benefit to us, the speakers. Montague writes: "The use of tongues, just as the exercise of any of the other gifts, is no infallible sign of charity and if a man does not have love in his heart, all his tongues do is to manifest the emptiness within him" (1976, 164). We become as empty as a noisy gong or clanging cymbal. Although it is paradoxical, we benefit when we act in love. We do not benefit when we act without love.

Second, in verse 2, Paul says: "If I have *the gift of* prophecy, and know all mysteries and all knowledge; and if I have all faith, so as to remove mountains, but do not have love, I am nothing." Here, Paul again mentions several of the gifts of the Spirit. He spoke previously about prophecy in 12:10, knowledge in 12:8, and faith in 12:9. Here Paul adds "mysteries," which he will write about again in 14:2. He does not specifically label "mysteries" as a gift of the Spirit, but the word obviously fits the category. In my view, it is a gift of the Spirit. Several points concerning verse 2 follow.

One, since I wrote earlier on prophecy, knowledge, and faith, and since prophecy will be a major topic in our discussion of 1

---

[59]Fee states that *chalkos ēchōn* (χαλκὸς ἠχῶν) literally means "echoing bronze." He says that "Of the two items, this is the more puzzling since there is no known evidence for its use as an 'instrument.' Recently it has been suggested that it reflects the bronze 'amplification' systems of the stone amphitheaters" (1987, 632).

Corinthians 14, I will only make brief comments on these topics here. The verb "know," in verse 2, includes both mysteries and knowledge. No doubt knowledge is interchangeable with "word of knowledge." This is true especially when the broader meanings of each term are accepted. When Paul mentions faith, he explicitly says that he is referring to faith that "removes mountains," not to saving faith.

Two, sometimes Paul uses the word "mysteries" to refer to truths previously hidden but now revealed. Mysteries, knowledge, and revelation are interrelated. We can obtain knowledge of truth that is not mysterious or knowledge of hidden or mysterious truth. Either type of knowledge can be based on revelations by the Spirit to us.

The mysteries have to do with God's future purposes as well as with current situations. With regard to 13:2, Fee writes: "Paul now uses this language to refer to God's present revelation of his ways, especially in the form of special revelations by means of the eschatological Spirit whom Christians have received (cf. 14:6)" (1994, 203). In Colossians 2:2, Paul indicates that the revelation of hidden truths includes "a true knowledge of God's mystery, *that is*, Christ *Himself*."

Three, Paul indicates in verse 1 what would happen to him if he acted without love. He says "I have become" a noisy gong or a clanging symbol. Here in verse 2, he declares that, without love, "I am nothing." The emphasis in both verses is on who he now is as a person. Even if he were to have "all mysteries," "all knowledge," and "all faith," he is nothing. No matter how gifted a person is, he is nothing without the motivation of love. Others may benefit from what a person does; but without love, he is nothing. We benefit only when love motivates our actions.

Third, Paul states (13:3): "And if I give (*psōmisō*, ψωμίσω) all my possessions to feed *the poor*." The words "the poor" are not in the Greek text; they are supplied based on the meaning of the verb *psōmisō*. Thayer maintains that *psōmisō* means "*to feed by putting a bit* or *crumb (of food) in the mouth*" (1962, 678). Bauer accepts this meaning, but gives a broader definition as well. He states that this verb means to "*give away all one's property bit . . . by bit*" (2000, 1100). When Paul says "possessions," it suggests that he has the broader meaning in mind. The broader sense, of course, may include the narrower meaning. One could give away possessions in order to obtain food to feed the poor. With regard to 13:3, I would note these points:

One, Paul does not identify "giving" as a gift of the Spirit in 13:3, but he does in Romans 12:8. Whether or not we identify the giving in 13:3 as a gift of the Spirit, we know that it is an act of great personal sacrifice. As far as I am concerned, we can call this a gift of the Spirit. As with the other gifts, this giving should be motivated by love.

Two, with regard to the second clause of verse 3, whether Paul means "that I may be burned" or "that I may boast" is much discussed. Just which verb Paul uses is an issue because of variant readings in the manuscripts (cf. Thiselton 2000, 1042 and Taylor 2014, 308).

According to one reading, Paul uses the verb *kauchēsōmai* (καυχήσωμαι). This is a form of the verb *kauchaomai* (καυχάομαι) which means "to boast" or "to glory" (Bagster, 226). Fee favors this reading and points out that boasting is not always negative. He says that, as long as the boasting is brought under the gift of grace, it can be positive. He cites, as examples, Paul's comments in 2 Corinthians 1:14 and Romans 5:2-3 (1987, 634-635).

Two variant readings change the Greek letter χ (*chi*) to θ (*theta*). With this change, Paul writes either *kauthēsōmai* (καυθήσωμαι) or *kauthēsomai* (καυθήσομαι). Both of these verbs are forms of *kaiō* (καίω) which means "to burn." Bauer says that scholars may view this as martyrdom, voluntary self-burning, or being marked as a slave by branding (2000, 499). In any case, whoever gives his body acts with great personal sacrifice.

Both approaches have their supporters, but either burning or boasting without love is empty. Paul says that such action "profits me nothing." As Lim states, "With either reading, the point is the same and the result is the same" (1991, 117).

Paul statement that "but [if I] do not have love, it profits me nothing" may surprise us. How can anyone give away all that he has and it profit him nothing? How can anyone surrender his body to be burned and it profit him nothing? Are not such acts, by definition, acts of love? Without hesitation, Paul makes it clear that these acts can be done out of other, less worthy, motivations. When done in love, it is a huge example of what God can do through us.

Characteristics of Love

In 13:4-7, Paul gives a list of characteristics of love. His teaching applies to believers of all ages, but the occasion for the letter was the behavior of the believers at Corinth. As Hummel states, Paul does not present an abstract ideal of love; rather, he tells us how love "acts and *reacts* in the rough and tumble of life" (1979, 143).

Because Paul's teaching on love is set in the context of his teaching on spiritual gifts, Harold Horton relates all these characteristics to the gifts. For example, he maintains that love is kind "to those who, like Paul and thousands today, speak with tongues; to those who, on the contrary, do not speak with tongues though they might (xiv. 5)" (1962, 98). Similarly, Stanley Horton says, "Since the word 'love' is used in so many different contexts, Paul identifies twelve characteristics that describe the kind of love needed in the seeking and manifesting of spiritual gifts" (1999, 126). All this is true, but the kindness should extend to all people and in every way, whether or not a gift of the Spirit is involved.

In just four verses, Paul lists 15 characteristics that include both positive and negative traits. The positive traits indicate what the believers should be doing and imply that they were not. The negative statements identify what they should not do and suggests that they were. Moreover, as Lenski avers, "The negatives used in Paul's description suggest corresponding positives. Instead of being envious love is satisfied with its own portion and glad of another's greater portion" (1946, 556).

Without attempting to categorize the characteristics of love, I will present them in the order that Paul employs. His order seems to be more random than systematic. He states:

> 4 Love is patient, love is kind *and* is not jealous; love does not brag *and* is not arrogant, 5 does not act unbecomingly; it does not seek its own, is not provoked, does not take into account a wrong *suffered*, 6 does not rejoice in unrighteousness, but rejoices with the truth; 7 bears all things, believes all things, hopes all things, endures all things.

First, Paul mentions five traits of love in verse 4. These are being patient, being kind, not being jealous, not bragging, and not being arrogant. These traits are not unrelated to each other. They tend to go together as a part of a life that is dedicated to being like Christ.

One, love is patient (*makrothumei*, μακροθυμεῖ).[60] The present tense of the verb indicates that we should continuously be patient. God provides the example for us. As He seeks to draw us to Himself, He is patient with us. We should desire to be a channel of His patience in our interaction with others. When we truly love others, we will overlook moments that might seem to warrant impatience. Even when we have a right to be impatient, patience can overrule.

Two, love is kind (*chrēsteuetai*, χρηστεύεται). Not only should we be patient with others, but we should be kind. According to Lim, "Early Christians saw the relationship between the word *chrēsteuetai* and Christ (*christos*, Χριστὸς), whose very nature is to show kindness. Jesus' greatest act of kindness was at Calvary" (1991, 119). Kindness comes in various forms. At its highest level, kindness asks nothing in return.

Three, love is not jealous (*zēloi*, ζηλοῖ). Paul uses the present tense of the same Greek verb that he uses in 1 Corinthians 12:31 and 14:1. This verb can be used concerning either noble or base motivation. As Bauer explains, *zēloi* means "in a good sense *strive, desire, exert oneself earnestly*" and "in a bad sense *be filled with jealousy*" or "*envy toward someone*" (2000, 427). In 13:4, Paul uses the word in a bad sense. When believers are filled with love, they are not jealous of others. With regard to spiritual gifts, Harold Horton gives this example: love "envieth not the doorkeeper because he prophesies nor the elder because he has the Gifts of Healings" (1962, 98).

---

[60]Thiselton adds this thought: "Love, Paul urges, waits patiently not only because it deals patiently with the loved one but also because it recognizes that *the right timing* plays a huge part in securing the welfare of the other. Love does not blunder in. The Corinthians, by contrast, were all too ready to jump the gun both in their assumptions about Paul and other ministers (1 Cor. 4:5) and in anticipating their own triumphs (4:8)" (2000, 1047).

Four, love does not brag (*perpereuetai*, περπερεύεται). The Greek verb, according to Bauer, means "boast," "brag," "behave as a braggart" or "be a wind bag" (2000, 808). Whenever people are blessed of God in ministry, it is a temptation to forget the source of the blessing and start bragging on oneself. This can happen with any of the spiritual gifts. Unfortunately, some might be tempted to also brag about how much love they show. When this happens, both the gifts and the fruit of love are diminished.

Five, love is not arrogant (*phusioutai*, φυσιοῦται). The meaning of this verb, says Robertson, is "to puff oneself out like a bellows" (1931, 178). With regard to this verse, Thayer gives this definition: "to be puffed up, to bear oneself loftily, be proud" (1962, 660). This applies to people in all aspects of life, including in their exercise of spiritual gifts. Love avoids arrogance and embraces humility. As Lenski states, "in this case the positive virtue is Christian humility and lowliness of mind" (1946, 556).

Second, in verse 5, Paul lists four more characteristics of love. He says that love "does not act unbecomingly; it does not seek its own, is not provoked, does not take into account a wrong *suffered*."

One, love does not act unbecomingly (*aschēmonei*, ἀσχημονεῖ). According to Bauer, this verb means "*behave disgracefully, dishonorably, indecently*" (2000, 147). One only has to read Paul's entire letter to the Corinthians to see that this church had many behavioral problems. Some of their problems had to do with the way they exercised the spiritual gifts in the worship services. Whatever the reasons are for their unbecoming behavior, the antidote is love. As Montague states, love "is not ill-mannered or lacking in propriety. It acts with respect, delicacy, with an instinct for what is most appropriate" (1976, 166).

Two, love does not seek its own (*zētei ta heautēs*, ζητεῖ τὰ ἑαυτῆς).[61] The verb *zēteo* (ζητέω) means "*seek*" or "*look for*" (Bauer 2000, 428). Paul adds *heautēs*, a reflexive pronoun meaning

---

[61]Kistemaker comments as follows: "Translators differ on the meaning of this clause. The one says that love 'does not insist on its own way' (NRSV), another that 'it never seeks its own advantage' (NJB), and still another that it 'does not claim its rights' (*Cassirer*). Even though their emphases differ, all these versions convey the same message. In shortened form the clause simply connotes '[Love] is not selfish' (NCV)" (1993, 460).

"its own." Seeking one's own interests is a natural trait that is common to all mankind. Christ does not demand that we give up all self-interest, but He does challenge us to avoid negative self-interest and to go beyond legitimate self-interest in our actions toward others. As Calvin states:

> For Paul does not mean that we must have no care and anxiety about our own affairs at all; but he is condemning excessive care and anxiety about them, which, in turn, spring from excessive blind love of our selves. But the excessiveness actually consists in neglecting others through thinking about ourselves, or being distracted by concern for our own interests from that consideration, which God commands us to have for our neighbors. (Trans. Fraser, 1960, 277)

Three, love is not provoked (*paroxunetai*, παροξύνεται). The Greek verb, says Thayer, means "*to rouse to wrath, to provoke, exasperate, anger*" (1962, 490). The circumstances and people who can exasperate us are many. Not many would claim to have never been provoked. It is the motivation of love that leads us to improved behavior. With the help of the Spirit, we can overcome and become far less easily provoked. Regarding verse 4, Fee states, "This is a further expression of the forbearance [*makrothumei*, μακροθυμει, v.4] with which the list began" (1987, 639).

Four, love does not take into account (*logizetai*, λογίζεται) a wrong suffered (*kakon*, κακόν). Thayer states that the verb *logizetai* means "to reckon" or "to take into account" (1962, 379). The noun *kakon* means "wrong" or "evil" (Bauer 2000, 501). Fee makes these comments:

> Literally this says that love "does not reckon the evil." Since the language is very close to the LXX of Zech. 8:17, it is possible, as the KJV does ('thinketh no evil'), to understand this to mean "love does not devise evil against someone else." (1987, 639)

However, like most scholars, Fee favors the view that love does not take into account the evils inflicted by others upon us. Lenski, another author who holds this view, points out that the verb *logizesthai* (λογίζεσθαι) "is the very verb used to describe the pardoning act of God: he does not impute to us our guilt, Ps. 32:2;

Rom. 4:8; II Cor. 5:19; but imputes to us righteousness for Christ's sake, Rom. 4:6-11; 22-25; James 2:23" (1946, 558-559).

Third, in verse 6, Paul lists additional characteristics of love. Up to this point, Paul has listed by itself either a negative or a positive characteristic of love without stating the opposite. Here, he puts together in one sentence both a negative and a positive aspect. We could consider this to be one characteristic that is twofold or simply two characteristics.

Either way, "love does not rejoice (*chairei*, χαίρει) in unrighteousness, but rejoices with (*sunchairei*, συγχαίρει) the truth." Love does not rejoice in any form of wrongdoing or evil, no matter who commits the wrongs. Love does not rejoice in evil done by others or evil that befalls others.[62] In contrast, love does rejoice with the truth. The truth not only has to do with propositional truth, but also with what is morally righteous. Although Paul does not specifically personify "truth" in this verse, Jesus is the truth, He taught the truth, and He asks us to live the truth. When we do this, we will rejoice with the truth.

Fourth, in verse 7, Paul adds four more characteristics of love. Love "bears all things, believes all things, hopes all things, endures all things." As Lenski explains, the first and last statements should be understood in the sense of "all that is worst" while the second and third statements should be taken in the sense of "all that is best" (1946, 560).

One, love bears all things (*stegei*, στέγει). The verb *stegō* (στέγω) has several meanings. Among them, Thayer lists "to protect," or "to keep secret," and "to endure" (1962, 586). These meanings give rise to at least two interpretations.

The majority opinion seems to be that love "endures" all things. Those who love can endure great suffering and wrong doing that are inflicted on them. Calvin agrees with this interpretation, but he suggests a limitation with these comments: "By Paul's reference to 'all things' we must understand things that must be endured, and in the right way. . . . this endurance does not

---

[62]Concerning truth, Morris writes: "It is all too characteristic of human nature to take pleasure in the misfortunes of others. . . . Plainly there is that in man to which reports of this kind appeal. But love is not like that. Love takes no joy in evil of any kind. Rather its joy is *in the truth*" (1958, 185).

cut out disciplinary measures and punishments which are deserved" (Trans. Fraser, 1960, 278). It should be said, however, that most people are more in danger of not enduring enough rather than too much.

Another option has to do with keeping things confidential. Concerning 13:7, Bauer gives this interpretation: *"of love that throws a cloak of silence over what is displeasing in another person"* (2000, 942). Although using a different verb (*kaluptei*, καλύπτει), a similar statement is made in 1 Peter 4:8. Peter says, "Above all, keep fervent in your love for one another, because love covers a multitude of sins." The two approaches are not contradictory. Keeping a wrong confidential is sometimes a way of enduring, but not all wrongs should be kept confidential. When things are legally wrong, for example, it is important to act with good legal advice.

Two, love "believes (*pisteuei*, πιστεύει) all things (*panta*, πάντα)." Paul uses the Greek word *panta*, which means all things, in connection with all four of the traits of love listed in verse 7. When thinking about others, love motivates us to believe the very best about them. There are occasions when constructive evaluation is necessary, but love will inspire us to highlight the good qualities in others and overlook characteristics that might irritate us. Without love, the temptation is to headline any weakness that surfaces. As much as possible, through love, we should relate to others on the basis of confidence and trust.

Three, love "hopes (*elpizei*, ἐλπίζει) all things (*panta*)." The hope that love inspires should not be limited by a narrow definition. Given the context, we know love will move us to hope for the best for others and from others. This hope would be for the best in all aspects of life.

Four, love "endures (*hupomenei*, ὑπομένει) all things (*panta*)." Here, Paul uses a different verb than he uses in verse 4 (*makrothumei*, μακροθυμεῖ) and previously in this verse (*stegei*). These words have some overlapping significance, but also each has its own special focus. According to Bauer, the verb *hupomenei* means *"patience, endurance, fortitude, steadfastness, perseverance"* especially "as they are shown in the enduring of toil and suffering" (2000, 1039). Lenski comments that "love 'endures all things' in the sense of brave perseverance" (1946, 561). When life is difficult, love helps us keep alive our courage.

Conclusion

The apostle Paul is writing to the Corinthians about spiritual gifts. Apparently, there were problems with the way that they were exercising the gifts, so he writes to correct them and encourage them to use them in the right way. He says in 12:31 that love is the most excellent way to earnestly desire the spiritual gifts. Then, in 13:1-3, he writes about exercising gifts without love. Such an approach may benefit the recipient of the ministry, but not the minister. Next, in 13:4-7, Paul gives a rather lengthy list of characteristics of love. These traits apply to those who minister with spiritual gifts, but also, in a very general way, to all of a believer's life.

In chapter eight, I will discuss 13:8-13. In 13:8-12, Paul draws a contrast between the present age and the age of the future. In contrast to the temporary nature of gifts, love never fails. Finally, in 13:13, Paul maintains that faith, hope, and love abide. All three abide in the present; in some ways, faith and hope will cease, but in other ways, they will abide in the future; love abides both now and in the future. Paul ends with the strong proclamation that love is the greatest. Next, in 14:1, he again encourages us to "pursue love, yet desire earnestly *spiritual* gifts." The ideal is not gifts without love or love without gifts, but to exercise the gifts motivated by love.

CHAPTER EIGHT

THE GREATEST IS LOVE

Introduction

In 1 Corinthians 13:8-13, Paul continues his discussion of love. He has made the point in 12:31 that the highest way to earnestly desire spiritual gifts is through love. In 13:1-4, he makes the point that spiritual gifts without love profit us nothing. Then, in 13:4-7, he gives a list of the characteristics of love. All believers should demonstrate these traits in all aspects of their lives, including in the way they exercise spiritual gifts.

Next, in 13:8-13, Paul shows us how spiritual gifts and love fit into the present age and the age to come. He begins verse 8 with the statement that "love never fails." In the rest of 13:8-12, he presents the temporal nature of prophecies, tongues, and knowledge. These gifts will pass away when that which is perfect comes. He uses two analogies, childhood and looking in a mirror, to explain that our knowledge is partial, but we will have full knowledge in the future. Finally, in 13:13, he extols the abiding nature of faith, hope, and love, with love being the greatest. Paul writes:

[8]Love never fails; but if *there are gifts of* prophecy, they will be done away; if *there are* tongues, they will cease; if *there is* knowledge, it will be done away. [9]For we know in part and we prophesy in part; [10]but when the perfect comes, the partial will be done away. [11]When I was a child, I used to speak like a child, think like a child, reason like a child; when I became a man, I did away with childish things. [12]For now we see in a mirror dimly, but then face to face; now I know in part, but then I will know fully just as I also have been fully known. [13]But now faith, hope, love, abide these three; but the greatest of these is love.

Love Never Fails

Paul's declaration in 13:8 that "love never fails (*piptei*, πίπτει)" could be viewed as either the end of the previous paragraph (13:4-7) or the beginning of the new one, or both. As the end of the previous paragraph, it lists another characteristic of love. As the beginning of the new paragraph, it presents love that never ceases in contrast with spiritual gifts that will pass away. This statement is transitional and belongs with both the previous paragraph and the new one.

Bauer gives several meanings of *piptei*, including "fall" as in fall down, fall in a religious or moral sense, and in the sense of perish or disappear (2000, 815-816).[63] The latter two meanings are metaphorical. With regard to whether Paul was referring to falling in a moral sense or in the sense of never ending, Fee states:

> Perhaps Paul's intent is to be found in the very ambiguity of such figurative language, so that both are in view. There is a sense in which love is never brought down; it reflects God's character, after all, and cannot fluctuate from what it is. Yet that very reality is what also gives it eternal character, so that it "remains" even after all other things have come to their proper end. (1987, 643)

When scholars say that love does not fail in a moral sense, they mean God's love. Obviously, this point is true. Thus, we can include this point in the meaning of "love never fails." In addition, this declaration stands in contrast to the temporal nature of spiritual gifts. Given this contrast, the predominant meaning of the statement seems to be that love abides without end.

Now and Then

In the rest of 13:8-12, Paul focuses on the present age and the age to come. He deals with what exists now and what will exist then. It is important to study what he says in the immediate context

---

[63] Garland recognizes that "love never falls" can mean different things. He says, "Paul may mean that love never collapses in defeat, is never destroyed (cf. Luke 6:49), never falls apart, never falls short, or never fails to have an effect. . . . But Paul is introducing an eschatological perspective on love and spiritual gifts. . . . It means that love 'never ceases to exist, even in heaven' . . . and usually is translated as love 'never fails' or 'never ends'" (2003, 621).

and also in the larger context of his theology in general. The larger context is Paul's "already-not yet" approach to his theology.[64]

Many scholars hold that the Kingdom of God has "already" come in the person of Christ, but that the full realization has "not yet" taken place. This will happen when Christ returns. Meanwhile, we live "between the times," between the resurrection and the consummation, and the church is a creation of the Kingdom. During this time, the Holy Spirit enables the church to experience the power of the Kingdom. Moreover, the power of the Spirit is available to every believer.

Ladd is representative of those who maintain that the "already-not yet" approach is central to Paul's thinking. In his view, the church is a creation of the Kingdom. Ladd presents his "central thesis" as follows:

> Our central thesis is that the Kingdom of God is the redemptive reign of God dynamically active to establish his rule among men, and that this Kingdom, which will appear as an apocalyptic act at the end of the age, has already come into human history in the person and mission of Jesus to overcome evil, to deliver men from its power, and to bring them into the blessings of God's reign. The Kingdom of God involves two great moments: fulfillment within history, and consummation at the end of history. (1974, 91)

With this in mind, the spiritual gifts are ways to work with God "between the times." Between now and the return of Christ, the Holy Spirit of God works through us to exalt Christ and to minister to people everywhere. The Holy Spirit distributes the gifts among

---

[64] According to Ridderbos, a growing consensus exists among scholars that the "main entrance" to Paul's theology is found in "the *redemptive-historical, eschatological character of Paul's proclamation*" . . . It is this great redemptive-historical framework within which the whole of Paul's preaching must be understood and all of its subordinate parts receive their place and organically cohere" (1975, 39). Ridderbos identifies this "main entrance" as an "already-not yet" approach (1975, 29, 43), but he also uses the terms "already now" and "even now." He writes: "It is this remarkable ambivalence of the 'now,' which can have the sense of the '*already* now' of the time of salvation that has been entered upon as well as of the '*even* now' of the world time that still continues, which imparts to Paul's eschatology its wholly distinctive character" (1975, 52).

118

us. Obviously, the gifts will be useful until Christ returns. Now, we will examine 13:8-13 verse-by-verse.

First, Paul continues verse 8 by contrasting love with spiritual gifts. He states: "but if *there are gifts of* prophecy (*prophēteiai,* προφητεῖαι), they will be done away (*katargēthēsontai,* καταργηθήσονται); if *there are* tongues (*glōssai,* γλῶσσαι), they will cease (*pausontai,* παύσονται); if *there is* knowledge (*gnosis,* γνῶσις), it will be done away (*katargēthēsetai,* καταργηθήσεται)." The NASB[95] has changed "prophecies" to "*gifts of* prophecy."

One, as 13:8 indicates, prophecies, tongues, and knowledge all are spiritual gifts. Paul has mentioned prophecy and kinds of tongues in 12:10 and the word of knowledge in 12:8. Prophecies contain messages to man or praises to God. In 13:8-12, Paul especially emphasizes knowledge and our expression of it to the body of Christ. In these verses, Paul does not discuss the impact of tongues with and without interpretation. He will do this in 1 Corinthians 14. Speaking in tongues with interpretation communicates to man as well. All of these terms are very flexible and capable of including a variety of meanings.

Two, these gifts will cease to exist and will be done away. The temporal nature of the gifts is an important point in Paul's thinking. Concerning the gifts ceasing in verses 8-11, Blomberg writes:

> The NIV renders the same verb *katargeō* ('to destroy or abolish') four different ways in verses 8-11 ('cease' [v. 8a]. 'pass away' [v. 8c], 'disappears' [v. 10], 'put . . . behind' [v. 11]), but each of these captures an important nuance of the term. Paul uses a different verb (*pauomai*) with tongues (NIV 'be stilled'—v. 8b) but probably for stylistic variety (creating an ABA pattern for the three parallel statements of v. 8). Although it is a middle voice (sometimes translated as action done to, by, or for oneself), this particular verb has become a virtual deponent (a verb without active voice endings) in the Greek of the New Testament, so it is dangerous here to read anything much into this specific grammatical form.[65] (1994, 260)

---

[65] As Carson points out, some scholars hold that *pausontai* (παύσονται), the verb used with tongues, means "will cease of *themselves.*" Carson counters this position as follows: "There is something [they say] intrinsic to their

As many put forward, the gift of tongues will cease, but so will prophecies and knowledge. Indeed, all the spiritual gifts are temporal and will cease when Christ returns. The three gifts that Paul mentions are representative of all the spiritual gifts.[66] All of them are valuable in this present age, but they are all temporal. All will pass away when the conditions of our text are met.

Second, in 13:9, Paul says, "For we know (*ginōskomen*, γινώσκομεν) in part (*ek merous*, ἐκ μέρους) and we prophesy (*prophēteuomen*, προφητεύομεν) in part (*ek merous*)." The verbs *ginōskomen* and *prophēteuomen* are in the present tense. We are still in this "present age" when these gifts are valuable. The Corinthians know and express partial knowledge in their current experience and prophesy from time to time. Bauer says that *merous* means "*part*, in contrast to the whole" (2000, 633).[67] Our current knowledge is partial in contrast to the full knowledge that we will have.

The views of Calvin and Fee are representative of scholarly approaches to this verse. Calvin holds that "in part" applies to us as believers, while Fee holds that the phrase applies to our knowledge and prophecies. Calvin states:

> Most people explain this verse in the wrong way, viz., that our knowledge is not yet perfect, but that we are making daily progress in it; and that the same thing applies to prophecy. But Paul's meaning is that the fact that we have knowledge and prophecy [as gifts] is precisely because we are imperfect. Therefore "in part" means that we are not yet made perfect.

---

character that demands they cease—apparently independently of the cessation of prophecy and knowledge. This view [Carson maintains] assumes without warrant that the switch to this verb is more than a stylistic variation" (1987, 66).

[66] On this point Taylor writes: "These three gifts are not the only gifts that will cease, but rather represent all gifts and are chosen because of their relevance to the Corinthian context" (2014, 315).

[67] With regard to *ek merous* in 13:9, Thayer gives this definition: "in part, partially, i.e. *imperfectly*" (1962, 401). Thiselton posits that "The idiom [*ek merous*] has the force of *piece by piece, bit by bit, or* **part by part** in many contexts, including here" (2,000, 1064). For stylistic reasons, he translates the first *ek merous* as "in fragmentary ways" and the second as "part by part" (2000, 1064-1065).

Knowledge and prophecy will therefore have a place in our lives, so long as imperfection clings to us, for they help us in our incompleteness. (Trans. Fraser 1960, 280)

In my judgment, the phrase "in part" has to do with the knowledge and prophecies, not the believers themselves. The comments by Fee on this point give the right perspective. He states:

Even though Paul says "we know in part," the emphasis is not on the immaturity of the Corinthians, but on the relative nature of the gifts. This is demonstrated (1) by the γὰρ (*gar*) that ties it to v. 8, where it is said of these gifts that *they* will pass away, not that the Corinthians need to grow up, and (2) by the clause "we prophesy in part," which makes sense only as having to do with the prophecies, not with the prophets. (Transliteration Mine, 1987, 645)

Third, in verse 10, Paul says, "but when the perfect (τελειον, τελειον) comes (*elthē*, ἔλθῃ), the partial (*ek merous*) will be done away (*katargēthēsetai*, καταργηθήσεται). Thayer indicates that the verb *teleioō* (τελειόω) means "to make perfect or complete" (1962, 618). Here, the adjective *teleion* is used as a substantive to refer to that which is complete or perfect. Also, this word often means "mature."[68]

Paul is writing about knowledge (verses 9 and 12). The partial knowledge of the Corinthians will be replaced "when the perfect comes." With regard to the "perfect" coming, there are three main ideas: (1) that Paul was referring to the completion of the New Testament canon; (2) that he had in mind the maturity of the believers; and (3) that he refers to the consummation. Under the third view, we will have perfect knowledge when Christ returns. I will comment briefly on the first view; then consider the second and third views.

Some scholars argue that the gifts ceased when the New Testament canon was completed. The New Testament provides our

---

[68]Kistemaker says that "The literature of the New Testament usually equates the Greek expression *teleion* with maturity" (1993, 467). He cites: 1 Cor. 2:6; 14:20; Eph. 4:13; Phil. 3:15; Col. 1:28; 4:12. Even so, Kistemaker argues that the reference in 13:10 is to the consummation.

"perfect" knowledge. According to them, the gifts of knowledge, prophecies, and tongues will not be needed. According to Hummel, this interpretation has two major difficulties. He writes:

> First, Paul describes the perfection as the time when "we shall see face to face" and "know fully, even as I am fully known," that is, perfectly (13:12). This condition did not exist at the end of the first century, and will not occur until the end of the age at the coming of Christ. Second, this view narrows the function of these gifts to the apostles and prophets through whom inspired Scripture was written. Paul, however, teaches a wider purpose for these charisms—constantly building the body of Christ. These three gifts, as well as the others, are needed as long as the church continues its pilgrimage. (1979, 145)

Fourth, in verse 11, Paul deals with the subject of "why" spiritual gifts will pass away. He says, "When I was a child, I used to speak like a child, think like a child, reason like a child; when I became a man, I did away (katērgēka, κατήργηκα) with childish things." In Greek, all the verbs for "was," "speak," "think," and "reason" are in the imperfect tense, signifying continuous actions in the past. The verbs "became" and "did away" are in the perfect tense.

Here, Paul uses the nouns "child" and "man" in a metaphorical sense. Some scholars focus their interpretation on spiritual maturity. They may hold that, as believers mature, they will stop exercising at least some of the spiritual gifts. Very often, speaking in tongues is named as one of the gifts that will cease. The implication often is that speaking in tongues is for those who are immature. Another approach is that the gifts are appropriate to this age, but that the Corinthians were exercising them in an immature way. Their childish actions should cease in favor of a mature manner.[69]

---

[69] Arrington states: "The point of 13:11 is not that the church on the earth will become so mature that it will no longer need such gifts as prophecy, tongues and knowledge. On this earth the church needs these gifts because its knowledge remains incomplete. An accurate understanding of the idea of spiritual gifts passing away at maturity (or perfection) is this: regardless of how magnificent gifts may be the partial knowledge they provide now must be seen as childish in comparison to the fuller knowledge that believers will

However, Paul uses the metaphors of "child" and "man" to refer to this present age and the age to come. In context, he is drawing a contrast between this present age and the consummation. Just as the way the things of the child are appropriate to the child's age, so the spiritual gifts are appropriate to this present age. When Christ returns, there will be no need for the gifts; they will have fulfilled their role. Spiritual gifts will be inappropriate in the future age, so they will cease. Nevertheless, this approach does not totally lose sight of the concepts of maturity as life in the age to come is in a sense more mature.[70]

Fifth, Paul says in verse 12, "For now (*arti*, ἄρτι) we see in a mirror dimly (*en ainigmati*, ἐν αἰνίγματι), but then (*tote*, τότε) face to face; now (*arti*) I know in part, but then (*tote*) I will know fully just as I also have been fully known." Thayer writes that the noun *ainigmati* means "*an obscure saying, an enigma*" (1962, 16). Now, we see in a mirror "dimly." The result is that our knowledge is not complete. In this verse, the two Greek adverbs, *arti* and *tote*, guide us in interpreting what Paul means. According to Fee, *arti* is used in the New Testament predominately to mean "the present time" and can mean nothing else when set in contrast to *tote* (then)" (1987, 647). Given these adverbs, we conclude that Paul contrasts this present age with the age to come. We note the following two points.

One, in the first clause, Paul contrasts seeing in a mirror with seeing face-to-face. According to Thiselton, a key question with regard to this clause is: "Does *en ainigmati* (dimly) "allude to *obscurity, distortions*, or *puzzles* caused by the limitations of the mirrors in the ancient world (cf. AV/KJV, *darkly*) or to indirectness as signifying the difference between secondhand reflections and interpretations, and direct face-to-face vision and complete knowledge?" (2000, 1068).[71] Actually, it does not really

---

possess at the return of the Lord, when their faith gives way to sight" (2003, 256-257)

[70] As Keener avers, "The present experience is immature by comparison, just as the present body is a mere seed of future glory (15:36-37)" (2005, 110).

[71] According to Robertson, "Ancient mirrors were of polished metal, not glass, those in Corinth being famous;" moreover, he says: "To see a friend's face in a cheap mirror would be very different from looking at the friend" (1931, 179). Lenski contends: "The ancients used metal mirrors, yet we should not

matter about the mirror. No matter how well they could see in the mirror, or how obscure it might be, it was partial knowledge in comparison with the knowledge resulting from face-to-face communication.

Two, Paul closes verse 12 with these words, "Now, I know (*ginōskō*, γινώσκω) in part, but then I will know fully (*epignōsomai*, ἐπιγνώσομαι) just as I have been fully known (*epignōsthēn*, ἐπιγνώσθην)." The verb *ginōskō* means to know, and *epiginōskō* (ἐπιγινώσκω), according to Bauer, means "*know exactly, completely, through and through*" (2000, 369). The NASB[95] uses the translation "fully" know.

Three different verb tenses are used in this sentence: (1) present, *ginōskō*; (2) future, *epignōsomai*; and (3) aorist, *epignōsthēn*). The change in verb tenses is significant. With the present and future tenses, Paul writes about two ages. When Paul uses the aorist, as Lim explains, he "places himself at a future standpoint, looking back at the point of his present condition" (1991, 133).[72]

During this present age, our general knowledge is partial and incomplete. In the future, our knowledge will be complete. This verse does not put limits on what kind of knowledge we will have. Our increased knowledge of God is the main point, but knowledge of ourselves may be included. Montague says, "one of the promised joys of the future life is to know ourselves as God knows us, that is, to see in him not only the mystery of his own nature but also everything else that he sees and knows, particularly the mysterious depths of our self" (1976, 172).

---

suppose that these mirrors were dull and offered only a dim reflection; they were bright enough. The *tertium comparationis* [common quality] is found in the fact that as we see only the reflection and not the person or the object itself in a mirror, so we, who are children and know only in part, now see the divine realities only as they are reflected in the mirror of the Word and not directly as they are in fact" (1946, 568).

[72]Lenski writes: "The aorist 'have been known fully' is constative and includes all of God's knowledge regarding Paul and sums all of it up in one point. Commentators mention especially Paul's election and his conversion as being included in this knowing. Yet we should be careful not to restrict the force of this verb in any way" (1946, 571).

Our knowledge of God will be vastly expanded. MacGorman makes this comment, "Partial knowledge will yield to a full understanding of him, even as we have been fully understood by him" (1974, 78). Having a full understanding, however, does not mean that we will know everything that God knows. His knowledge is infinite and always will be greater than ours. According to Lenski,

> As God's direct and all-penetrating knowledge takes into account every one of his children already in eternity and, of course, through all of life, so we, too, shall at last know God directly and completely to the highest degree in which this is possible for his children." (1946, 571)

With regard to knowing fully, Fee stresses how we will know rather than what we will know. He says, "By this Paul intends to delineate the difference between the 'knowing' that is available through the gift of the Spirit and the final eschatological knowing that is complete" (1987, 648). God's way of knowing is immediate, direct, face-to-face. In the future, we will know in that way, not just knowing as in looking in a mirror.

Faith, Hope, and Love Abide

Paul says in verse 13: "But now faith, hope, love, abide (*menei*, μένει) these three; but the greatest of these is love."[73] In 13:8-12, the concepts of the present and future ages stand out. In 13:13, the abiding nature of faith, hope, and love and the superlative rank of love are the dominant chords that Paul strikes. What this means in connection with the two ages is often discussed.

First, Paul begins 13:13 with these words, "But now" (*nuni de*, νυνὶ δὲ). With regard to the adverb now (*nuni*), there are two major views. Many hold that *nuni* has a temporal force meaning "now, in this present age." Under this approach, faith, hope, and love abide in this age. Nothing is explicitly said, based on this

---

[73.]The triad of faith, hope, and love, occurs frequently in the New Testament: see Romans 5:1-5; Galatians 5:5-6; Colossians 1:4-5; 1 Thessalonians 1:3; 5:8; Hebrews 6:10-12; 10:22-24; 1 Peter 1:3-8, 21-22. Fee says, "Together these words embrace the whole of Christian existence, as believers live out the life of the Spirit in this present age, awaiting the consummation" (1987, 650).

phrase, about the future. However, the phrase itself does not preclude the idea that faith, hope, and love abide both now and in the future.

The other major view is that *nuni* should be taken in a logical sense. In other words, the adverb "now" introduces what comes next after discussing the temporary nature of the gifts. Without specifying when or how long faith, hope, and love abide, Paul just states the fact that they abide or remain. Nevertheless, the logical sense often is used to support the view that faith, hope, and love abide forever. Both views are sometimes modified to say that faith and hope abide in this age, but that love abides forever.

My view is that the words "but now" introduce a contrast between spiritual gifts and faith, hope, and love with regard to when they abide. Under the temporal view, faith, hope, and love, as well as the spiritual gifts, abide in this present age. Moreover, the word "these three" hold faith, hope and love together. So faith, hope, and love in some way abide in contrast to the gifts that pass away. It seems likely to me that the meaning is that faith, hope, and love will abide both now and in the future.

Second, let us consider what Paul means by faith and hope. In 13:2, Paul mentions "all faith, so as to remove mountains." In 13:7, he states that love "hopes all things." At this point, he mentions faith and hope with different connotations than in the earlier passages. Barrett avers, "Faith is now no longer the miracle-working faith of verse 2, but faith in its full Pauline sense" (1971, 308). It is saving faith in God, and faith that sustains us in our ongoing walk with God. There are many aspects to this faith. To this, we can add that hope is not just hoping for the best in considering others, but hope is maintaining our faith in God and in the fulfillment of His promises. With faith, we hope for all that God has promised.

Third, the Greek verb *menei* is in the present tense and can be translated "abide" or "remain." The present tense tells us that faith, hope, and love remain at least in this present age. Verse 13 neither explicitly says that these qualifies will abide forever nor that they will not. With regard to the context of 13:1-12, verse 8 says that "Love never fails." Usually this is interpreted to mean now and in the eternal future, love will not fall so as to disappear. Given the fact that Paul connects faith and hope with love, we can conclude that all three abide forever.

Fourth, when Paul writes, "the greatest (*meizōn*, μείζων) of these is love." Bagster says the adjective *meizōn* is the comparative form of *megas* (μέγας), which means "great" (n.d., 261). The superlative of *megas* is *megistos* (μεγίστος). Citing 13:13, Robertson says that in the New Testament, there is a "blurring of distinction between the comparative and the superlative" (1934, 668). It appears, therefore, that *meizōn* can mean either "greater" or "greatest." Most English translations opt for "greatest."

In this clause, Paul shifts his primary emphasis from when and how long faith, hope, and love abide to which one is the greatest. In other words, Paul speaks about the ranking of these qualities. Paul says that love is the greatest, but he does not say why. Much of the discussion about this clause focuses on why love is the greatest. Two points are germane.

One, some scholars hold that love is the greatest because, unlike faith and hope, it lasts eternally. In support of this, many cite 2 Corinthians 5:7. Now, it is said, "we walk by faith, not by sight," while in the future we will walk by sight. In addition, Romans 8:24 says, "but hope that is seen is not hope." It is true that some aspects of faith and hope will cease when the present age is folded into the future, but other aspects will not. In the future age, we apparently will not need faith "so as to remove mountains." However, we will continue to rely on and trust in God. There is no sufficient reason to separate faith and hope from love by saying that faith and hope abide only in this present age and that love abides now and forever.

Two, the other view focuses on who God is. Supporters cite 1 John 4:8 which says, "God is love." As Barrett declares: "But if God did not have love he would not be God. Love is an activity, the essential activity, of God himself, and when men love either him or their fellow-men they are doing (however imperfectly) what God does" (1971, 311). Love is God's motivation in His dealings with us, and it is the motive that we should have in relating to others. The God who is love exists eternally. Given this, we know that love is the greatest of all great qualities.

Fifth, scholars will no doubt continue to have different views with regard to whether or not faith and hope abide into the future age, but the opinion that love endures eternally is virtually unanimous. With regard to faith, hope, and love, Drummond expresses his view as follows:

Some think the time will come when two of the three things will also pass away—faith into sight, hope into fruition. Paul does not say so. We know little now about the conditions of the life that is to come. But what is certain is that Love must last. God, the Eternal God, is Love. Covet therefore that everlasting gift, that one thing which it is certain is going to stand, that one coinage which will be current in the Universe when all the other coinages of all the nations of the world shall be useless and unhonoured. You will give yourselves to many things, give yourselves first to Love. (n.d., 50)

With all these issues obviously in mind, but without giving the details of various views, Stanley Horton makes a very helpful statement in concise form. He holds that faith and hope, as well as love, will remain in eternity. He gives an excellent presentation of the sense of 13:13, where he writes:

In contrast to temporary blessings of charismatic gifts given for this age, three things we have now are permanent: faith, hope, and love. Even when faith becomes sight, faith in the sense of trustful obedience will always be the right attitude toward God. Even when the promised hope is realized, hope in the sense of expectation of future good will remain, for God is the God of hope (Rom. 15:13). But love, though mentioned last, is the greatest. We shall never forget John 3:16 and the glory of the Cross. Love was and is God's primary motive and must become ours, for God is love (1 John 4:8). (1999, 130)

Conclusion

Paul begins 1 Corinthians 13:8-13 with the comment that "Love never fails." This statement both concludes his list of characteristics of love and introduces his comments on the passing nature of spiritual gifts in contrast with love that never fails. In 13:8-12, Paul draws a contrast between the present age and the age of the future. In this present age, we need the gifts of prophecy, tongues, and knowledge, but in the future age, we will have complete and perfect knowledge.

In 13:13, Paul maintains that faith, hope, and love abide. All three abide in the present; in some ways, faith and hope will cease, but in other ways, they will abide in the future; love abides both now and in the future. Paul ends with the strong proclamation that love is the greatest. It is greatest because God is love and is the highest motivation for service. In language similar to 12:31, Paul encourages us in 14:1 to "pursue love, yet desire earnestly *spiritual gifts*." The ideal is not gifts without love or love without gifts, but to exercise the gifts motivated by love.

CHAPTER NINE

TONGUES, INTERPRETATION, AND PROPHECY

Introduction

In his letters to the churches, Paul lays down comprehensive spiritual principles that have guided the life of the church through the centuries. In 1 Corinthians 12-14, he discusses some of the key aspects of spirituality. He tells us how to be truly spiritual people, to exercise spiritual gifts through love, and to be a spiritual church in the way that we conduct our services.

In these chapters, Paul puts a special emphasis on the issue of spiritual gifts and their exercise in the church. He deals broadly with many gifts in chapter 12, inserts chapter 13 about love, and then turns more specifically in chapter 14 to tongues, interpretation of tongues, and prophecy. In addition, he comments briefly on having a psalm, a revelation, and a teaching.

Based on what Paul teaches, it is apparent that the spiritual gifts were being unwisely used and with the wrong motivation. So Paul writes to correct the believers at Corinth. Although this was true of the gifts in general, Paul gives special attention to the gift of speaking in tongues. He places a high value on speaking in tongues, but wants the gift to be used properly in the assembly.

The main problem at Corinth was that the believers were speaking in tongues to the church without interpretation. Without interpretation, tongues do not edify the body. Therefore, Paul stresses the importance of tongues being interpreted. In addition, he compares the greatness of the one who speaks in tongues with the one who prophesies. He explains that, in the church, the one who prophesies is greater than the one who speaks in tongues without interpretation.[74] In other words, unless tongues are interpreted, prophecy has greater value.

---

[74]Paul refers to the church 8 times in 1 Corinthians 12-14. Seven of the eight times are in chapter 14. Thus, it is clear that, in this chapter, Paul is concerned about the use of tongues and prophecy in the church, when the

While addressing this subject, Paul also places a high value on speaking in tongues in private.[75] In private, an interpretation is possible but not necessary. Another usage is for people to pray quietly in tongues in the church without intending to speak to the audience. Essentially, this is a "private" usage. The issue is intelligibility. When we wish to communicate with the assembly, tongues should be interpreted.

In chapter 14, Paul picks up the theme he struck in 12:31 where he said, "But earnestly desire (*zēloute*, ζηλοῦτε) the greater gifts (*charismata*, χαρίσματα). And I show you a still more excellent way." After 12:31, Paul inserted his chapter on love. Love is the most excellent way to desire spiritual gifts, the proper motivation. Then, after an admonition to pursue love, he picks up his theme of spiritual gifts. In 14:1-5, Paul writes:

[1]Pursue love, yet desire earnestly spiritual *gifts*, but especially that you may prophesy. [2]For one who speaks in a tongue does not speak to men, but to God; for no one understands, but in *his* spirit he speaks mysteries. [3]But one who prophesies speaks to men for edification and exhortation and consolation. [4]One who speaks in a tongue edifies himself; but one who prophesies edifies the church. [5]Now I wish that you all spoke in tongues, but *even* more that you would prophesy; and greater is one who prophesies that one who speaks in tongues, unless he interprets, so that the church may receive edifying.

Desire Spiritual Gifts

In 14:1, Paul exhorts: "Pursue (*diōkete*, διώκετε) love, yet desire earnestly (*zēloute*, ζηλοῦτε) spiritual gifts (*pneumatika* πνευματικά), but especially (*mallon de*, μᾶλλον δὲ) that you may

---

people were assembled. The eight references are: 12:28; 14:4, 5, 12, 19, 23, 28, and 35. Also, he mentions churches in 14:33 and 34.

[75]Balfour asserts: "Let us be clear. There is not more than one gift of speaking in tongues. Rather, the one gift of speaking in tongues has a dual function: private and public. It can be either interpreted or not interpreted. When it is not interpreted, it is intended for private edification—the person using the gift is speaking not to other people, 'but to God'" (2009, 32).

prophesy."[76] This is a transitional statement that both concludes what Paul says about love and introduces his comments about tongues and prophecy. Paul makes several points in this opening verse.

First, when Paul says "pursue" love, he uses the present imperative form (*diōkete*) of the verb *diōkō* (διώκω). Fee indicates that "The present imperative implies continuous action, 'keep on pursuing love'" (1987, 654). According to Bauer, this word can mean "*persecute*." However, with regard to 14:1, he indicates that Paul uses the verb in a figurative sense meaning to "pursue, strive for, seek after, aspire to" love (2000, 254). Taylor points out that "Paul frequently uses the verb 'to pursue' to refer to persecution but he also uses the verb metaphorically of spiritual effort in some contexts, as in 1 Cor. 14:1" (2014, 322).[77]

Second, Paul exhorts the Corinthians to "desire earnestly (*zēloute*) spiritual gifts." This form of the verb can be translated in the indicative or imperative mood. In both 14:1 and 14:39, Paul obviously intends the imperative mood.

Paul uses the same verb in 12:31 where he says "earnestly desire the greater gifts." Scholars debate whether *zēloute* in this verse should be translated in the imperative or the indicative mood. In my view, as expressed earlier, Paul is urging the Corinthians to desire the greater gifts. The Corinthians are zealous (14:12) for spiritual things, but they must seek to abound for the edification of the church. Their motivation must be right.

We are to earnestly desire spiritual gifts. The fact that wrong attitudes and unwise usage developed in connection with them does not mean that we should be reluctant to exercise them. We must be motivated by love and exercise them for the benefit of the body. Just because wisdom is needed in the exercise of a gift does

---

[76]Kistemaker notes the following: "The three verbs in this verse are directives: the first two are imperatives (Pursue love! Strive eagerly!), and the third is an indirect command (that you may prophesy). All of them are in the present tense to indicate that the readers should always seek to obey these injunctions" (1993, 476).

[77]According to Taylor, "All occurrences of the term in Paul include Rom 9:30-31; 12:13-14; 14:19; 1 Cor 4:12; 14:1; 15:9; 2 Cor 4:9; 5:11; 6:12; Phil 3:6, 12, 14; 1 Thess 5:15; 1 Tim 6:11; 2 Tim 2:22; 3:12" (2014, 322-323).

not mean that it should be prohibited. Rather, the proper usage of the gift should be encouraged.

Third, in 14:1, Paul exhorts the believers to "desire earnestly *pneumatika* (literally "spirituals"). This term is a neuter plural adjective used here as a noun. In our English translations, we normally supply the noun. It could mean either spiritual gifts or spiritual things. Because Paul immediately deals with prophecy and tongues, the term spiritual gifts in this verse seems preferable. This would harmonize with 12:31 where Paul refers to the *charismata*, a neuter plural noun meaning spiritual gifts.

However, the term *pneumatikos* is flexible.[78] Paul announces in 12:1 that he is writing "concerning *pneumatikōn* (πνευματικῶν)." This is a neuter or masculine plural adjective meaning spiritual gifts, spiritual persons, or spiritual things. The term *spiritual things* is broad enough to include both spiritual gifts and spiritual persons. In 14:37, Paul uses a masculine singular adjective, *pneumatikos* (πνευματικός), to refer to a spiritual man. In both of these cases, Paul uses the adjectives as substantives.

Fourth, Paul says the believer should "earnestly desire spiritual gifts, but especially that you may prophesy." With this statement, he draws a contrast not only with tongues but also with other gifts. Paul stresses prophecy because it is a way to deliver a message to the body of Christ. The vocal gifts include word of knowledge, word of wisdom, teaching, and revelation that is spoken. In 14:1, Paul highlights the gift of prophecy. He is especially eager that they exercise this gift.

Speaking in Tongues

Verse two deals with speaking in tongues. Paul declares, "One who speaks in a tongue (*lalōn glōssē*, λαλῶν γλώσσῃ) does not speak to men, but to God; for no one understands, but in his spirit he speaks mysteries."

---

[78]Thiselton acknowledges that the term *ta pneumatika* is flexible, that it normally means "spiritual gifts," but he suggests the meaning may be narrower here. He says that "in this specific context it may well mean more specifically *spiritual utterances* or *gifts of the Spirit for utterance* within contexts of worship" (2000, 1083). Naturally, we can include these gifts without limiting the meaning of the term.

As I indicated in chapter four, the one who speaks in tongues, speaks in various forms that he has not learned and does not understand. The forms may be human languages, the language of angels, or special purpose tongues or languages. By special purpose languages, I mean expressions that are not humanly intelligible. While some might call this gibberish, it is not gibberish to God. He does understand.[79] Here, Paul tells us who is addressed, the source of the tongues, and the content of what is spoken.

First, who is addressed? Without ambiguity, Paul tells us that tongues are addressed to God. But why is this true? Many emphasize the content of what is said. Is the content of speaking in tongues for God, for man, either, or both?

Many hold that everything that is said is addressed to God. In most cases, this would be praise. As it turns out, this has direct implications for interpretation of tongues. If utterances in tongues are always praises or other comments to God, then the idea of an "interpreted message" to man seems untenable. When tongues are not intended to be interpreted, we may assume that the content is for God.

However, Paul gives the reason why tongues are addressed to God. He says "for no one understands." Neither the speaker nor those around him can understand what the tongues are saying. This comment implies that God does understand what is said when one speaks in tongues. The communication is intelligible to God, but not to man. Therefore, the message is to God. Putting this another way, the reason why the tongues are addressed to God is that He does understand. The content, however, may be addressed to God, to man (as 14:6 will show), or both. With regard to content, the message may contain praise, a prayer request, a message to man, or anything else that the Spirit inspires.

Later, in verses 27-28, Paul says that one who speaks in a tongue speaks "to himself and to God." This phrase can be translated "by

---

[79]With regard to the nature of speaking in tongues, Carson presents several possibilities, but he favors the following: "speech patterns sufficiently complex that they may bear all kinds of cognitive information in some coded array, even though linguistically these patterns are not identifiable as human language" (1987, 84-85). This may be, but I would include this option under "special purpose" languages. Whether a speech code exists or not, God understands the utterances.

himself and to God," but "to himself" is the generally accepted view. It might seem that there is some tension between this statement and the comment that "no one understands." My understanding is that the speaker may understand the intent or burden of what he says, but not the words. In contrast, God fully understands the speaker and what he is saying.

Second, Paul states, "but in *his* spirit (*pneumati*, πνεύματι) he speaks mysteries (*mustēria*, μυστήρια). The words "in *his* spirit" focus our attention on the source of what the speaker in tongues says. The question is: What does "in spirit" mean?[80]

In the English translation, the possessive pronoun "his" has been added by the translators. The word "spirit" could refer to the speaker's spirit, to the Holy Spirit speaking, or to the speaker's spirit inspired by the Holy Spirit. Because the gift of tongues is a manifestation of the Spirit (12:7, 11), and the speaker is the instrument the Spirit uses, the last option is best. The Spirit of God inspires (cp. 14:14) the human speaker to speak in tongues. Speaking in tongues involves both the divine and the human aspects.

Third, now, what does "mysteries" mean? In a sense, any content not understood by the hearers is a mystery to them. Sometimes, Paul uses the word "mystery" to refer to truths, previously unrevealed, but now being revealed. These truths can include the gospel (1 Cor. 2:1, 7) and events that will happen at the end (1 Cor. 15:51). "Here," according to Barrett, "the meaning is simply 'secrets'; the speaker and God are sharing hidden truths which others are not permitted to share" (1971, 315-316). Even though the one who speaks in tongues does not understand the sounds that express "mysteries," he can be edified. As Fee states:

---

[80] As Lim explains: "The phrase 'in the spirit' is not always used to mean speaking in tongues in Paul's writings. Further it is not necessary in Paul's writings to conclude that all prayer in the Spirit had to be in tongues and that prayer in understanding could not be 'in the Spirit.' See, for example, Romans 8:26 where the Spirit prays with 'groans that words *cannot* express' (emphasis added). Ephesians 6:11 says 'all kinds of prayers and requests should be 'in the Spirit,' implying even times of silence or prayer in the understood language" (1991, 140).

Although one may wonder how "mysteries" that are not even understood by the speaker can edify, the answer lies in 14-15. Contrary to the opinion of many, spiritual edification can take place in ways other than through the cortex of the brain. Paul believed in an immediate communing with God by means of the S/spirit that sometimes bypassed the mind; and in 14-15 he argues for his own edification he will have both. But *in church* he will have only what can also communicate to other believers through their minds. (1987, 657)

Whether or not we classify the content of tongues as a mystery, we need not limit its scope. The content might be the mighty works of God, a personal burden, prayer, praise, or something else. When considered a mystery, such content would only be a mystery until it is interpreted.

Prophecy

Verse three deals with prophecy. Paul writes: "But one who prophesies speaks to men for edification and exhortation and consolation?" Concerning this verse, we will consider who is addressed, the purpose and content of prophecy, and the relationship between revelation and prophecy.

First, who is addressed? Prophecy, like tongues, is inspired (12:10) by the Holy Spirit. The Holy Spirit inspires the speaker to utter words that are relevant to the congregation. In contrast to speaking in tongues (verse 3), Paul says, "one who prophesies speaks to men." When one prophesies, one addresses the people in the congregation. He speaks in a language they all understand. Because they can understand what is said, they can all benefit.

Second, what are the purpose and the content of prophecy? With regard to purpose, the prophecies are for the edification, exhortation, and consolation of the believers. Obviously, the spoken content suits the purposes. Although this is not an exhaustive list of purposes, it highlights the points Paul wishes to make. We will examine each of these purposes.

One, *edification* is a translation of the noun *oikodomēn* (οἰκοδομὴν). According to Thayer, this noun means "builder" or "architect" (1962, 439-440). Paul uses both the noun (*oikodomēn*) and the verb (*oikodomeō*, οἰκοδομέω) in a spiritual sense. Those who are edified are built up and strengthened in the faith. All of the believers in the assembly can be edified (14:12). Collectively, we who believe in Christ are God's building (1 Cor. 3:9). Thus, prophecy is Spirit-inspired utterance which builds up the body of Christ.

Two, *exhortation* is a translation of the noun *paraklēsin* (παράκλησιν). Bauer says this word means *"encouragement, exhortation,"* *"comfort, consolation"*, and *appeal, request"* (Bauer 2000, 766). To this list, Thayer adds *"admonition"* (1962, 483). In the NASB[95] translation, the word *exhortation* was selected. A prophetic word can be an exhortation. The exhortation can include a variety of content, including words that are encouraging, admonitions of various types, and requests. Whatever is said, the intent should be to build up the people in the assembly.

Three, *consolation* is a translation of the noun *paramuthian* (παραμυθίαν). Bauer indicates that it means *"encouragement,* esp. *comfort, consolation"* (2000, 769).

To some extent, the meanings of *paraklēsin* and *paramuthian* overlap. It may be that, to some degree, these words represent distinct categories; but some scholars think of these words as near synonyms. In Philippians 2:1, for example, they are respectively translated *encouragement* and *consolation*. A prophecy can console one who is sad, disappointed, or in need. The consolation will build up his spirit.

Four, as we have seen, prophecy is a gift given to build up, encourage, and challenge the church. However, Paul does not overlook the impact of prophecy on the unbeliever. An unbeliever (14:24-25) may be "called into account" by prophecy and fall on his face and worship God. The term *prophecy*, as we have noted, is very flexible.

Third, prophecy and revelation are very closely related. Both in the Old and the New Testaments, revelation often provides the basis of the message to be delivered. This close relationship is seen in 14:26-32. Revelation may be the basis for a teaching or a psalm or any other vocal presentation. Moreover, the "revelation" may consist simply of the speaker knowing that the message is relevant and applicable to the audience. The term *revelation* is broad enough to be flexibly used.

The verb *prophesy* is broad and flexible as well.[81] As Lenski points out, to prophesy extends much farther than direct revelation "and includes all of the uses that are to be made of the divine truth that has been revealed to us" (1946, 579). The scope of prophecy may include declarations of previously revealed information as well as new revelation. In addition, many think of prophecy as messages to men, but the term is broad enough to include praises to God also. Prophecies that include Spirit-inspired praise many times are a great blessing to the gathered believers. God does wondrous things in the midst of praise.

Edification

Paul continues in verse 4 with this comment: "One who speaks in a tongue (*lalōn glōssē*, λαλῶν γλώσσῃ) edifies himself; but one who prophesies (*prophēteuōn*, προφητεύων) edifies the church (*ekklēsian*, ἐκκλησίαν)." Here, Paul compares speaking in tongues and prophecy with regard to edification. We will consider each of these two gifts in turn.

First, in this verse, when Paul says "one who speaks in a tongue," he is referring to a person speaking in tongues without interpretation. Clearly, the people in the congregation do not understand the tongues; thus, they are not edified. When one speaks in tongues, without interpretation, only he is edified.

When one speaks in tongues, he speaks in words he has never learned. How, then, can the speaker be edified?[82] The speaker would not understand the *words* he utters. However, as previously

---

[81] Thiselton broadens the meaning of prophecy to include preaching. He writes: "We shall argue . . . that here prophecy amounts to healthy preaching, proclamation, or teaching which is pastorally applied for the appropriation of gospel truth and gospel promise, in their own context of situation, to help others" (2,000, 1084).

[82] Some scholars argue that Paul means "edifies himself" in a negative or derogative sense. However, Fee and many others disagree. Fee writes: "But Paul intended no such thing. The edifying of one's self is not self-centeredness, but the personal edifying of the individual believer that comes through private prayer and praise . . . Contrary to the opinion of many. Spiritual edification can take place in ways other than the cortex of the brain" (1994, 219). I would add that few would deny that an individual can be legitimately edified through private prayer and praise.

noted, the spirit may understand (verse 14) even when the mind does not. Thus, he is not edified solely on the basis of the words or sounds spoken.

Because he is the speaker, other criteria besides intelligibility enter in. The speaker is edified because he knows he is speaking to God, and God hears. This fellowship does not require specific knowledge of the words spoken. The speaker benefits even from the expression of his feelings to God. Also, he knows his voice is an instrument of the Spirit and that he is harmonizing with the will of God (Rom. 8:26-27).

Although speaking in tongues, without interpretation, does not bring edification in the church, it is important. Speaking in tongues brings edification to the believer. We must learn the proper exercise of speaking in tongues and speak as the Spirit gives utterance!

Second, who is edified by prophecy? Paul says that "one who prophesies edifies the church (*ekklēsian*, ἐκκλησίαν)." The word *ekklēsian* is used without an article. Because of this, Lenski says that Paul means "a church" or "an assembly" (1946, 579). Similarly, Barrett says that, without the article, Paul means "literally, *an assembly*, but the sense is *the assembly of which he is one member*." All of the members of the church in Corinth would be edified. In addition, we must keep in mind that whatever blesses one assembly in another sense blesses the entire body of Christ. The assembly is edified by prophecy. Both the speaker and the audience are lifted up and blessed.

Paul's Wishes

Building on what he has said, Paul declares in verse 5: "Now I wish that you all spoke in tongues, but *even* more that you would prophesy; and greater is one who prophesies than one who speaks in tongues, unless he interprets so that the church may receive edifying."

First, Paul expresses his wishes concerning speaking in tongues and prophesying.[83] He wishes that all would speak in tongues, but

---

[83]Some commentators hold that Paul was making a concession to the Corinthians rather than expressing a heartfelt wish. However, many believe it was actually the real wish of Moses. Some link Paul's wish to the wish of

"even more" that they would prophesy. Thayer indicates that *mallon* (μᾶλλον) is an adverb meaning "*more, to a greater degree; rather*" (1962, 387).[84] As I see it, Paul was expressing a preference for prophecy without precluding speaking in tongues.

One, Paul expresses his wish concerning speaking in tongues. He says: "Now I wish that you all spoke in tongues."[85] In this clause, Paul expresses his wish without qualification. He does not mention public and private speaking or speaking with and without interpretation. However, the context does deal with these issues.

With regard to public speaking, three points can be made. One, based on 14:28, we know that Paul would not wish that they would all speak in tongues in the church without interpretation. Two, because speaking in tongues and interpretation are equal in value to prophecy, Paul could wish that they exercised both gifts rather than only speaking in tongues. Three, his wish probably applies to the

---

Moses in Numbers 11:29 (Kistemaker, 1993, 481; Thiselton, 2000, 1097; Garland, 2003, 635). In Numbers 11:29, Moses said, "Would that all the Lord's people were prophets, that the Lord would put His Spirit upon them!" The outpouring of the Spirit on the Day of Pentecost was a fulfillment of this wish.

[84] A key word in interpreting Paul's wish is *mallon*. In 1 Corinthians 12-14, this word occurs four times. The Scripture references and the NASB[95] translations are as follows: 12:22, much truer; 14:1, especially; 14:5, even more; and 14:18, more. In 14:1 and 14:5 the phrase Paul uses is *mallon de.* The NIV translations respectively are "especially" and "rather." According to Bauer, *rather* can mean *instead* (2000, 613-614). Thayer classifies 14:5 under this description: "it does not do away with that which it is in opposition, but marks which has the preference: *more willingly, more readily, sooner* (1962, 388). The translation "even more" by the NASB[95] fits the context in 14:5.

[85] Thiselton holds that various kinds of tongues refers to "species" of tongues. He says that, in chapter 14, to speak in a tongue "almost always denotes an upwelling of praise or praising, joyful acclamation to God" (2000, 1085). Citing Romans 8:26-27, he concurs with the view that tongues can be the "language of the unconscious" released in sighs too deep for words (2000, 985, 988). He argues that the verbs *hermēneuō* (ἑρμηνεύω, explain, interpret) and *diermēneuō* (διερμηνεύω, translate, interpret) frequently mean not to interpret but "*to put into words, i.e., to render in articulate intelligible speech*, what is difficult to express" (2000, 1098). In my view, a "species" of tongues can be inarticulate groaning. Because the groaning has meaning to God, I would call this a "special purpose" language. Therefore, "putting into words" may also be called "interpretation".

person who speaks in tongues with the intent of the tongues being interpreted. He exhorts him to pray that he may interpret (14:13) the tongues.

Paul's wish definitely applies to speaking in tongues in private. When spoken privately, an interpretation is possible but not necessary. With regard to private tongues, Paul is referring to a life of prayer and the blessing that tongues can be in prayer. No doubt this is his intent in 14:18 as well where he says, "I thank God, I speak in tongues more than you all." Far from putting down speaking in tongues, Paul upholds the blessing that speaking in tongues brings in personal devotions. He does not limit the private use of tongues in any way.

Two, Paul expresses his wish concerning prophecy. He says, "but even more (*mallon*) that you would prophesy." When Paul speaks about prophecy, he has the assembly in mind. In the church, Paul prefers prophecy over speaking in tongues without interpretation. The reason is that prophecy edifies the church. Because speaking in tongues with the interpretation is equivalent in value to prophecy, the phrase "even more" does not apply when tongues are interpreted.

Paul's primary concern was what was being said in public. Using 14:18-19 as a guideline for interpreting these wishes, we could insert "in the church" before "that you would prophesy." If we do this, then Paul is comparing prophecy with tongues without interpretation in the assembly. He may not have been comparing prophecy and private tongues. However, if we apply the "even more" wish to private tongues, then it would not be on the basis of being intelligible. It would be on the basis of people other than the speaker being edified. Both approaches are possible.

Second, Paul declares, "and greater is one who prophesies than one who speaks in tongues, unless he interprets, so that the church may receive edifying." In 12:31, Paul speaks about the "greater gifts," but here he writes about "the one who prophesies" and the "one who speaks in tongues." Here, Paul gives equal stature, on the basis of intelligibility, to the one who prophesies and the one who speaks in tongues and interprets what he says. Because he can be understood by the body, the one who prophesies is greater in the assembly than the one who speaks in tongues without interpreting what he says.

Does Paul mean that the one who prophesies is greater than the one who speaks privately in tongues? As indicated above, Paul may not be comparing prophecy with private tongues. However, on the basis of what edifies the body, as opposed to the speaker alone, prophecy edifies more people. When the church is edified, the speaker is edified as well. According to Paul, Jesus said, "It is more blessed to give than to receive" (Acts 20:35). Perhaps we can capture Paul's intent with this paraphrase, "It is more blessed to edify than to be edified."

Third, Paul speaks about the potential all believers have. He clearly wishes that all would speak in tongues in private devotions (14:5). His wish is a strong encouragement to do so. Moreover, potentially all could speak in tongues in public. Concerning prophecy, Paul exhorts everyone to earnestly desire to prophesy (14:1) and wishes that all would (14:5). He repeats this exhortation to desire earnestly to prophesy in 14:39. Therefore, potentially all believers can speak prophetically. However, in 12:29-30, Paul rhetorically points out that all are not prophets, nor do all speak in tongues in the church.

Unless He Interprets

Here we will continue our discussion of verse 5. Paul declares that the one who prophesies is greater than the one who speaks in tongues "unless (*ektos ei mē*, ἐκτὸς εἰ μὴ) he interprets (*diermēneuē*, διερμηνεύῃ)." Literally, the words *ektos ei mē* mean "except if not." It is an idiomatic way of saying "unless." Unless one interprets, the one who prophesies is greater.

First, who is addressed? When one speaks in tongues without interpretation, he speaks to God. When the tongues are interpreted, we may still say the tongues are addressed to God. However, the interpretation is understood by men. Thus, we may say that tongues and interpretation, taken together, are designed for communication to man. Even when an interpretation is addressed to God, men may learn from it.

Second, what is the content? Here, there is considerable disagreement. One view is that interpretation simply gives the sense of the prayer and praise uttered to God in tongues. Another view, based in part on 14:6, is that the content can be intended as a message for men. We will study this verse in our next chapter.

We need not place any limits on the content. The content may be for God, man, or both. It is difficult to draw a sharp line between praise and a message for man. On the Day of Pentecost, the disciples, speaking in tongues, spoke "the mighty deeds of God" (Acts 2:11). When spoken, these words were words of praise. However, they became words of witness to the audience.

The word "interprets" is a translation of *diermēneuē*. This word may mean to explain, interpret, or translate (Bauer 2000, 244). Interpret appears to be the best choice. Words spoken in tongues are "to God" because God understands. However, when interpreted, they may well be addressed to men. The content of what is said in tongues, when tongues are intended for interpretation, may well be addressed to God, man, or both. To whom the content applies will be made clear when the interpretation is given. The content may be praise, prayer, illumination of gospel truth, or anything else the Spirit has prompted one to say.

Third, the question sometimes arises, "Why have the two stages approach of tongues plus interpretation? Or, to put the question another way, "Why would someone speak in tongues at all, even with interpretation?" Montague posits the following answer:

> Paul equates interpreted tongues with prophecy. This gives us an insight into the relationship between the experience of tongues and that of interpretation or prophecy. The prophetic word to the community is prepared, it seems, by the gift of tongues, very much in the way pregnancy prepares for birth. The non-rational experience of the Spirit has a great advantage precisely because it temporarily at least puts the mind to rest and seeks a deeper union with God in faith and love without words. But just as pregnancy is frustrated without birth, so that activity of tongues in not an end in itself but should normally terminate in some clear message for the community. (1976, 176)

Fourth, who is edified? When the church understands what was said in tongues, just as when one prophesies, the church is edified. The words "unless he interprets" (verse 6) indicate that tongues and interpretation are equal in edification and value to prophecy. Once again, this judgment is made on the basis of what is intelligible. When tongues are interpreted, the content is understandable to the assembly.

Conclusion

Paul begins the chapter 14 by saying, "Pursue love, yet desire earnestly spiritual gifts, but especially that you may prophesy" (14:1). So right away, he signals that prophecy has special value in the church. Paul ends the chapter, verses 39-40, by saying, "Therefore, my brethren, desire earnestly to prophesy, and do not forbid to speak in tongues. But all things must be done properly and in an orderly manner."

In the first paragraph (14:1-5), Paul draws a contrast between speaking in tongues without interpretation and prophecy. Because prophecy communicates to the people, the one who prophesies is greater than the one who speaks in tongues that are not interpreted. However, tongues with interpretation, like prophecy, communicates with the people in the assembly. When the tongues are interpreted, the one who speaks in tongues has the same edification value for the assembly. Moreover, when the body is edified, the speaker is edified as well.

In addition, Paul puts a high value on tongues in devotional life. He writes about the one who, inspired by the Spirit, speaks mysteries. When the mysteries are spoken privately, there is no need for interpretation. The speaker utters words that God understands. He may understand the intent of the messages, but he does not understand the words. The communication is nevertheless valuable. Because private tongues edify the individual, Paul urges all to speak in tongues.

In our next chapter, we will discuss 14:6-12 which is a paragraph about clear communication. In verse 6, we will begin with a study of what content an interpretation of tongues might contain. Without interpretation, the sound of the bugle is unclear. With interpretation, the message is understandable. Paul's emphasis is on clear communication for the edification of the church.

CHAPTER TEN

THE BUGLE SOUND

Introduction

In 1 Corinthians 12-14, Paul gives his most extensive discussion of spiritual gifts. The twelfth chapter is devoted to a broad presentation of the gifts. Then Paul inserts his chapter on love—the thirteenth chapter. After this chapter, he narrows his focus to tongues, interpretation of tongues, and prophecy. While discussing these gifts, he speaks also about related matters such as revelation, knowledge, a psalm, and teaching.

Paul begins in 14:1-5 with comments on tongues and prophecy. He declares that tongues without interpretation, while personally edifying, do not communicate to the assembly. Prophecy, on the other hand, does. Therefore, as far as the edification of the body is concerned, prophecy is greater than tongues without interpretation.

Another theme woven into the text by Paul is interpretation of tongues. In 14:5, Paul says prophecy is greater "unless he interprets." Through the gift of interpretation, speaking in tongues stands equal to prophecy in value for the edification of the body. With interpretation, the criterion of being intelligible to the members of the assembly is met.

With the way that Paul makes transitional statements, it is not easy to form paragraphs. Quite a few verses are transitional and can go with what precedes or what follows. We notice this in connection with the gift of interpretation. Verses 5 and 13 explicitly mention interpretation of tongues. Verse 5 could go with verses 6-12, or verse 6 could go with verses 1-5. Verse 13 could go with verses 6-12 or with verses 14-17. No matter how the paragraphs are formed, verses 5, 6, and 13 highlight interpretation of tongues. When a tongue is interpreted, it makes the content intelligible. Paul continues his thoughts on intelligibility in 14:6-12. He writes:

> 6But now, brethren, if I come to you speaking in tongues, what shall I profit you, unless I speak to you either by way of

revelation or of knowledge or of prophecy or of teaching? [7]Yet even lifeless things, either flute or harp, in producing a distinction in the tones, how will it be known what is played on the flute or on the harp? [8]For if the bugle produces an indistinct sound, who will prepare himself for battle? [9]So also you, unless you utter by the tongue speech that is clear, how will it be known what is spoken? For you will be speaking into the air. [10]There are, perhaps, a great many kinds of languages in the world, and no kind is without meaning. [11]If then I do not know the meaning of the language, I shall be to the one who speaks a barbarian, and the one who speaks will be a barbarian to me. [12]So also you, since you are zealous of spiritual gifts, seek to abound for the edification of the church.

Interpreted and Independent Messages

Now, let's examine the question Paul asks in verse 6: "But now, brethren,[86] if I come to you speaking in tongues [without interpretation], what shall I profit you, unless (*ean mē*, ἐὰν μὴ) I speak to you either by way of (*en*, ἐν) revelation or of (*en*) knowledge or of (*en*) prophecy or of (*en*) teaching?" Here, Paul mentions vocal gifts that can be independently exercised, but the question is whether or not they can also represent interpretations of tongues.

First, in this verse, Paul writes about tongues without interpretation and, as I maintain, tongues with interpretation. Based on verse 5, it is speaking in tongues in the church *without* interpretation that is unprofitable to the church. When Paul says (verse 5), "unless he interprets," he implies that tongues with interpretation does edify the church. Having already said this, the opening clause of verse 6 can only refer to tongues without interpretation.

Second, the key word in this verse is the conjunction "unless." Our English conjunction "unless" is a translation of the Greek words

---

[86]With regard to "But now, brethren," Kistemaker says: "*Now* transmits not a temporal connotation but a logical one: 'but because things are so.' On the basis of practices in the congregation, Paul is challenged to give his own view on tongues. He addresses the Corinthians with the word *brothers,* which in the parlance of that day included the sisters in the church" (1993, 483).

ean mē, which literally means "if not." Here, instead of saying "unless he interprets," Paul says, "unless I speak to you either by way of revelation or of knowledge or of prophecy or of teaching?" The question for us is: What meaning does the conjunction "unless" signal for us? We will consider three possibilities.[87]

One, the conjunction *unless* could mean "unless in addition." In other words, speaking in tongues without interpretation is not acceptable "unless in addition" the person speaks by way of revelation, knowledge, prophecy, or teaching. A person could speak in tongues and also deliver a message in a language known by those present without interpreting the tongues. However, this approach does not solve the problem that the tongues are still not intelligible.

Speaking intelligibly will bring benefit to the church, but the tongues by themselves are still unprofitable. Unless the intelligible speaking is an interpretation of the tongues, speaking in tongues is

---

[87]Scholars hold different views with regard to 14:6. One line of thought is represented by Fee who holds that speaking in tongues "is speech directed basically toward God (14:2, 14-15, 28); one may assume, therefore, that what is interpreted is not speech directed toward others, but the 'mysteries' spoken to God" (1996, 169). Others who hold this view are Palma (2001, 236-238) and Brandt (1981, 54-55).

Other scholars hold that an utterance in tongues is addressed to God because only He understands. The interpretation, however, can be addressed to man. With variations, representatives of this approach include Brumback (1947, 303), Harold Horton (1962, 174-175), Boyd, (1970, 114-115), Barrett (1971, 319), Gee (1980, 76), and Rea (1998, 234).

Some authors maintain that the content of an interpretation can be in the form of the items mentioned in 14:6. Stanley Horton states that "tongues when interpreted may bring insight into spiritual truths (a 'revelation'); 'knowledge,' including spiritual understanding; a message to strengthen, encourage, and comfort ('prophecy'); or a 'word of instruction' (not in the sense of establishing new doctrine but clarifying spiritual truth and helping the hearers to apply it)" (1999, 133; cp. 1976, 226).

The New English Bible and the Twentieth Century New Testament translations are as follows: NEB: "Suppose, my friends, that when I come to you I speak in tongues: what good shall I do you, unless what I say contains something by way of revelation, or enlightenment, or prophecy, or instruction?" TCNT: "This being so, Brothers, what good shall I do you, if I come to you and speak in 'tongues,' unless my words convey some revelation, or knowledge, or take the form of preaching or teaching?"

still unprofitable to the church. Without interpretation (14:28), the speaker in tongues is to keep silent in the church. We have to conclude that the word "unless in addition" solution does not give the proper sense of the passage.

Two, another view commonly held is that Paul means "unless, instead of" speaking in tongues. In other words, he is saying: "I will not come speaking in tongues without interpretation because it is unprofitable to you, but *instead* I will come speaking through one of the intelligible gifts." Under this view, the inspired messages of revelation, knowledge, prophecy, and teaching are to be directly delivered. The messages do not come by way of interpretation of tongues. Speaking in tongues without interpretation remains unprofitable to the church.

Whatever Paul meant to signal by the conjunction *unless*, revelation, knowledge, prophecy, and teaching are gifts in their own right. They can be exercised (cp. 14:26) directly in the language of the audience. They may be exercised without any connection to tongues. Also, being intelligible, they benefit the church. This interpretation is possible, but the conjunction *unless* suggests that something will happen that makes speaking in tongues edifying to the church. It seems to say that the speaker speaks in tongues as well as exercising the other gifts.

Three, under another view, Paul means "unless, by interpretation," I speak to you either by way of revelation, knowledge, prophecy, or teaching." In other words, he means, "unless I add the interpretation, you will not profit." As he has pointed out already (verse 5), tongues with the interpretation would bring edification to the church. Barrett gives this translation and comment: "if I come to you speaking with tongues, what good shall I do you, unless I speak to you (in addition, that is, or perhaps by an interpretation of the tongue) in revelation, or in knowledge, or in prophecy, or in teaching?" (1971, 317).

As we discussed above, the "unless in addition" approach does not provide for the interpretation of the tongues. The "unless "instead of" view does away with the tongues rather than making them profitable. The best view is "unless by interpretation" the tongues convey revelation, knowledge, prophecy, or teaching. The interpreted tongues take on the *form* of one of these gifts. Even when these expressions are interpretations of tongues, we may still regard them as *gifts* of the Spirit. The gifts overlap in their operation.

Looked at in this way, verse 6 amplifies verse 5. In verse 5, Paul says, "greater is one who prophesies than one who speaks in tongues, unless he interprets, so that the church may receive edifying." Verse 6 then tells us that the interpretation could contain revelation, knowledge, prophecy, or teaching. Later, in verse 13, Paul adds, "Therefore let one who speaks in a tongue pray that he may interpret." Putting all this together, the best way to read verse 6 is: "But now, brethren, if I come to you speaking in tongues, what shall I profit you, unless [*by interpretation*] I speak to you either by way of revelation or of knowledge or of prophecy or of teaching?"

Third, there are several additional reasons that support the view that an interpretation of tongues can contain revelation, knowledge, prophecy, or teaching. Other content is possible, but these are the gifts that Paul mentions in 14:6. The reasons are as follows:

One, the context leads us to expect interpretation. In verse 5, the one who prophesies is greater than the one who speaks in tongues "unless" he interprets. Then, in verse 13, Paul exhorts the one who speaks in tongues to pray that he might interpret. A very natural conclusion is that the gifts mentioned in verse 6 are ways to interpret speaking in tongues.

Two, we note that prophecy is directed to men (14:3). Because the words are in the vernacular, men understand. However, prophecy can include praises to God as well as messages to man. Even the praise speaks to the hearts of men. In any case, God understands. Similarly, tongues spoken to God, because He understands, can be interpreted for men to understand.

Three, an interpretation gives the sense of what an utterance in tongues means. The interpretation simply makes the utterance understandable to the church. When only God understands, people speak to God and not to man. On the same basis, when man understands the message, it is also for man. God, of course, always understands. An interpreted praise to God ministers both to God and man. In some cases, a praise to God may be transposed into an exhortation for men to praise Him. The exhortation, in such cases, is still an interpretation.

Fourth, clearly, the intelligible gifts can be independently exercised. However, we cannot exclude revelation, knowledge, prophecy, or teaching by means of tongues and interpretation. The "unless by interpretation" view is less limiting. It takes nothing from the direct exercise of the intelligible gifts. It adds something in that interpreted tongues may also contain revelation, knowledge, prophecy, or teaching. Or, we could say that an interpretation, while still being an interpretation, "becomes" one of these gifts.

Gifts that Communicate

The gifts mentioned by Paul in the last part of verse 6 are marked by intelligibility. He says, "unless I speak to you either by way of (en, ἐν) revelation or of (en) knowledge or of (en) prophecy or of (en) teaching." All of these gifts can be exercised independently or through interpretation of tongues. Four times Paul repeats the preposition en and thereby highlights the listed gifts. We note that he does not precisely define them. Indeed, they interlock, overlap, and merge with each other. We should not, therefore, try to define the terms too narrowly.

A spiritual gift can be labeled in more than one way.[88] For example, a gift of healing can be called a miracle, and a revelation could be called a word of knowledge. The common core of all of the gifts is that they are manifestations of the Spirit. Normally, they include natural aspects to some degree. Each of the gifts has its own distinctiveness as well. The thrust of Paul's writings about spiritual gifts does not depend on the precision of narrow definitions, but rather upon the empowerment of the Spirit in a variety of ways.

First, the word *apokalupsei* (ἀποκαλύψει) means revelation or disclosure (Bauer 2000, 112). The Bible is God's revealed Word. Now the canon of Scripture is closed, and nothing more is being added. All knowledge, prophecy, and teaching now is based on that revelation. Although the canon is closed, the gift of revelation remains operational. Apart from adding to the Word of God, we

---

[88]Barrett writes: "All these activities, which shade too finely into one another for rigid distinctions to be profitable or even accurate, are of advantage to the Christian assembly, but, without them, speaking with tongues is (as far as the assembly is concerned) sheer sound, signifying nothing" (1971, 317).

need not limit what God may disclose. Our understanding of the Word may be enriched through Spirit-inspired revelation spoken to the assembly.

There is an important relationship between revelation and knowledge, prophecy, and teaching. When a speaker receives a revelation, he receives knowledge. The same is true for prophecy and teaching. Also, independent of revelation, the other gifts have a knowledge component. In other words, the other gifts can operate without a specific revelation, but all of them include knowledge.

Second, Paul says, "unless I speak by way of knowledge (gnōsei, γνώσει)." Many scholars agree that this is the same gift as the word of knowledge listed in 12:8. The "word of knowledge" emphasizes the expression of knowledge as well as the knowledge itself. The word *knowledge*, by itself, probably does not stress the expression of knowledge as much. However, the expression of knowledge is not excluded. All of this is inspired by the Spirit. Without any evidence to the contrary, it is best to maintain the broad scope of these words.

We often think of a word of knowledge as a body of content revealed to us. Without doubt, such knowledge is included here. However, the gift of knowledge may refer also to the interpretation of knowledge after it has been accumulated. An element of illumination, and even revelation, may be involved here as well. Knowledge may refer to the understanding of divine truth and to clear insight into what truth contains. As with revelation, we should not limit the term too much. Paul's concern is intelligibility. Clearly, there is an overlap between revelation and knowledge.

Third, the word *prophecy* (prophēteia, προφητεία) can be both narrowly and broadly used. Used in a very narrow sense, a prophecy is based on a revelation from God to the prophet who delivers a message to man. The term broadens to a degree when you include prophetic praises to God. With even more inclusive meaning, a message or praise sometimes is deemed to be prophetic because of the empowered way it is delivered. The gift of prophecy can be independently exercised without an interpretation of tongues being involved. Or, a prophecy can be given by means of interpretation. The interpretation expresses and, in a sense, becomes a prophecy.

The breadth of the term *prophecy* is readily seen in the way Paul uses it in 1 Corinthians 14. In 14:3, Paul says that the "one who prophesies speaks to men for edification and exhortation and consolation." This statement, alone, gives a broad scope to prophecy. As 14:5 indicates, "greater is the one who prophesies than one who speaks in tongues unless he interprets, so that the church may receive edifying." Messages and praises in known languages edify the assembly. In 14:24, Paul declares, "But if all prophesy, and an unbeliever or an ungifted man enters, he is convicted by all, he is called to account by all." Thus, prophecy has an evangelistic impact. Then, in 14:31, Paul says, "For you can all prophesy one by one, so that all may learn and all may be exhorted." This verse highlights learning and the gift of teaching. Given this statement, we know that prophecy can have an instructional value.

The gift of prophecy and the gift of revelation are interrelated. Some scholars believe that prophecy is always based on new revelation. It very often is, but as Leon Wood asserts:

This is not to say that all prophets received revelations. No doubt, many did not, but found the information they were to proclaim either in the revealed law or from what had been revealed to other prophets. Many did, however; they were told what to say and when, how, and where to say it. (1976, 117)

Prophecy can include new revelation or old revelation applied to current situations. The revelation may simply be the leading of the Spirit to speak forth a given message or praise. When both the words *prophecy* and *revelation* are understood broadly, there are many possibilities. Concerning prophecy and revelation, Lenski makes these comments:

Paul's brief description of the gift of prophecy shows that it does not deal only with special direct revelations from God in certain chosen instruments (prophecy in the narrow sense as revelatory) but that it extends much farther and includes all of the uses that are to be made of all of the divine truth that has been revealed to us. Thus all true preachers and teachers of the gospel are prophets in the general or broader sense because they offer edification, admonition, and consolation to their hearers. All true Christians who are able to impart the gospel truth privately in a similar manner exercise the gift of prophecy to this extent. Here, too, we see how one may use zeal and more and more acquire this precious gift for fuller and more effective use in the church. (1946, 579)

Fourth, Paul includes teaching (*didachē*, διδαχῇ) as a gift. The gift of teaching includes instruction in any portion of divine truth. The Spirit inspires and uses natural talent to present truth. At times, however, a special revelation may be involved. The teacher may be moved by the Spirit to punctuate his normal lessons with special moments of divine insight. No doubt, some teaching came by way of tongues and interpretation. This teaching, too, would be in the form of Spirit-inspired utterances rather than just through natural talents.

The gift of teaching is related to the gifts of revelation, knowledge, and prophecy. These gifts overlap, but each has its own unique characteristics as well. They overlap in that all four are inspired by the Spirit, and they have a knowledge component, but they are also different. Scholars differ over how much they overlap and to what extent they are different.

As an illustration, we will consider the gifts of prophecy and teaching. Grudem draws a distinction between prophecy and teaching with regard to revelation. He holds that prophecy "must be based on a 'revelation'; if there is no revelation, there is no prophecy" (1982, 146). Then, he says, "Teaching, on the other hand, is always based on an explanation and/or application of Scripture or received apostolic doctrine; it is never said to be based on revelation" (1982, 146).

The view of Grudem encounters some difficulty with 14:31. Paul says, "For you can all prophesy one by one, so that all may learn and all may be exhorted." To overcome this difficulty, Grudem says that people learn from such things as prayer, kind behavior, and an encouraging smile. Then he says, "These activities may be called 'teaching' in some broad sense, but they are not 'teaching' in the sense in which Paul uses the word in the New Testament to refer to the explanation and application of Bible passages to the church" (1982, 138).

With regard to this view, I would agree that the most characteristic traits of prophecy and teaching are respectively revelation and the exposition of the Scriptures. However, not all prophecy contains new revelation, and some teaching can include revelation; moreover, some prophecy teaches, and some teaching is delivered with prophetic impact. In other words, the gifts of teaching and prophecy are alike in some ways but different enough to be distinct gifts.

According to Dunn, Paul recognizes two modes of teaching: (1) the normal approach to the exposition of the Word of God without any particular or special revelation and (2) a mode that includes charismatic insights. By charismatic insights, Dunn means revelation. Dunn makes the following comments:

> In Paul's view the activity of teaching διδάσκων (*didaskōn*) is also a charismatic act (Rom. 12.7). Paul certainly uses the noun in a non-charismatic sense for a body of teaching, something his readers already accept and can therefore use as a check on beliefs and life (Rom. 6.17, 16.7). But in I Cor. 14.6, 26 he obviously has in mind *particular teachings*. That a charismatic insight [revelation] is in view is strongly suggested by the companion contributions to the assembly's worship listed in vv. 6 and 26 (1975, 236-237). (Transliteration Mine)

The companion gifts, mentioned by Dunn, include revelation, knowledge, prophecy, a psalm, a tongue, and an interpretation. The Spirit of God inspires all of these forms of communication. Teaching is listed by Paul in keeping with this company.

Concerning Dunn's view, I would hold that the divide between the two modes that he proposes is not sharp. Surely the Spirit uses natural expository talent, but He also lights up the instruction with His divine presence and, on occasion, persuasive revelation. Even the seemingly "natural" teaching can come alive with the Spirit's inspiration. Most of the time, the exercise of spiritual gifts includes natural and supernatural dimensions.

Fifth, the above four gifts are the keys to communicating with the people in the assembly, and they are interrelated. With regard to communication, they may be exercised independently or through interpretation of tongues. In the church, it is the expression of tongues without interpretation which does not profit the hearers. When messages are interpreted, they do edify the body.

Analogies about Intelligibility

Paul is eager for believers to speak clearly to the people in the assembly. Speech that is understood by the people, or intelligible speech, is what edifies the believers. Paul illustrates his point about intelligibility with some very graphic analogies to musical instruments and to languages.

First, Paul refers to musical instruments, which are inanimate objects, to illustrate his point. Because musical instruments are known to nearly everyone, such illustrations communicate readily to the people in the assembly. Paul writes:

> [7]Yet even lifeless things, either flute (*aulos*, αὐλὸς) or harp (*kithara*, κιθάρα), in producing a sound, if they do not produce a distinction in the tones, how will it be known what is played on the flute or on the harp? [8]For if the bugle (*salpinx*, σάλπιγξ, trumpet) produces an indistinct sound, who will prepare himself for battle? [9]So also you, unless you utter by the tongue (*glōssēs*, γλώσσης) speech that is clear, how will it be known what is spoken? For you will be speaking into the air.

Even musical instruments must make distinctions in tones to be of value. The flute (*aulos*) represents wind instruments, and the harp (*kithara*) stands for stringed instruments. Without distinctions in tones, all we receive is an aimless clatter of noise. Sometimes, when musicians are warming up, their instruments sound like this. It is like speaking into the air.

The trumpet, or bugle (*salpinx*), was an instrument used to summon men into battle.[89] Calvin writes that "the trumpet is designed to stir the blood in such a way that it excites not only men but horses also" (Trans. Fraser 1960, 289). An indistinct bugle sound would not give a recognized signal, and the call for battle

---

[89]According to Garland, "The trumpet (σάλπιγξ, *salpinx*) can be a musical instrument (Rev. 18:22), but in 1 Corinthians refers to a military bugle. It sounded the alarm of a coming attack (Jer. 4:19; 6:1, 17; Ezek. 33:3-6; Hos. 5:8; Joel 2:1), the beginning of an attack (Judg. 3:27; Jer. 51:27), and the end of an attack (2 Sam. 20:1)" (2003, 636).

would not be understood. Thus, no one would prepare for battle. Harold Horton expounds on this point as follows:

> Martial bugles must make sense as well as sound, if others are to respond and react. I think I could myself produce a bugle's authentic sound on a bugle. But nothing would happen as the result—except perhaps a certain gratification of my personal sense of achievement. But listen to that bugler sounding the same instrument and see how perfectly he makes himself understood! The sounds are similar to mine, but now others are reacting. Men now arise and dress, or come to the cookhouse door, or fall in, or charge, or dismiss, or retire! There is meaning in the bugle because of the interpretation! (1962, 200-201)

In verse 9, Paul says, "unless you utter by the tongue (*glōssēs*, γλώσσης) speech that is clear, how will it be known what is spoken?" Most commentators hold that the word (*glōssēs*) refers to the physical tongue.[90] Fee, who concurs that "tongue" in this verse refers to the physical tongue, comments as follows concerning speaking in tongues without interpretation:

> The analogy is clear. Tongues, Paul is arguing, is like the harpist running fingers over all the strings, making musical sounds but not playing a pleasing melody, or like a bugler who blows the bugle without sounding the battle cry. In both cases sounds come from the instrument, but they make no sense; hence they do not benefit the listener. So it is with tongues. (1987, 664)

When believers speak in tongues without interpretation, what they say is indistinct, not understandable, and therefore without edification for the people in the assembly. Therefore, we must utter

---

[90]Kistemaker provides this explanation: "Further, the phrase *with your tongue* can mean either the physical speech organ, a known language, or ecstatic speech. Of these three, the first explanation appears to be the best. First, the noun *tongue* is rather personal, as it is modified by the pronoun *your*. Next, the noun serves as the counterpart of the musical instruments mentioned earlier (vv. 7-8). And last, the preposition *with* signifies instrumentality that applies more to the organ of speech than to a language as a whole" (1993, 486).

speech that is clear. This can be a direct expression of various gifts or speaking in tongues with interpretation. The main point is that one must speak with meaning.

Second, Paul comments (verses 10-11) on languages to illustrate his point. He uses the Greek word *phōnōn* (φωνῶν) (*phōnēs* (φωνῆς), singular) which means sounds, voices, noises, or languages.[91] Usually, the term *languages* is chosen by the translators for verse 10 and *language* for verse 11. Without doubt, this is the primary meaning in this context. We must speak intelligibly in order to edify the church. He writes:

> [10]There are, perhaps, a great many kinds of languages (*phōnōn*) in the world, and no kind is without meaning (*aphōnon*, ἄφωνον). [11]If then I do not know the meaning (*dunamin*, δύναμιν) of the language (*phōnēs*), I shall be to the one who speaks a barbarian (*barbaros* (βάρβαρος), foreigner), and the one who speaks will be a barbarian to me. [12]So also you, since you are zealous of spiritual gifts (*pneumatōn*, πνευμάτων), seek to abound for the edification of the church.

In verse 10, Paul points out that there are many kinds of languages in the world. All these languages have meaning to the speakers. In verse 11, our English word *meaning* is a translation of the Greek word *dunamin* which is that normal word for power.[92] When we do not understand a language, we do not realize its power. The speaker and the hearer become foreigners to each other. The analogy applies fully to one who speaks in tongues and to those who hear but do not understand what is said.

Third, in verse 12, Paul recognizes that the Corinthians are zealous for *pneumatōn*. Literally, *pneumatōn* is a noun meaning "spirits."[93] Normally, our translators supply the noun *gifts* and treat

---

[91]Taylor suggests the following: "The lexical choice of 'sound' may be rhetorical wordplay or may link with the preceding analogies of the sounds of musical instruments" (2014, 328).

[92]Kistemaker: "A literal translation of the phrase the meaning of the language is 'the power of the language.' The Greek term *dynamis* (power) can also be translated 'force,' which makes good sense in this text" (2003, 487) Compare Bauer (2000, 262-263) and Fee (1987, 665).

[93]Garland reports that: "Most think that he [Paul] refers to spiritual gifts by metonymy by referring to the Spirit" (2003, 638). Taylor (2014, 329) and Fee

pneumatōn as an adjective. This does give the proper interpretation, but so does the noun *spirits*. Lenski says, "This term 'spirits' designates the different manifestations of the one Holy Spirit in the individual Christians" (1946, 590).

Although the Corinthians already value spiritual gifts, they should earnestly seek the gifts for the right reason. They should "seek to abound for the edification of the church."[94] This edification can be accomplished when they communicate clearly. Therefore, the greater gifts in the assembly are the ones which communicate intelligibly and edify the members.

Conclusion

In 1 Corinthians 14:6-12, Paul's theme is intelligibility. While stressing this theme, he deals with speaking in tongues, interpretation of tongues, and several gifts. These gifts include revelation, knowledge, prophecy, and teaching. They can be exercised independently or as interpretations of tongues. When the interpretations of tongues contain these elements, the interpretations, in a sense, become one or more of the other gifts. In the final analysis, what is said is more important than how we label it.

We do not have a meaningless religion based on ritual, but rather one in which communication is essential. Both the heart and the mind must be involved. The mind cannot be involved unless the messages are pronounced in a language that is understood by the people in the assembly. When it is, the body of Christ will be edified. If the believers speak in tongues, they should pray that they will interpret. Unless tongues are interpreted, the speaker will produce indistinct sounds as instruments do when they do not play

---

(1987, 666) hold a similar view. Kistemaker maintains that Paul's intention is to say that the Holy Spirit reveals himself in distributing a multitude of spiritual gifts to his people" (1993, 488). Thiselton says "spirits" means "powers of the Spirit." He writes: "It is best to retain Spirit wherever possible, since Paul never speaks of 'spirituality' in the sense widely used today without implicitly alluding to the Holy Spirit as what makes 'spirituality' *spiritual*" (2000, 1107).

[94]Blomberg makes this point: "Verse 12 concludes by repeating the point with which the first paragraph of this chapter ended (v. 5). The NIV misleads us here; 'Excel in gifts that build up the church' reads as if some gifts do not build up the church! But the Greek merely says, 'Seek that you abound towards the edification of the church'" (1994, 269).

distinct tones. Or, the sounds will be like a foreign language that the people do not understand.

The three topics of tongues, interpretation of tongues, and prophecy are woven together in the text. Like verse 5, verse 13 is a transition verse. It could go with verse 6-12, but is put by NIV with verses 13-18. We will study verse 13 in our next chapter. However, the connection with verses 6-12 should not be lost. Although Paul excludes tongues without interpretation in the assembly, he describes other ways to communicate in a way that the people will be edified.

CHAPTER ELEVEN

PRAYING AND SINGING

Introduction

Paul continues with his theme of intelligibility in 14:13-19. It will be helpful, as background, to recall what he has already said in the fourteenth chapter. In 14:1-5, Paul introduces his theme. Some of the people in the church apparently were speaking in tongues without any interpretation. Because others could not understand the tongues, they were not edified. To offset this, Paul names prophecy as the preeminent gift of communication. Also, he indicates that, as far as edification is concerned, tongues with interpretation is equal in value to prophecy. Then, in 14:6-12, he stresses communication via revelation, knowledge, prophecy, and teaching, whether spoken directly or by means of tongues and interpretation. Also, he exhorts the believers to seek to abound for the edification of the church.

Now, in 14:13-19, Paul applies his theme of intelligibility to praying, singing, and to blessing and giving thanks. He can do each of these spiritual exercises "with the spirit" and "with the mind." Essentially, this means he can speak or sing in a tongue or in the vernacular. Again, he states his general principle of intelligibility. He explains that, even though he frequently speaks in tongues privately, in the church he would rather speak five words in a language they understood than ten thousand words in tongues. Paul, in verses 13-19, states:

[13]Therefore let one who speaks in a tongue pray that he may interpret, [14]For if I pray in a tongue, my spirit prays, but my mind is unfruitful. [15]What is the outcome then? I shall pray with the spirit and I shall pray with the mind also; I shall sing with the spirit and I shall sing with the mind also. [16]Otherwise if you bless in the spirit only, how will the one who fills the place of the ungifted say the "Amen" at your giving of thanks, since he does not know what you are saying? [17]For you are giving thanks well enough, but the other man is not edified. [18]I thank God, I speak in tongues more than you all; [19]however, in the church I

desire to speak five words with my mind, that I may instruct others also, rather than ten thousand words in a tongue.

We will examine what Paul says in 13-19, verse-by-verse. The key point throughout the passage is that we are to worship and communicate intelligibly with our spiritual gifts. Although Paul does not explicitly deal with every possible usage of our spiritual gifts, he does give us guidelines that will help us make decisions. The Spirit will help us as we apply Biblical principles to the life of the church.

Pray That He May Interpret

Paul states in verse 13, "Therefore (*dio*, διὸ) let one who speaks in a tongue pray that he may interpret." The NIV begins the new paragraph with verse 13. However, verse 13 concludes what Paul has said in verse 6-12, but it also introduces verses 14-19. Thus, it is a transition verse. It goes well with both paragraphs.

First, the word "therefore" is a translation of the Greek conjunction *dio*. According to Bauer, this is an "inferential conjunction meaning "therefore, for this reason" or "therefore . . . also" (2000, 250). As Bauer explains, it denotes that the inference is self-evident. Paul has built his case and what he now says follows from that case. In the verses that follow, he further builds up his premise about the importance of intelligibility.

Second, Paul has instructions for the speaker in a tongue (*glōssē*, γλώσσῃ). He should pray that he may interpret. Interpretation of tongues is, in itself, a gift of the Spirit. Thus, when one speaks in a tongue, he should pray to exercise this additional gift. Others in the body may have this gift also. Nevertheless, the speaker in a tongue has a responsibility to pray for it. Concerning this verse, Fee writes:

> In light of the total argument to this point, one might have expected, "For this reason let the one who speaks in tongues seek rather to prophesy." But prophecy is not Paul's concern, intelligibility is; thus he moves toward that concern by urging that "the person who speaks in a tongue should pray that he may interpret what he says." The point is that of v. 5. The interpretation of the tongue makes it intelligible utterance;

therefore it can satisfy the concern of v. 12, the edification of the church. (1987, 668-669)

The subject of interpretation of tongues is woven into the entire text of 1 Corinthians 12-14. In 12:10, Paul lists the gift of "interpretation of tongues." He asks in 12:30: "All do not interpret, do they?" In 14:5, he mentions that one who prophesies is greater than one who speaks in tongues, "unless he interprets." Here, in 14:13, Paul exhorts the one who speaks in a tongue "to pray that he may interpret." He mentions, in 14:26, one who "has an interpretation" in a service. Finally, as Paul says in 14:28, when someone speaks in a tongue, "one must interpret." With all this as the context, we will explore below whether or not interpretation of tongues is involved in 14:15-16.

Third, the speaker in a tongue should pray that he may interpret, not for his own benefit, but for the understanding of the church. The speaker in a tongue (14:4 and 28) is himself edified without the interpretation. For the benefit of the church, he should pray that he may interpret. Only through interpretation will the church be edified. This prayer might precede or follow the utterance in a tongue.

Praying in a Tongue

Sometimes, speaking in tongues takes the form of a prayer. In verse 14 says: "For if I pray in a tongue (glossē, γλώσσῃ), my spirit (pneuma mou, πνεῦμά μου) prays, but my mind (nous mou, νοῦς μου) is unfruitful." Several points can be made.

First, in this verse, Paul focuses on prayer in a tongue. If he prays in a tongue, His prayer is addressed to God in every way: his intent is to address God, only God understands, and the content is addressed to Him. God is the One with whom we interact, and it is He who answers our prayers.[95]

Speaking in a tongue does not always take the form of a prayer. Paul says in 14:2 that, when one speaks in a tongue, "he speaks mysteries." The "mysteries" could include prayer, but also a broader

---

[95] As Lenski explains: "This 'praying with a tongue' is different from the praying for ability to interpret mentioned in v. 13. The prayer mentioned in v. 13 is spoken in ordinary language, here in v. 14 the prayer is made in a tongue or a foreign language" (1946, 501).

range of content. As we earlier concluded, it is not wise to put limits on what the mysteries might be. In verse 14, Paul's concern is prayer, and the prayer may contain content that is described as a "mystery."

Second, using a possessive pronoun, Paul says, "my spirit prays." What does Paul mean by *my spirit*? Whether "my spirit" refers to the human spirit, the Holy Spirit, a gift of the Spirit, or the human spirit inspired by the Holy Spirit is debated. Barrett's view is as follows:

> Paul's language lacks clarity and precision here because he is compressing into a few words the thoughts (1) that it is the Holy Spirit of God that is at work, inspiring Christian worship and prayer; (2) that the work of the Spirit is crystallized into a specific gift; (3) this gift is given in such personal terms to me that I can speak of it as mine—in short as my spirit, which, being what it is, operates through appropriate psychological channels independently of my mind. (1971, 320)

It is possible to include all these ideas, yet put the greater emphasis on the human spirit. In other words, our human spirit prays, but this does not preclude the presence of the Spirit. Therefore, we may say that "my spirit" refers to the human spirit, but it is the human spirit inspired by the Holy Spirit and expressing the Spirit's power through a spiritual gift.[96] This, I believe, gives the best sense of the passage.

Third, Paul then says, "but my mind is unfruitful (*akarpos*, ἄκαρπός)."[97] Here, Paul refers to praying in tongues (without interpretation) in the assembly. When he prays in tongues, his mind

---

[96]Concerning "my spirit," Fee writes: "The most viable solution to this ambiguity is that by the language 'my spirit prays' Paul means his own spirit is praying as the Holy Spirit gives the utterance. Hence, 'my S/spirit prays'" (1987, 670). Barrett (1971, 320) and Thiselton (2000, 1113) object that the Holy Spirit is never called "my" Spirit in Paul's writings. However, the relationship between the human Spirit and the Holy Spirit is always very close in Paul's writings. Given this, the use of "my" is just another way to describe the close relationship.

[97]According to Bauer, the adjective *akarpos* means "*unfruitful, fruitless;*" figuratively, it can mean "*unproductive;*" with regard to 14:14, Bauer says "*(my) mind is unproductive* because it is not active" (Bauer 2000, 35).

does not produce fruit. The question is: Does Paul mean that his mind is unfruitful for his own benefit or for those who are in the audience? Some scholars hold that Paul means that speaking in tongues is of no benefit to him as the speaker. We can agree that it does not enlighten his mind. However, we must keep in mind that engaging the mind is not the only way to edify or benefit the speaker. Paul already has said (14:4) that "one who speaks in a tongue edifies himself." Other scholars argue that Paul means that his mind is not productively engaged in edifying the church. Without an interpretation, the audience is not edified.[98] As long as we do not exclude the fact that one who speaks in tongues is thereby personally edified, we can include both options.

Here, Paul stresses the importance of the mind. With the mind, one speaks in the language of the people present. Morris comments on this point as follows:

> The Christian life is considerably more than a mental exercise. But the man whose mind is *unfruitful* is not being true to his Christian calling. This passage is very important for the insistence on the rightful place of the intellect. Notice that this is secured without any diminution of the spiritual fervor. (1958, 194-195)

The mind is important, but this does not mean that the Holy Spirit is not involved. The Spirit inspires us to pray in known languages as well as unknown. One can pray with the mind without involving a gift of the Spirit, but earnest prayer is often directly inspired by the Spirit.

Fourth, Paul, in verse 14, makes a distinction between praying with the *spirit* and with the *mind*. This distinction applies to singing, blessing, and giving thanks as well as to praying. Paul is not giving a lesson in psychology with psychological terms. The essential distinction is simply between unintelligible and intelligible speech and singing. Paul expands on this in the verses that follow.

---

[98]Thiselton makes this statement: "Paul's point is not that the tongue-speaker misses out, but that the *church community* misses out. Of the major translations NRSV's *my mind is unproductive* is best at this point since *produce* can serve others. . . . However, it may perhaps still more clearly convey Paul's logic to translate but *my mind produces no fruit from it*, i.e., means by which to benefit others" (2000, 1111).

Praying and Singing

Next, Paul asks a question and answers it. Based on what he has just said, he asks (verse 15): "What is the outcome then?" His answer is: "I shall pray with the spirit (*tō pneumati*, τῷ πνεύματι) and I shall pray with the mind (*tō noi*, τῷ νοΐ) also; I shall sing (*psalō*, ψαλῶ) with the spirit (*tō pneumati*) and I shall sing (*psalō*) with the mind (*tō noi*) also."

First, Paul uses the future tense four times to say what he will do. He declares that I *shall* sing and pray with the spirit and with the mind. According to Lenski, "The future tenses are volitive; they state a determination on Paul's part" (1946, 874). Paul's singing and praying in tongues and with the mind are not just an occasional spontaneous outburst; he is determined to pray and sing with both the mind and the Spirit.

Second, Paul deals with praying and singing "with the Spirit" and "with the mind." When Paul prays and sings with the mind, he prays and sings in a language known to the speaker and the hearers. His intellect, and the intellect of the audience, is fully engaged. When he prays and sings with the Spirit, he prays and sings in tongues. Although Paul does not say "my spirit," as in verse 14, the meaning does not dramatically change. In both cases, the human spirit is inspired by the Holy Spirit. However, "with the Spirit" possibly puts a stronger emphasis on the Holy Spirit than "my Spirit" does. Both expressions mean that the Spirit inspires the person to pray and sing.

Third, Paul says "I will sing (*psalō*)," using the future tense of *psallō* (ψάλλω). Concerning this verse, Bauer says *psallō* means: "*sing praise in spiritual ecstasy* and *in full possession of one's mental faculties*" (2000, 1096). In addition, he says that, in accordance with Old Testament usage, *psallō* means to "*sing (to the accompaniment of a harp) sing praise*" (2000, 1096). As the usage of the word developed, *psallō* came to include unaccompanied singing as well. According to Robertson and Plummer:

> *Psallō* originally meant playing on a stringed instrument; then singing to the harp or lyre; finally, singing without accompaniment, especially singing praise. . . . It is possible that the ecstatic utterances sometimes took the form of an

inarticulate chant, songs without intelligible words or definite melody. (1914, 312)

Modes of Singing and Praying

What modes of praying and singing does Paul have in mind? How does interpretation of tongues fit in? As we study this verse (15), let us consider three sets of situations to which his comments might apply. Praying and singing could be: (1) private prayers and songs, (2) solo prayers and songs in public, or (3) unison prayers and songs. Let us consider these various forms.

First, any believer can pray or sing privately in a devotional way. Many people testify to the blessing they receive through this form of praying. Later in our text (verse 18), Paul gives his own testimony about speaking in tongues in private.

One, in private, a person may pray in tongues and pray with the mind also. When he prays privately with the spirit, he may also pray the interpretation, but it would seem that usually he does not. The one who prays in tongues is edified by such praying even without interpretation. Thus, praying with the mind is not, in this case, an interpretation of prayers with the spirit. Praying with the mind would be an additional form of expressing one's prayers.

Two, similarly, a person may sing in tongues privately and also sing with the mind. A person may sing an interpretation, but private devotional songs in tongues are meaningful without interpretation. Thus, as with private prayers with the Spirit, singing privately with the Spirit is probably not often interpreted. I say "probably" because, unless people report what they do in private, we do not know.

Second, we can be sure that Paul was concerned about praying and singing in the public services. He expresses this concern very well in verse 16. His attention is focused, I believe, on solo praying and singing. He illustrates by saying what he himself has determined to do. Then, in verse 26, he speaks of "each one" exercising a gift. Others, in turn, will manifest the presence of the Spirit.

One, Paul is not saying, "I will pray in tongues, leave such prayers without interpretation, and then pray with the mind also." Instead, as instructed in verse 13, the one who prays in tongues should pray that he may interpret. The solo praying in tongues without interpretation would not be in harmony with Paul's own preferred guidelines. The audience would not view these prayers as being intended for them. Because the audience would not understand such prayers, they would not be edified. When Paul prays in tongues, he will interpret such prayers *by* praying with the mind.[99] Through interpretation, the audience will be edified. He may, of course, pray with the mind without having prayed in tongues. This point is not in question.

Two, some commentators move to congregational singing when Paul says, "I will sing." We will consider this below, but the main focus, it seems to me, is on solo singing in the church.[100] When Paul says, "I will sing with the spirit," he means he will sing in tongues. This is spontaneous, Spirit-inspired singing.

As with prayer (verse 13), the one who sings in tongues should pray that he may interpret. In the church, Paul will sing in tongues, but also he will interpret the song by singing with the mind.

Paul will sing with the spirit, but he will sing with the mind as well.[101] As with prayer, this point is not in question. Obviously, he may sing with the mind without singing in tongues. The songs sung with the mind include prepared songs, such as psalms, and possibly spontaneous songs.

Three, many people hold that believers pray and sing in tongues then, in addition, pray and sing in the vernacular with the

---

[99] Carson holds that verse 15 probably means something like this: "What then shall I do? Well, having prayed for the gift of interpretation, I will pray with my spirit (that is, I will continue to speak in tongues), but I will also pray with my mind (that is, the prayer will be repeated, this time with the mind engaged-presumably the interpretation of the prayer with the spirit). The same is true for singing with the spirit (apparently this is a more melodious or metrical form of tongues-speaking/praying)" (1987, 104).

[100] Fee posits that: "The present passage [v. 15], as well as v. 26, indicates that some of this kind of singing was 'solo.' This text also adds a dimension to our understanding of 'speaking in tongues.' Not only did one pray in this way, but one also praised God in song in this way. Hence the verbs in vv. 16-17 that pick up this theme are 'bless' and 'give thanks'" (1987, 671).

[101] Garland makes this point: "Paul's conclusion is that he will do both: he will pray and sing with spiritual ecstasy, and pray and sing in full possession of his mental faculties. That implies that the spiritual ecstasy will be complemented by rational interpretation that communicates to others and produces fruit" (2003, 640).

two modes not being connected. With regard to this approach, Brandt counters with these comments on 14:15:

> Does he [Paul] mean, as we have for so long thought, that he would pray supernaturally in tongues, and that he would also pray from his own mind on the natural plane? No way! He plainly, in light of his previous instruction relating to the gift of interpretation, says, "I will pray in tongues, and then I will interpret what I have prayed. The exact same thing would apply to his singing with the spirit. "I will sing with the spirit and I will interpret what I sing." (1981, 60)

Third, let us consider praying and singing in unison. One, although Paul is not directly discussing unison prayers, we may apply his guidelines to this type of praying. The key criterion is edification. We have no evidence that the Corinthian church all prayed together in tongues. Nevertheless, it would be possible for this to happen. It would be a collective act of worship not intended for communication to each other. Unlike when a single person speaks in tongues, the audience is not sitting by, uninvolved. Even an unbeliever (14:24) probably could recognize unison prayer in tongues as a collective act of worship. Thus, intelligibility would not be an issue. Interpretation of such prayers would not be feasible nor would there be a need for it. The people would be collectively edified.

Paul does not say whether or not the Corinthian church prayed in unison with the mind. Such praying is common in our churches today. Because all pray at once, this form of praying does not communicate well with others. However, as a collective act of worship, it would be permitted. Indeed, unison praying has been a great blessing to many churches.

Two, obviously, the church at Corinth did sing in unison. Although solo singing seems to be what Paul chiefly had in mind, we can apply what he says to congregational singing. Here, to "sing with the spirit" means to sing in tongues. As with praying, unison singing in tongues without interpretation would be permitted.[102] Such singing is not intended to convey a message to

---

[102] Rea writes about congregational worship in spiritual songs (Eph. 5:18-19): "This is the beautiful, unrehearsed, extemporaneous singing in the Spirit by

the assembly. All are engaged in an act of worship without any needing to sit by, uninvolved. No interpretation is needed. The congregation would be collectively edified.

During times of renewal, it is common for congregations to sing "with the Spirit." This form of singing can be very heartwarming and expressive of our adoration of our Savior. The congregation, of course, may sing with the mind as well. Paul mentions "spiritual songs" in both Ephesians 5:18-19 and Colossians 3:16. To the Ephesians, he writes:

[18]And do not get drunk with wine, for that is dissipation, but be filled with the Spirit, [19]speaking to one another in psalms and hymns and spiritual songs, singing and making melody with your heart to the Lord. (5:18-19)

Similarly, he says to the Colossians: "Let the word of Christ richly dwell within you, with all wisdom teaching and admonishing one another with psalms *and* hymns *and* spiritual songs, singing with thankfulness in your hearts to God" (Col. 3:16).

In these passages, spontaneous songs in one's own language and previously prepared songs may be included. Although the term "spiritual songs" may be used more broadly in these passages, songs in tongues are certainly included. As these passages indicate, the believers taught and admonished others through songs. This would be through songs sung in a known language. Although people are singing "with the mind," the Spirit inspires them as they sing.

When people in the congregation pray or sing in unison, all have the opportunity to be engaged in this activity. Thus, it would seem that, when the congregation sings or prays with the spirit, an interpretation would not be necessary. When they sing with the mind, all are singing the same words. When praying in unison, they are praying individual prayers in a collective setting.

---

all or many of the believers assembled in worship. Often it takes the form of singing praise to God in various tongues, which need not be interpreted because all are participating in the adoration. If only one person sings aloud in a tongue, then an interpretations should follow, perhaps also in song" (1998, 237).

The One Who Does Not Understand

As verses 16 and 17 show, Paul's main concern is praying and singing in the public worship services. He is concerned both with blessing God, blessing others, and being blessed. He writes:

[16]Otherwise if you bless (*eulogēis*, εὐλογῇς) in the spirit ([*en*] *pneumati*, [ἐν] πνεύματι) *only*, how will the one who fills the place (*topon*, τόπον) of the ungifted (*idiōtou*, ἰδιώτου) say the "Amen" at your giving of thanks (*eucharistia*, εὐχαριστίᾳ), since he does not know what you are saying? [17]For you are giving thanks (*eucharisteis*, εὐχαριστεῖς) well enough, but the other man is not edified.

First, the Greek word here translated *bless* is *eulogia* (εὐλογία). It can mean praise, bless, or the act of blessing. To bless can signify to bless God, to call down God's grace upon others, and to give thanks to God. Paul uses the noun *eucharistia*, or giving of thanks, to describe the activity of blessing. In verse 17, he uses the verb *eucharisteis*, meaning "you are giving thanks." One may bless, praise, and give thanks through prayer, song, and speech, but the word *eulogia* is not limited to these ways.

Paul speaks to those who would bless in the spirit *only*. The verbs in verses 16-17 are all in the singular. This would suggest that each person in turn blesses and gives thanks. His comments in this verse mean that they bless in tongues but not with the mind. Because they bless in tongues, the people do not know what they are saying. The word "only" is not in the Greek text, but this is clearly the intended sense. The principle that people who pray in a tongue should pray that they would interpret would apply to blessing others as well. If they bless in a tongue, they should pray to interpret. An interpretation is needed for people to understand.

Second, Paul speaks about the one "who fills the place (*topon*) of" the *idiōtou* (genitive singular of *idiōtēs*, ἰδιώτης). Bauer indicates that *topon* can refer to a literal location or in a figurative sense to a position (2000, 1011). With regard to 14:16, he holds that there was a special place for the *idiōtai* (ἰδιῶται, plural) in the room where Christians assembled (2000, 468). However, the majority opinion seems to be that *topon* should be taken in a figurative sense, referring to the role or position an *idiōtēs*.

Whether *topon* is taken in a literal or figurative sense, the questions still arises as to whom the term *idiōtēs* refers. Palma provides a concise summary paragraph about the various views on this topic. He writes:

An interpretation is needed because of the presence of an 'ungifted' (*idiōtēs*) person (1 Cor. 14:16; NASB[95]). The identity of such a person is much disputed. Some suggest he may be a proselyte or a catechumen, or a member of the congregation who is not endowed with the gift of tongues or interpretation of tongues. But it does not seem that Paul has in mind only people of those types, for even full-fledged members do not know what the tongue-speaker has said and whether they must respond with the "Amen." A different meaning for *idiōtēs* may be present in verses 23-24, however, where Paul speaks of the possibility of such persons and unbelievers entering a service. They would then be no different from the unbelievers, and the two terms would express one idea— unbelieving outsiders. (2001, 243)

Third, Jewish and early Christian congregations showed their agreement with blessings, prayers, and thanksgiving by saying "Amen." With a rhetorical question, Paul makes the point that people will not be able to say "Amen" when a speaker blesses "in spirit" only. He speaks about an *idiōtēs* in particular, but the point applies to all who are present. Therefore, the one who blesses in tongues should bless, through interpretation, with the mind also.

Based on 14:15, Brandt holds that that those who pray and sing in tongues should interpret by praying and singing in the vernacular. With regard to verse 16, Brandt states: "There Paul says, 'Else,' that is, 'otherwise,' the idea being that if you fail to follow these guidelines requiring you to interpret in the public meeting what you have prayed or sung in a tongue, how shall those who can't understand what you are saying say 'Amen' and be edified?" (1981, 60)

Fourth, in verse 17, Paul says, "For you are giving thanks well enough, but the other person is not edified." When translating this verse, some scholars use an English subjunctive, meaning "you may be giving thanks well enough." Some go further and presume that Paul is speaking ironically. The context, however, indicates that they actually are giving thanks when they pray or sing in tongues.[103] Paul is not prohibiting this; he is just pointing out that, without interpretation, others are not blessed.

Speaking in the Church

Paul expresses the value he places on speaking in tongues in private but contrasts this with the importance of speech that is intelligible in the public worship services. He writes:

[18]I thank God, I speak in tongues more than you all; [19]however, in the church I desire to speak five words with my mind, that I may instruct others also, rather than ten thousand words in a tongue.

First, once again, Paul puts the key issue in focus. The issue is not the validity of tongues. Privately, Paul speaks in tongues more than all of them. By saying so, Paul shows that speaking in tongues is very valuable to him in his private prayer life.[104] The issue is one of intelligible speaking in the church. This is why, in the church, he would rather speak five words with his mind than ten thousand words in a tongue.

Second, in verses 18-19, Paul does not mention speaking in tongues with interpretation. He already has made it clear that tongues with interpretation meet the criterion of intelligibility. Therefore, the gift of interpretation has a significant role in the meetings of the assembly. The value and utility of speaking in

---

[103]Fee declares: "There is no good reason to translate the first clause with an English subjunctive, 'You may be giving thanks well enough. Paul is simply affirming what he has already said in vv. 15 and 16: 'To be sure, you are giving thanks.' But that is not adequate in the assembly, he is telling them. What is needed is to give thank intelligibly, so that others may benefit as well" (1987, 674). Compare Barrett (1971, 321).

[104]With regard to 14:19, Carson avers, "There is no stronger defense of the private use of tongues, and attempts to avoid this conclusion turn out on inspection to be remarkably flimsy. If Paul speaks in tongues more than all the Corinthians, yet in the church prefers to speak five intelligible words rather than ten thousand words in a tongue (which is a way of saying that under virtually no circumstance will he ever speak in tongues in church, without quite ruling out the possibility), then where does he speak them? It will not do to suppose Paul is counseling private, quiet use of tongues during the assembly when another is ministering" (1987, 105).

tongues with interpretation is well established in the context that Paul presents. He does not have to repeat the principle each time that it applies.

Conclusion

As we study Paul's message in 1 Corinthians 14, we understand even better why he wrote chapter 13, the chapter on love. Love is the highest motive for exercising spiritual gifts. When we love others, we will want to edify them. We can do this by speaking intelligibly. We will not want to shut out our audience and talk with God just for our own benefit. Our attention will be focused on their edification.

In 14:13-19, Paul deals with praying and singing as well as blessing and giving thanks with the mind and with the Spirit. Even though he does not deal explicitly with every situation, he gives us very good guidelines to help us deduce principles that will be effective in our church services. The principle that tongues should be interpreted applies to both solo praying and singing. Paul does not discuss praying and singing in unison in this passage, but he does write about "spiritual songs" in Ephesians 5:18 and Colossians 3:16. These spiritual songs include singing in tongues. Because all are engaged in singing and praying, an interpretation is not necessary. The people are edified by their participation.

All this does not preclude our own edification. We can privately talk with God in a public service as well as when we are alone. When we are privately praying in tongues, an interpretation is possible but not necessary for us to be edified. In public, when we bless others through tongues and interpretation, we are blessed as well. Let us, therefore, earnestly desire the spiritual gifts which will communicate intelligibly to others. Let us submit ourselves to the guidance of the Spirit and pray that God will use us in a wonderful way to bless others. The church will be abundantly enriched.

CHAPTER TWELVE

TONGUES AND PROPHECY AS SIGNS

Introduction

Many pastors are concerned with the use of tongues and prophecy in the church. With regard to the gifts of the Spirit, perhaps no other issue is debated as much as this. What Paul says in 1 Corinthians 14:20-25 bears directly on the subject, so these verses provide important guidance for pastors.

In this passage, Paul writes about the role of tongues and prophecy as signs, respectively, for believers and unbelievers. When he mentions tongues, he means tongues without interpretation. In this paragraph, Paul does not mention interpretation of tongues. He corrects the Corinthians with regard to both tongues without interpretation and prophecy because their understanding was faulty. Paul writes:

[20]Brethren, do not be children in your thinking; yet in evil be babes, but in your thinking be mature. [21]In the Law it is written, "By men of strange tongues and by the lips of strangers I will speak to this people, and even so they will not listen to Me," says the Lord. [22]So then tongues are for a sign, not to those who believe, but to unbelievers; but prophecy is for a sign, not to unbelievers, but to those who believe. [23]If therefore the whole church should assemble together and all speak in tongues, and ungifted men or unbelievers enter, will they not say that you are mad? [24]But if all prophesy, and an unbeliever or an ungifted man enters, he is convicted by all, he is called to account by all; [25]the secrets of his heart are disclosed; and so he will fall on his face and worship God, declaring that God is certainly among you.

A key word in these verses is "sign." In general terms, a sign is anything that represents or points to something else. A sign can be positive or negative in its content, its impact on people, and the responses it evokes. In addition, a sign may mean different things to different people. This can be true of the same sign at the same time and place. Thus, the word itself is very flexible. Speaking theologically, a sign can point to the presence of God and, going further, to His favor or disfavor. A sign can confirm faith or point to judgment. The disfavor of God can be expressed in judgment. Moreover, a sign can evoke responses from the hearers. It is God's desire that the people listen to Him and obey, but many do not.

The word "sign" occurs in verse 22 which sets the agenda for the entire passage. This verse makes four assertions about tongues and prophecy as signs. These assertions are: (1) tongues are not for a sign to those who believe, (2) tongues are for a sign to unbelievers, (3) prophecy is not for a sign to unbelievers, and (4) prophecy is for a sign to believers. A major issue develops over how to reconcile Paul's comments in verses 23-25 with the assertions in verse 22. Our study in this chapter will include an examination of all four of these assertions.

Monologue and Dialogue Views

Expositors generally agree that Paul expresses his own views in verses 20 and 23-25. He rebukes the Corinthians in verse 20 for their immature thinking. Then, in verses 23-25, he declares his own views. With regard to these verses, some exegetical issues may be raised, but there is considerable harmony with regard to the broad outlines.

Problems arise, however, over interpretations of verses 21-22. With regard to verse 21, Paul cites, but does not precisely quote, Isaiah 28:11-12. The issue is whether Paul cited Isaiah directly or quoted the Corinthians who, in turn, cited Isaiah. Another issue comes up over verse 22. The question is whether Paul makes the assertions in this verse or was citing the view of the Corinthians. Whether he quoted a Corinthian declaration or their rhetorical question is debated. In any case, scholars usually agree that the assertions of verse 22 are presented as following from the information given in the Isaiah passage.

Three views emerge over these issues: (1) the monologue view, (2) the dialogue view, and (3) the diatribe view. The diatribe view is really a form of dialogue. Thus, sometimes my use of the term *dialogue* includes the diatribe form. Where needed, I distinguish the terms. Under all these approaches, Paul sets out to correct the thinking of the Corinthians.

First, the monologue view is the most common. This view holds that Paul is expressing his own positions throughout this passage. Proponents hold that he rebukes the Corinthians in verse 20, cites Isaiah 28:11-12 in verse 21, gives his conclusions in verse 22 that are based on verses 20-21, and then amplifies his view in verses 23-25. Advocates of this view do not, of course, agree on all points. Given my purpose, I will deal mainly with their general points of agreement.

Second, an alternative approach is the dialogue method. Using this approach, Paul rebukes the Corinthians in verse 20, quotes their citation of Isaiah in verse 21, presents their declaration in verse 22 with its four assertions, then refutes some of their assertions in verses 23-25. The dialogue view has points of agreement as well as disagreement with the monologue view. This is the view that I support.

Paul was noted for his dialogic preaching. According to Stott, Paul was the "past master" of this art, and the best example is the book of Romans. Stott states, "Throughout its early chapters, as he dictates to Tertius, he is conscious of Jewish objections to his argument. Many times he voices their objection and answers it" (1964, 63).

Moreover, in 1 Corinthians 7:1, Paul uses the phrase *peri de* (περὶ δὲ, concerning moreover) to acknowledge issues raised by the Corinthians. He uses this phrase again in 7:25, 8:1, 12:1, 16:1; and 16:12. Also, he uses *peri* in 8:4. Paul clearly uses the method of dialogue. The question is: Does he use it here? As I see the passage, Paul presents the thinking of the Corinthians in verses 21-22. By interpreting 14:20-25 dialogically, the reader avoids the internal contradictions.

Third, Johanson contends that Paul uses the method of diatribe (1979, 194), which, in my view, is a form of dialogue.[105] He maintains that Paul rebukes the Corinthians in verse 20 for their

---

[105] Concerning diatribe, Johanson states: "It is typical of diatribe for an objection or opinion to be put forward and then refuted inferentially by a question (i.e. v. 23, 'will they not say you are mad?') or an example immediately following it" (1979, 194). Even so, diatribe is still a form of dialogue. The assumption is that the imaginary opponent represents some of the Corinthians with whom Paul is interacting.

immature thinking. Then, in verses 21-25, Paul presents his argument against their immature thinking. In verse 21, he quotes Isaiah 28:11-12. In response to the Isaiah passage, Paul puts the assertions of verse 22 in the mouth of an imaginary opponent in the form of a rhetorical question.[106] The opponent speaks for the group of Corinthians who would answer "yes" to the question. Then, in verses 23-25, Paul counters their view with his own.

My view and Johanson's are in agreement that Paul counters some of the points made by the Corinthians in verse 22, but there are two main differences. One, Johanson argues that Paul cites Isaiah 28:11-12 to use it as a springboard to his argument, but that this passage may or may not have been known to the members at Corinth. Against this, it seems to me that Paul could have refuted their views without citing Isaiah. Two, placing the assertions of verse 22 in the mouth of an imaginary opponent seems unnecessary. To me, it appears that Paul was directly quoting a declaration by the Corinthians, but either way, the end result is that Paul is making known the conclusions of the Corinthians.

Paul's Exhortation

The dialogue interpretation of verse 20 harmonizes with the monologue view. In verse 20, Paul rebukes the Corinthians with this comment: "Brethren, do not be children (*paidia*, παιδία) in your thinking; yet in evil (*kakia*, κακία) be babes (*nēpiazete*, νηπιάζετε), but in your thinking be mature (*teleioi*, τέλειοι)." With this exhortation, Paul introduces what he will say about the proper roles of tongues and prophecy as signs to believers and unbelievers.

First, it is clear that Paul is addressing a twofold problem in the church at Corinth. One, it seems that some of them felt that speaking in tongues made them spiritually elite. Some scholars hold that all of the Corinthians had this problem, but others believe

---

[106]Johanson notes the following: "For this particular insight I am indebted to Professor M. Black, who was so kind as to suggest it to me in a letter. At first I had come to the conclusion that v. 22 constituted a slogan quoted by Paul" (1979, 194). Verbrugge (2008, 383) has the same view as Johanson. Talbert (1987, 87-88) cites Johanson in support of his view that verse 22 presents the view of the Corinthians.

they were divided between those who highly valued tongues and those who favored prophecy. As a result, a power struggle may have developed. My dialogue view is not significantly affected by this debate. Two, in any case, the problem was made worse because some of them were speaking in tongues without interpretation. They failed to see the implications of their improper use of this gift.

Second, Paul prescribes a solution to the problem that has three aspects: One, he says that they should not be children (*paidia*) in their thinking. No doubt, they were proud of their wisdom and knowledge, but they were children in their thinking about tongues. Spiritually, instead of being elite, they were just in the early formative stages of spiritual development.

Two, Paul appeals to the Corinthians to be "mature" (*teleioi*) in their thinking. Their maturity depends, in part, on a proper understanding of the gifts of tongues and prophecy. At the heart of the matter, as 1 Corinthians 13:1-13 makes clear, is the importance of having love as the proper motive and doing what edifies all the members of the assembly. When they are motivated by love, the edification of the body will be paramount. Maturity can be reached only when we are motivated by love.

Three, Paul makes a parenthetic statement in between exhorting the Corinthians not to be children and to be mature. He says, "yet in evil (*kakia*) be babes (*nēpiazete*)." According to Thayer, the word *kakia* means wickedness, depravity, ill-will, and malice; the verb *nēpiazete* refers to being little children or babes (1962, 320). Bauer says the meaning in this verse is to "have as little wickedness as a child" (2000, 671). Fee says the clause means being innocent in behavior with regard to evil (1994, 238).

Without changing the basic meaning, Lenski relates this clause to the wrong use of a spiritual gift. He holds that Paul means using a spiritual gift so that it does not serve its true purpose. He says, "To use it with a display of vanity is childish; to ignore its purpose by disregarding edification is wrong" (1946, 598). Thus, wrong usage of a spiritual gift leads to wrongdoing. This is true, but the wrongdoing is not limited to this.[107]

---

[107]Thiselton says: "However, to be innocent of wickedness entails rejecting knowledge of devious strategies which may promote one's own evil

178

Isaiah and the Assertions

Verses 21-22 consist of a citation of the Law[108] from Isaiah 28:11-12 and the related four assertions that Paul lists. The citation and the assertions, as written by Paul, are as follows:

[21]In the Law it is written, "BY MEN OF STRANGE TONGUES AND BY THE LIPS OF STRANGERS I WILL SPEAK TO THIS PEOPLE, AND EVEN SO THEY WILL NOT LISTEN TO ME," says the Lord. [22]So then tongues are for a sign, not to those who believe but to unbelievers; but prophecy *is for a sign*, not to unbelievers but to those who believe.

First, verse 21 is a citation of Isaiah 28:11-12, but it is not an exact quotation of either the Greek LXX (Septuagint) or the Hebrew MT (Masoretic Text). Also, it varies from the NASB[95] and NIV[109] versions of Isaiah 28:11-12 in English. The NASB[95] version states:

---

purposes, including here perhaps a hint that even religious contexts can offer subtle temptations to manipulate them on behalf of self-interests in ways which ultimately may come to be *wicked*" (2000, 1119).

[108]Taylor notes that: "On Paul's other uses of 'It is written' followed by a scriptural citation in 1 Corinthians see 1:19, 31; 2:9; 3:19; 9:9; 10:7; 15:45" (2014, 339). He presents this analysis: "The formula 'It is written' introduces Isa 28:11 into the argument. Even though the text is from the Prophets, Paul refers to what is written 'in the Law,' indicating a broadened sense of the term 'law' in this context. Paul will refer again to what the 'law' says in 14:34, but there is no citation of a specific text. This is the only place in his letters that Paul does not link the formula, 'It is written,' to what precedes with a conjunction. This does not mean that the scriptural citation is disconnected altogether from 14:20 but implies that Paul is not drawing support from the Old Testament for the preceding command to 'become mature' but rather to establish the claim that follows in 14:22, namely, that tongues are a sign to unbelievers rather than believers, which is amplified by the illustration in 14:23-25." (2014, 339) Although Taylor does not hold that Paul is quoting the Corinthians in 14:21-22, his line of thought fits very well with that position. The Corinthians would agree that Paul is not drawing support from the Old Testament for what he says in 14:20.

[109]Some of the differences are listed by Kistemaker. With the NIV as the basis for comparison, he states: "Paul has reversed the two parts of the first line, 'foreign lips' and 'strange tongues.' In the second line he substitutes 'I' for 'God'—in other words, God speaks directly to the people. He deletes the

[11]Indeed, He will speak to this people through stammering lips and a foreign tongue, [NIV, "with foreign lips and strange tongues"] [12]He who said to them, "Here is rest, give rest to the weary," And, "Here is repose," but they would not listen.

There are several differences between verse 21 and the Isaiah passage. For my purpose, the main difference is that Isaiah reports (28:12) that God had previously spoken a message of comfort to Israel in their language, but they would not listen. Verse 21 omits this report. The focus of Paul's comment in 14:21 is on unintelligible speech as a sign of judgment, not on a message of comfort in the vernacular.

Second, according to the Isaiah passage, the nation of Judah would not listen to the prophets and mocked Isaiah. Therefore, God will judge the Judeans by speaking to them through "stammering lips" and a "foreign tongue." Young says that the "stammering lips" appear to be unintelligible mutterings, but the words "another tongue" show that the reference here is to another language. The men of strange tongues were Assyrians speaking their language. Because the people of Judah did not understand them, their words sounded like vain babblings (1969, 277). God judged them by turning them over to men speaking a foreign language. The foreign language became a negative sign of God's judgment. As it turns out, this sign was not effective in motivating people to listen to God and obey.

Third, commentators hold various views with regard to verses 21 and 22, but they usually agree that these verses belong together. Paul says, "So then (hōste, ὥστε) tongues are for a sign, not to those who believe, but to unbelievers; but prophecy *is for a sign*, not to unbelievers, but to those who believe" (verse 22). Robertson says that *hōste* means "and so" (1934, 999). According to Bauer, when introducing an independent clause, this conjunction (*hōste*) means "for this reason, therefore, so" or "so that" (2000, 1107). He

---

third and fourth lines and half of the fifth. And last, he adds 'even so' and 'says the Lord' to the second half of line five" (1993, 499). The deleted lines in verse 21 say: "to whom he said, 'This is the resting place, let the weary rest'; and 'This is the place of repose'." God had previously spoken to them in their language.

lists 14:22 as an example. I concur that this conjunction means that verse 22 is connected with verse 21.

Johanson contends that the conjunction *hōste* (verse 22) introduces a rhetorical question. He believes this is analogous to Paul's use of *hōste* in Galatians 4:16. Against this view, Fee says: "the alleged analogous usage in Gal. 4:16 is not similar" (1987, 682). However, without reference to 14:22, Lenski maintains that *hōste* in Galatians 4:16 introduces a question rather than a declaration (1946, 223). Either approach is grammatically possible, but my view is that Paul was quoting a Corinthian declaration. Even if verse 22 expresses a rhetorical question, it still makes known the Corinthian view.

Fourth, according to the monologue view, Paul was stating his own view in verses 21-22. In verse 22, Paul declares his own assertions concerning tongues and prophecy as signs. In verse 21, he cites Isaiah 28:11-12, but he tailors the citation to his own purposes. As noted above, he does not mention that God had already spoken to Israel in its own language and that Israel did not listen. With regard to the Corinthians, he has in mind their speaking in tongues and the impact it was having on the unbelievers. The end result, as stated by Paul, is that "Even so, they will not listen to me." In this way, tongues becomes a negative sign to the unbelievers, not to the believers.

Fifth, in the dialogue view, Paul is quoting the Corinthians in verses 21-22. They have cited the Isaiah passage and applied in to the impact of tongues on the unbelievers. Based on their faulty application, the believers at Corinth reached the conclusions set forth in verse 22. Although Paul does not say, "You have quoted Isaiah 28:11-12 and have wrongly applied it," we can assume that this was his position. In support of this assumption, we might ask, "Why would Paul cite Isaiah as a basis for his argument and then make assertions of his own that he would proceed to refute?" The contradictions are difficult to overcome.

Three additional reasons favor the dialogue view. One, a very strong reason is that this view easily resolves the apparent contradictions that arise out of the monologue view. Two, a convincing argument for this assumption is that Paul has just rebuked the Corinthians for their immature thinking. This leads us to anticipate that he will tell us what their immature thinking is. In verses 21-22, this is precisely what he does. Unless he does it here, we have to deduce his disagreement with the Corinthians from the implications of verse 22. Three, it appears that Paul was not concerned with exactly quoting Isaiah. He was quoting the Corinthians with regard to their citation of Isaiah and the conclusions they drew from this. This point does not prove my position, but it does harmonize with the fact that Isaiah 28:11-12 was not cited with precision.

Sixth, the assertions in verse 22 bring into focus four cases for us to consider. By cases, I mean topics for discussion. Each case is based on one of the four assertions. The cases are: (1) tongues as a sign for believers, (2) tongues as a sign for unbelievers, (3) prophecy as a sign for unbelievers, and (4) prophecy as a sign for believers.

Case One: Tongues and Believers

Case one has to do with whether or not tongues are a sign to believers.

Verse 22 makes an assertion with regard to this case. It says: "So then tongues are for a sign, not to those who believe."[110] In other words, verse 22 asserts that tongues are *not* a sign for believers. The monologue view regards this as Paul's stated view, but the dialogue view holds that Paul was citing the view of the Corinthians. This is a major difference between the views.

First, Paul does not discuss this case further in verses 22-25. He does not explicitly refute or affirm the assertion that tongues are not a sign for the believer. In verse 23, he says nothing about the believer. We may wonder why. One reason is that Paul has already discussed the impact of tongues on believers. In addition, the greater problem in Corinth had to do with the impact of tongues on unbelievers, not on believers.

---

[110]The NASB[95] translation of 14:22 is: "So then tongues are for a sign [*eis sēmeion eisin*, εἰς σημεῖόν εἰσιν], not to those who believe but to unbelievers; but prophecy *is for a sign*, not to unbelievers but to those who believe." With regard to "are for a sign," Grudem says that "this construction (Greek *eis* + accusative with the verb 'to be') often can replace a predicate nominative with no real change in meaning. Paul simply says, 'Tongues are a sign.'" The NIV translation is "are a sign."

Second, those who hold the monologue view have various ideas about the statement that tongues are not a sign to believers. Keep in mind that the subject is tongues without interpretation. Dunn holds, for example, that Paul is refuting the idea that tongues are a proof of pneumatic status and authority (1975, 230). Similarly, Fee maintains that Paul is countering the view of the Corinthians that tongues are the divine evidence of the presence of God in the assembly (1994, 240).

These ideas are not stated in verse 22. They are suppositions derived from verse 22 on the assumption that verse 22 expresses Paul's view. Certainly, Paul does hold (1 Cor. 12:1-3) that the Holy Spirit upholds Jesus as Lord. This is the ultimate test of the Spirit's presence and activity. This does not, however, lessen the fact that the presence of the Spirit is an evidence of God's favor.

Third, in the dialogue view, what Paul says in the context and elsewhere contradicts the statement in verse 22; tongues can be a sign to the believer. From other passages, we learn that tongues alone are for private prayer while tongues and interpretation are for expression in the assembly. However, this does not lead us to the conclusion that tongues are not a sign to the believer. Clearly, tongues can be a powerful sign of the presence and approval of God for the believer. This is true both with regard to speaking in tongues in private and the proper use of tongues and interpretation in the assembly.

In verses 20-25, Paul is dealing with tongues in the assembly. Even so, the value of tongues in private usage is instructive. We learn in 14:4 that tongues edify the believer himself. Then, in 14:5, Paul says that he wishes all of them spoke in tongues. In 14:18, he testifies that he has spoken in tongues more than all of them. Given all this, it is clear that Paul values the impact of private tongues. Tongues are a sign of the presence and power of God. Also, through tongues, Paul can magnify the Lord.

Concerning tongues in the assembly, Paul mentions spiritual songs in Colossians 3:16 and Ephesians 5:18. Many scholars hold that this, at least, includes singing in tongues. When a congregation sings in tongues, they are not attempting to communicate a message to the audience. Even the unbelievers would recognize this. We could say the same for praying in unison in tongues. Unison praying in tongues is a part of worship. As Lim states, "The issue of this passage is not whether to deny worship in tongues but how to participate in worship to bless others" (1991, 161).

Case Two: Tongues and Unbelievers

The second case has to do with whether or not tongues are a sign to the unbelievers. If tongues are a sign, then the issue becomes whether or not the sign is positive or negative. Are they a sign of God's favor or disfavor? In verse 22a, Paul writes: "So then tongues are for a sign . . . but to unbelievers." Then, in verse 23, he declares: "If therefore (*ean oun*, ἐὰν οὖν) the whole church should assemble together and all speak in tongues, and ungifted (*idiōtai*, ἰδιῶται) men or unbelievers (*apistoi*, ἄπιστοι) enter, will they not say that you are mad?"

First, it is important to examine the situation that Paul is addressing. He makes two important points in verse 23. One, Paul asks a rhetorical question that addresses a specific situation. According to Barrett, this speaking in tongues was "not necessarily all at once, though verse 27 suggests that this sometimes happened, and made confusion worse confounded" (1971, 324). All of them speaking in tongues at once could have happened, but Paul may be asking a question about a hypothetical situation.[111] Paul expected that the people would answer: "Yes, the unbelievers would say you are mad."

Two, another feature of the situation is that "ungifted men (*idiōtai*) and unbelievers (*apistoi*)" may enter the meeting. The NIV says "inquirers or unbelievers." Grammatically, as Lenski points out, these two terms can refer to two persons, each by a different name, or to one person described by two different names (1946, 602-603). The *idiotai* are variously held to be proselytes, uninstructed persons, non-members, unbelievers, and inquirers. Barrett fuses the two terms into "unbelieving outsiders" (1971,

---

[111]With regard to 14:23-24, Fee expresses this view: "Both sentences take the same form: a present general condition in which the protasis expresses the hypothetical situation of the gathered church into which unbelievers enter and the apodosis expresses their response—first to tongues then to prophecy. Although hypothetical, and probably overstated, the protases must nonetheless be taken seriously as real possibilities; otherwise the argument is to no avail" (1987, 683).

324). It appears to me that these terms could apply to two different people but, in some cases, apply to just one person.

Second, a critical question is: Does verse 23 follow from or stand it contrast to verse 22a? Paul begins verse 23 with the conjunctions *ean oun*. These two conjunctions can mean "if therefore." The NASB[95] translation is simply "therefore." With regard to *oun*, Bauer says that its meaning varies with the context, and at times it may be left untranslated. Also, it can mean 'therefore,'" "consequently," and "accordingly." On the other hand, Bauer says that this conjunction can be used adversatively in the sense of "but" or "however" (2000, 737).[112] Assuming Paul intends the adversative sense, he is saying "however" rather than "therefore." With this interpretation, verse 23 stands in contrast to what precedes rather than following from it.

Third, according to the monologue view, Paul asserted that tongues function as a sign to unbelievers. However, this statement seems to be in contradiction to verse 23. In order to resolve this conflict, the monologue view maintains that Paul cites Isaiah 28:11-12 in order to make his case in verse 22. In Isaiah 28:11-12, God uses men of strange (or foreign) speech to judge Israel, but they did not listen. Most believe that Isaiah refers to the Assyrians speaking their language. Then, the proponents say that, as in Isaiah's day, unintelligible tongues are a negative sign to unbelievers of God's judgment. The unbelievers will react negatively to the sign.

In this way, the apparent contradiction between verse 22a and verse 23 is resolved by saying that God did not intend for the strange or foreign tongues to be effective in drawing people to God. The tongues were a sign of judgment on the people. The people were further hardened in their sins; therefore, tongues as a negative sign results in hardening rather than conversion. Fee, who holds the monologue view, comments as follows:

---

[112]Garland counters the view that 14:21-22 constitutes a Corinthian assertion and not Paul's own conviction. He says: "This interpretation founders because the text contains no signals that Paul cites a Corinthian position, and he does not state his own counter conviction. It fails to take into account the . . . (*oun*) in 14:23, which serves to point out the consequences of the statement in 14:22 rather than to contradict it" (2003, 649). However, as Verbrugge (2008, 383) holds, *oun* has an adversative connotation in this passage.

Because tongues are unintelligible, unbelievers receive no revelation from God; they cannot thereby be brought to faith. Thus by their response of seeing the work of the Spirit as madness, they are destined for divine judgment—just as in the OT passage Paul has quoted. This is, of course, is not the divine intent [conversion] for such people; hence Paul's urgency is that the Corinthians cease thinking like children and stop the public use of tongues, since it serves to drive the unbeliever away rather than to lead him or her to faith. (1987, 682)

It is possible that verse 23 represents a hardening of the unbelievers. As a hardening, what Paul says in verse 23 would be in harmony with verse 22a. However, because the sign is negative, it would not fulfill God's desire for the people to listen to Him. On the other hand, if the sign to unbelievers is supposed to be positive, then verse 23 is in direct contradiction with verse 22a.

Fourth, the dialogue view is that, in verse 22a, the Corinthians make the assertion that tongues are a sign to unbelievers. However, even if tongues can be a negative sign of the judgment of God, Paul argues against using this sign in the situation that he describes. The unbelievers will not only reject the tongues, but will say the Corinthians are mad. Because they will think the speakers are mad, tongues will not be a sign of judgment that the hearers will take seriously. Therefore, as far as the effectiveness of the sign is concerned, verse 23 stands in contradiction to verse 22a.

Under the dialogue view, the Corinthians cited Isaiah 28:11-12. What Paul says in verse 23 is not a fulfillment of that passage. The Assyrians spoke in their language which the people of Judah did not understand. However, it is not likely that they thought the Assyrians were "mad." They would have understood that a foreign power was present and that God was judging them. Thus, the foreign language could have been a sign of judgment. When the Corinthians spoke in tongues, it was not the equivalent of the Assyrians speaking in their language. The Corinthians situation was different than it was for Israel. The unbelievers in Corinth will not think of tongues as a sign of anything other than the "madness" of the people.

Fifth, the conclusion about madness reached by Paul in verse 23 applies with full force to the situation he describes, but it is not an absolute assertion that applies in very situation. In Luke's writings, tongues can be a sign of God's presence both to believers and unbelievers. Tongues were such a sign, for example, at the House of Cornelius (Acts 10:44-48). Given Paul's ministry in Ephesus (Acts 19:1-6), it is clear that the approaches of Luke and Paul to tongues were complementary. After reviewing tongues as a sign to believers and unbelievers in Luke's writings, Menzies states: "We may summarize our discussion by noting that Luke presents us with a formidable resume for speaking in tongues" (1994, 10).

Case Three: Prophecy and Unbelievers

We turn now to case three. In verse 22b, Paul says that "prophecy *is for a sign*, not to unbelievers but to those who believe." The words "is for a sign" in verse 22b are not in the Greek language in connection with prophecy, but it is appropriate to supply these words. As Fee states: "This is not specifically said in the Greek text; but the sentence is most likely an ellipsis, since the verb εἰσιν (*eisin*) is omitted as well. This means that the two sets of antitheses are to be understood as in perfect balance" (2014, 243, Transliteration Mine).[113]

In verses 24-25, Paul deals with prophecy as a sign to an unbeliever. As with case two, tongues as a sign to unbelievers, Paul is concerned about the impact on anyone who does not believe. The terms "unbeliever" and "ungifted man" are both singular. Paul shifts from the plural in verse 24 to the singular in verse 25.[114] This clearly is his main concern in verses 20-25. Paul comments as follows:

[24]But if all prophesy, and an unbeliever (*apistos*, ἄπιστος) or an ungifted (*idiōtēs*, ἰδιώτης) man enters, he is convicted by

---

[113]Grudem points out that words "is for a sign" are not in the Greek text of verse 22. However, he thinks it is best to retain the same subject that appears in the first half of the sentence. He says: "If we retain the idea of 'sign' in the second half, Paul's sentence means: 'Therefore, tongues are a sign not for believers but for unbelievers ... but prophecy *is a sign* not for unbelievers but for believers'" (1988, 173). He reads "is a sign" rather than "is for a sign."

[114]Lenski writes: "Paul very properly now has the singular 'one unbelieving or unlearned' and not the plural as he did in v. 23. Conversion is a personal and individual matter" (1946, 603).

all, he is called to account by all; [25]the secrets of his heart are disclosed; and so he will fall on his face and worship God, declaring that God is certainly among you.

First, the third assertion is very difficult for the monologue view. The problem is reconciling the fact that verse 22b says prophecy is not for the unbeliever with the positive impact described in verses 24-25. In Paul's illustration, the unbeliever is convicted, falls on his face, and recognizes God's presence. Because of verses 24-25, proponents of the monologue view acknowledge the impact of prophecy on the unbeliever, but they have difficult overcoming the contradiction with verse 22b.

One approach is posited by Jamieson, Faussett, and Brown. According to them, "prophesying has no effect on them that are radically and obstinately like Israel (Is 28:11, 12), unbelievers, but on them that are either in receptivity or in fact believers; it makes believers of those not wilfully unbelievers (1 Co 14:24, 25; Ro 10:17), and spiritually nourishes those that already believe" (1871). This approach, however, does not fully avoid prophecy being a sign to unbelievers in some state of mind prior to coming to faith; so the contradiction remains.

Second, the dialogue view holds that Paul is citing the Corinthian view in verse 22b. Paul corrects the Corinthians by pointing to the impact of prophecy in bringing men to Christ. In verses 24-25, he is presenting his argument against their line of thought. Or, to put this another way, he is presenting the strong impact that prophecy has on unbelievers. To those who refuse to believe, prophecy could be a sign of judgment, but to all those who believe, it is a sign of God's approval, presence, and blessing. This interpretation makes sense and avoids all the apparent contradictions which interpreters struggle to harmonize.

Paul begins verse 24 with *ean de* (ἐὰν δὲ, if however). The word *de* can be used as a connective meaning *and*. When used in this way, no contrast is intended. However, *de* is often used as a mild adversative. Both the NASB[95] and the NIV translate *de* as *but*. The usual interpretation is that verse 24 stands in contrast to verse 23. Surely it does. However, verse 24 also reaches back and stands in contrast to "not to unbelievers" in verse 22b.

According to verse 24, if an unbeliever or unlearned person enters the church and hears prophecy, he will be convicted and called into account. Then verse 25 says, "the secrets of his heart are disclosed; and so he will fall on his face and worship God, declaring that he is certainly among you."[115] Thus, prophecy is a sign to the unbeliever. The one who was an unbeliever will say that God is certainly among you.

Case Four: Prophecy and Believers

Case four deals with prophecy as a sign to believers. In verse 22b, Paul concludes that "prophecy *is for a sign*, not to unbelievers, but to those who believe." The majority view is that the phrase "is for a sign" should be supplied. Paul does not say more in verses 20-25 about prophecy being a sign to the believers unless the new convert is included. However, he has fully taught on this subject. In 14:3, he says that prophecy is for the believers. There, he says, "But one who prophesies speaks to men for edification and exhortation and consolation."

Obviously, Paul does not refute the assertion that prophecy is a sign for the believers. Neither does Paul limit the value of the sign of prophecy to the believers. Rather, he points out its value in persuading unbelievers to accept Christ. When people accept Christ, the full value of prophecy as a sign of God's favor becomes theirs.

Conclusion

Whether Paul is stating his own view or the view of the Corinthians in verses 21-22, his conclusions in verses 23-25 are the same. My understanding is that Paul was quoting the Corinthians in 14:21-22. In verse 22, he cites four assertions made by the Corinthians about the value of tongues and prophecy as signs to believers and unbelievers. Now, we can summarize Paul's comments on the four assertions.

- The first assertion is that tongues are not for a sign to those who believe. Paul does not comment on this assertion in

---

[115]Taylor states: "Prophecy not only brings about conviction and discernment of the things of the heart, but it is capable of bringing about the wholesale change of one's perspective. Instead of proclaiming, 'You are out of your mind!' the visitor proclaims 'God is really among you!' an echo of Isa 45:14" (2014, 346).

verse 23-25. Elsewhere in his writings, he does contradict this assertion. Tongues can be a sign of God's presence and favor to those who believe, both privately and in some forms of public worship.

- The second assertion is that tongues are a sign to the unbelievers. In verse 23, Paul maintains that tongues are not a sign to the unbelievers in the situation he describes. The unbelievers will say that the speakers are mad. This rule does not necessarily apply in all situations, but in this situation, his statement in verse 23 contradicts the assertion
- The third assertion is that prophecy is not a sign to unbelievers. In verses 24-25, Paul contradicts this assertion by showing the effectiveness of prophecy in persuading unbelievers to believe. They declare that God is certainly among you.
- The fourth assertion is that prophecy is a sign for believers. Unless we include the declaration by new believers that God is among you (verse 24), Paul does not mention this assertion again in verse 23-25. However, he already has dealt with this subject.

The gifts of the Spirit, including tongues and prophecy, are from God. The Spirit distributes them according to His will, but this does not eliminate our human involvement. We must desire to be used of God, so let us offer ourselves as candidates. Then, having received gifts, having been used of the Lord, let us remember that the "fire" must be maintained. Paul exhorted Timothy (2 Tim. 1:6) "to kindle afresh the gift of God which is in you." No doubt, the voice of the Spirit is speaking this same message to us today.

CHAPTER THIRTEEN

EDIFYING PARTICIPATION

Introduction

Paul writes in 1 Corinthians 12-14 about the exercise of spiritual gifts in the church. All the gifts, he maintains, should be exercised in a way that is edifying to all. Moreover, as Paul proclaims in chapter 13, love should be our motivation for using the gifts. In chapter 14, he focuses on the gifts of prophecy, tongues, interpretation of tongues, and other vocal gifts. To be edifying, he declares, the gifts should be expressed in an orderly, intelligible, and balanced way.

Although there are many spiritual gifts, the most controversial ones are the gifts of tongues and interpretation of tongues and the gift of prophecy. Pastors who do not identify themselves as Pentecostal or charismatic may feel that such gifts have ceased. Those who do not may not permit these gifts to be expressed in the church. Even among the Pentecostal and charismatic pastors, there is a wide range of attitudes toward these gifts. Many of them encourage, or at least permit, the expression of these gifts in the public meetings of the church. Other pastors maintain that these gifts should be expressed in meetings for believers only. Some pastors prefer to have these gifts exercised in home groups.

In 1 Corinthians 14:26-33, Paul describes a worship service that is characterized by the participation of the members who are present. The early church service was not a spectator event; it was an event designed for individual participation. Paul does not preclude the possibility of having other types of services, but this is the type that he describes in this passage. Moreover, the services Paul describes here do not include all the potential elements of a service. Rather the focus is on the vocal gifts and their proper usage. Paul writes:

> [26]What is the outcome then, brethren? When you assemble, each one has a psalm, has a teaching, has a revelation, has a tongue, has an interpretation. Let all things be done for edification. [27]If

anyone speaks in a tongue, it should be by two or at the most three, and each in turn, and let one interpret; ²⁸But if there is no interpreter, let him keep silent in the church; and let him speak to himself and to God. ²⁹And let two or three prophets speak, and let the others pass judgment. ³⁰But if a revelation is made to another who is seated, let the first keep silent. ³¹For you can all prophesy one by one, so that all may learn and all may be exhorted; ³²and the spirits of the prophets are subject to prophets; ³³for God is not a God of confusion but of peace, as in all the churches of the saints.

We will examine this passage verse-by-verse and thereby unfold a picture of an early church "participation" service. In such a service, all should be done for the edification of the body. In Corinth, some people seem to have been unthoughtful in their participation. Therefore, Paul provides guidance for the proper exercise of gifts. Today, by way of contrast, we need to encourage participation in many churches.

The Outcome

In verse 26, Paul opens his discussion of a "participation" service with these comments: "What is *the outcome* then, brethren?[116] When you assemble, each one has a psalm, has a teaching, has a revelation, has a tongue, has an interpretation. Let all things be done for edification."

First, as in verse 15, Paul asks the question *ti oun estin* (τί οὖν ἐστιν)? Literally, the words mean "what then is?"[117] Given the conclusions that Paul will now state, we understand the meaning of the question. The question does not mean, "What then is the condition of things among you?" Rather, as most scholars agree, it

---

[116]Kistemaker states: "Whenever Paul touches a sensitive topic that affects the Corinthians personally, he usually addresses them as brothers (see vv. 6, 20, 26, 39) and this verse is no exception. He corrects their disorderly behavior in the church services, where they thoughtlessly promote their individualism and neglect the other members" (1993, 505).

[117]In both 14:15 and 14:26, the NASB[95] translation is "What is *the outcome* then?" The words "the outcome" are not in the Greek text. The NIV translation of 14:15 is: "So what shall I do?" Its translation of 14:26 is: "What then shall we say?"

means, "What, then, is the inference to be drawn from what I have said to you?"

Translators supply words to clarify the meaning. As noted in footnote 116, the NIV translation is, "What then shall we say?" As translated by Barrett, the question means, "What is to be done, then, brothers?" (1971, 327). Paul will now lay down his guidelines for what is to be said or done.

Second, Paul continues with "when you assemble (*hotan sunerchēsthe*, ὅταν συνέρχησθε)." The verb is a present middle subjunctive. According to Thiselton, "arguably the present subjunctive here with ὅταν (*hotan*) [transliteration mine] signifies repetition: *whenever you assemble together*" (2000, 1133). Robertson also holds that the verb signifies repetition, and he provides this translation: "whenever ye come together" (1931, 184).

Where the church meets has an influence on the nature of the services. For example, a meeting in a stadium will be different that a meeting in a home.

It is not my purpose to explore fully what the early church did. However, we can illustrate the point that the church met in different places and under a variety of circumstances. The church, in some form, met in such places as the Temple, the synagogues, and in homes.

We know that the church met in places that they did not call church property. Concerning the church in Jerusalem, Luke writes: "And every day, in the temple and from house to house, they kept right on teaching and preaching Jesus *as* the Christ" (Acts 5:42; cp. Acts 2:46). When Paul was saying farewell to the church at Ephesus, he reminded them that he had taught them "publicly and from house to house" (Acts 20:20). The public meetings were no doubt different than the meetings in houses.

The story of Aquila and Priscilla stands out as an example for the early church meeting in homes. According to Acts 18:2, Aquila and Priscilla lived in Rome. Not long before Paul arrived in Corinth, they moved there and took up their tent making trade (Acts 18:2-18). Luke does not say whether or not the church met in their home. When Paul left Corinth and went to Ephesus, Aquila and Priscilla went with him. They were residing in Ephesus when Paul wrote to the Corinthians. The church was meeting in their home (1 Cor. 16:19). Sometime later, Paul wrote to the Romans from Corinth. He asked them to greet Aquila and Priscilla and the church that was in their house (Rom. 16:3-5). Also, Paul said, "Gaius, host to me [in Corinth] and to the whole church greets you" (Rom. 16:23). This could be a reference to the hospitality of Gaius toward all travelling church members, but it could also mean that the whole church in Corinth met in his house. Very likely both points are true.

As Paul traveled, he regularly spoke in the synagogues. The synagogue was not owned and operated by the local church, but it was a place to proclaim the gospel. As Luke says in Acts 17:2, it was Paul's custom to go to the synagogue and reason with the people from the Scriptures. Describing Paul in action at Corinth, Luke says: "And he was reasoning in the synagogue every Sabbath and trying to persuade Jews and Greeks" (Acts 18:4). Quite often, Paul met with serious opposition when he spoke in the synagogues.

Third, when the people come together, "each one" has something to contribute. The Greek word *hekastos* (ἕκαστος) is an adjective meaning "each." Used as a substantive, it means "each one" or "everyone" (Bauer 2000, 298). Several points stand out.

One, it was expected that everyone would participate in the services. Spirit-inspired participation was characteristic of the Corinthian church. As Paul said earlier, "But to each one is given the manifestation of the Spirit for the common good" (12:7). Then he said, "But one and the same Spirit works all these things, distributing to each one individually just as He wills" (12:11). It was not necessary to "pull" for participation in the meetings.

Potentially every member could participate, but, except with a small crowd, it would not be possible for everyone to participate in any given service. Most of the crowds, however, probably were small. This would be true especially of meetings in homes. Each one, however, could contribute at times in the services. In any case, strong participation was expected.

Two, one person would have one gift, and another person would have a different gift.[118] Each one did not have all the gifts,

---

[118]Thiselton writes: "As Conzelmann urges . . .ἕκαστος [*hekastos*] "naturally must not be pressed to the effect that every single individual has one of the gifts mentioned, but means: one has this—another has that." The hypothetical εἴτε

but each one has at least one. One has a psalm; another has a teaching. The following illustration by Chafin is helpful:

> The church to which Paul wrote had no full-time staff, no history of worship, and very few models to copy. They did have an exciting experience with God to celebrate and a loving fellowship to nourish, and so their worship service was sort of a spiritual "covered dish" affair in which each person brought something to be shared by the group. (1985, 175)

With all the participation that was expected, it is not surprising that Paul needed to lay down some guidelines. For example, he indicated that everyone should not speak at once.

Three, Paul uses the present tense of the verb "has" (*echei*, ἔχει) five times, once with each gift that is to be exercised. Grammatically, this could mean that the people arrived with content in mind and were prepared to deliver it in the assembly. Whether the content was new or not, the member was inspired to deliver it to the congregation. Or, the verb "has" could mean that the people were inspired spontaneously with their content and delivery on site. The verb allows for either or both meanings. In any case, their contributions were inspired by the Spirit.

No doubt much of the content was inspired during the service. This especially would be true of tongues and interpretation. A revelation could come to one of the members during the service. This could be true of a teaching and a psalm as well. However, many may have come to the services *with* a revelation or an inspired psalm (perhaps a song) or teaching. For example, Stanley Horton avers that some may have come with a psalm from the Book of Psalms which they sang under the inspiration of the Spirit (1976, 231). Paul's language does not limit us here. We should not put limits of our own on what to expect.

We should stress the importance of heart preparation before our worship services. All too often, we come to service almost in a "contest" mode. We come passively waiting to see whether or not anything can be said or done to inspire us. We want to gauge the

---

γλώσσῃ [*eite glōssē*] in the very next verse confirms this." (2000, 1134). However, the fact that "one has this—another that" gift does not preclude each person having at least one gift.

performance of the ones on stage. We judge whether or not they are doing a "good job." Instead, our hearts should be prepared so that the Spirit could speak through us, too!

Fourth, Paul lists five types of content. He says, "each one has a psalm, has a teaching, has a revelation, has a tongue, has an interpretation." This list is not exhaustive. For example, Paul does not mention praying as he did in 14:15. Neither does he mention the reading of Scripture. However, his list is long enough to illustrate well what he wants to say.

One, Paul says "each one has a psalm (*psalmon*, ψαλμὸν)." According to Zodhiates, the noun *psalmos* (ψαλμός) is from the verb *psallō* (ψάλλω) which means to sing. He says that, originally, it meant, "Actually a touching, and then a touching of the harp or other stringed instruments with the finger or with the plectrum; later known as the instrument itself, and finally it became known as the song sung with musical accompaniment. This latest stage of its meaning was adopted in the Septuagint" (1984, 1769).

As many contend, the Greek noun *psalmos* can refer to an Old Testament psalm (Acts 13:33) or a Christian song (1 Cor. 14:26). On this point, Fee makes these comments:

> The "psalms," for example, may well include the Old Testament Psalter, now taken over into the worship of the Christian communities; but one would be bold indeed to limit the word only to the Psalter. This same word is used for the (apparently) more spontaneous singing of 1 Corinthians 14:26, and its corresponding verb is likewise used in 1 Corinthians 14:15 to refer to Spirit-inspired "praise to God." . . . What is suggested by this word is a song that is in praise of God. (1996, 159)

Obviously, the word *psalmos* is quite flexible. Presumably, the participant could sing a psalm from the Book of Psalms. Or, he or she could have been inspired by the Spirit to prepare a song before or during the meeting. Or, the participant may have simply composed the song while singing.[119] Without any information to the contrary, it is better to be open to all the possibilities.

---

[119]Concerning *psalmos*, Verbrugge writes: "What is this gift? We do know that singing was a prominent feature of the early church (cf. Eph. 5:19-20; Col. 3:16; Rev. 5:9-14). Does the gift of song here mean the ability to write a song

What Paul says in 14:15 is germane to this discussion. Using the verb, Paul writes: "I will sing (*psalō*) with the spirit and I will sing (*psalō*) with the mind also." In other words, Paul says, "I will sing in tongues and I will sing in the vernacular also." Given this information, we can assume that the participant, in some cases, has a song in tongues. Palma states: "This type of singing may be called 'hymns of glossolalia,' or a kind of 'charismatic hymnody'" (2001, 240).

Paul does not say in this verse whether the participant leads the assembly in singing or sings a solo. The former is possible, but the latter is more likely. Paul does say in 14:15, "I will sing." The natural meaning is that Paul will sing a solo. It appears to me that this is what he means in verse 26.

Two, Paul continues with "each one has a teaching (*didachēn*, διδαχήν). The Greek noun *didache* (διδαχή) can refer to teaching as an activity or to what is taught. Here, the reference is to the content. Barrett translates *didachēn* here as "a piece of teaching" (1971, 327). Similarly Palma calls this teaching a "word of instruction" (2001, 239). The term *gift of the Spirit* can apply to the teachers, the activity of teaching, or to what is taught. When we study these meanings, we see how flexibly Paul uses these terms.

In 12:28, Paul writes that God has appointed teachers (*didaskalous*, διδασκάλους). Paul includes them among the charismata in 12:31. Similarly, in Romans 12:6, Paul refers to the charismata and lists several of them. In the next verse, he says, "he who teaches (*ho didaskōn*, ὁ διδάσκων), in his teaching (*en tē didaskalia*, ἐν τῇ διδασκαλίᾳ). The thought is that one who is a teacher should enthusiastically do his teaching. Both the one who teaches and the activity of teaching can be called charismata. Using a different term, Paul mentions gifts (*domata*, δόματα) in Ephesians 4:8 and includes teachers (*didaskalous*) among them

---

and perhaps through it to teach God's people his truth, or is it the gift of being able to sing well? We really do not know. But if I am correct that the spiritual gifts refer, at least in part, to the Spirit's working in tandem with the talents and abilities of his people, I suggest that those with the gift of song are those who are able to bless the congregation with their singing ability and especially those who are able to write their own songs and teach them to the church" (2008, 384).

(Eph. 4:11). In this case, the terms *domata* and *charismata* are used interchangeably.

As we read this, a host of questions arise. Did the members arrive with a prepared lesson or spontaneously receive the inspiration during the meeting? Was the teaching very short, perhaps just a word of instruction, or a longer treatise? How many could deliver a teaching in one meeting? Was the teaching the product of study and natural talent or a divinely inspired word? Was there a planned teaching in addition to what may have been spontaneous?

The questions are ours. Paul does not directly address them. He sets down some guidelines, but he does not cover every possible point. The answer to these questions, for the most part, can be "all of the above." Without specific regulations, we need not shut off any approach that reaches the goal of the edification of the body. His point that all should be done for edification of the body really covers a lot of the territory. The leaders of the church, guided by the Spirit, should be able to take care of the rest.

Three, Paul says that each one "has a revelation (*apokalupsin*, ἀποκάλυψιν)." Every single person does not have a revelation, but among the gifts that the members have is revelation. The gift of revelation has a place at the table. The revelation could be delivered in any of several forms. It could be a prophecy, a teaching, even a hymn. Thus, revelation is closely interrelated with the other gifts. Usually revelation is mentioned in connection with prophecy or one of the other gifts.

It appears from verse 30 that a spontaneous revelation could come at any moment in the service. The Spirit of God speaks to people on his time table and at places where He desires. Our role is to be responsive to the Spirit. It was possible, also, for someone to come to the service with a revelation of knowledge or truth. It would then be important for him or her to find the right time to disclose the revelation.

Four, Paul says that each one "has a tongue (*glōssan*, γλῶσσαν)." When Paul writes about speaking in tongues, he uses both the singular "tongue" and the plural "tongues." An individual can speak in "a tongue" (14:4) or "in tongues" (14:6). What he says in communication moments may be in just one "tongue" or in more than one "tongue." In some cases, only the plural "tongues"

198

fits. Paul speaks about various "kinds of tongues" (12:10) and about all members speaking in tongues (14:23) at the same time. He does not use the singular "tongue" when referring to people (plural) speaking.

Each "tongue" can be any language unknown to the speaker. This would include a human language, an angelic language, or a special purpose language. Whatever the nature of the language, God understands. Most commentators think of a "tongue" as being spontaneously inspired during the service. This, I believe, is normally the case, but this does not preclude the possibility of being inspired in advance. Even though the actual sounds are usually formed "on the spot," other approaches are possible.

Five, Paul declares that each one has an "interpretation (*hermēneian*, ἑρμηνείαν)." According to Bauer, the noun *hermēnia* (ἑρμηνεία) can mean translation or interpretation (2000, 393). The gift of interpretation of tongues is not operational unless it is preceded by an utterance in tongues. One would not come to a meeting with an interpretation because there would be nothing to base it on. The interpretation has to be spontaneous.

Speaking practically, someone may speak in a tongue of a given length. The interpretation may be much shorter or much longer. One might wonder how the interpretation is related to the "tongue." Paul does not deal with this issue or others like it. We are dealing with a spiritual exercise that has meaning to all who rely on the Spirit, so this kind of precision is not required. At the same time, the members are led of the Spirit in making judgments about the interpretations that the interpreter gives.

Fifth, Paul writes, "Let all things be done (*ginesthō*, γινέσθω)[120] for edification (*oikodomēn*, οἰκοδομὴν)." Edification, or building up, is the goal. Both the individual and the church should be edified. Paul gives two explicit guidelines which lead to edification. The first is intelligibility. This is why tongues should be interpreted. The second is to do things properly and in order. A third guideline is implicit. There was a need for balanced participation. With "each

---

[120]The verb *ginesthō* is an imperative. According to Taylor: "In 14:26-40 Paul sets forth clear guidelines for all speech when the church gathers so that all might be edified. Fourteen imperative verbs occur in the span of fifteen verses" (2014, 347).

one" having a way to participate, one or two forms of expression should not dominate the meetings.

Tongues and Interpretation

Now, in verses 27-28, Paul deals with the gifts of tongues and interpretation of tongues. He has said already that it is the gift of interpretation that gives meaning to the audience to what is said in tongues. Unless the tongues are in a language unknown to the speakers but known to the hearers, as at Pentecost, the people do not understand the tongues. Paul gives these guidelines:

> [27]If anyone speaks in a tongue, it should be by two or at the most three, and each in turn (*ana meros*, ἀνὰ μέρος), and let one (*heis*, εἷς) interpret (*diermēneuetō*, διερμηνευέτω); [28]But if there is no interpreter (*diermēneutēs*, διερμηνευτής), let him keep silent in the church; and let him speak to himself and to God.

First, just what Paul meant by these comments is open to different interpretations. One, some hold that there should be no more than two or three utterances in tongues *before* there is an interpretation. Each one should speak in turn. Then, after the three have spoken in tongues, the interpretation of the utterances should be given. Grammatically, this view is possible.

Paul says, "Let one (*heis*) interpret. The Greek word *heis* can mean either the number *one* or the indefinite pronoun *someone* (Bauer 2000, 291). The NIV translation is "someone." Whether we say one or someone, it is possible that all the utterances in tongues would be interpreted by the same person. Another possibility, using either translation, is that there would be three interpreters, one or someone for each respective utterance. The interpreter or interpreters could even be one or more of those who spoke in tongues.

Two, many others believe that there should be no more than two or three utterances in tongues in any given service. Moreover, each utterance should be interpreted by just one person.[121] This view is held by Palma who states:

---

[121]David Petts provides this insight: "Apart from the possibility, suggested by the NIV translation, that Paul simply meant that someone should interpret, it is also possible to suggest that Paul meant that *one* person should interpret *each*

With respect to glossolalia there is the insistence that the church is not edified if the utterance remains uninterpreted (1 Cor. 14:5). But prior conditions are that these expressions of glossolalia must be given serially, not simultaneously, and that there will be a maximum of three in one worship service (vv. 27-28). . . . In addition, 'someone must interpret" (v. 27). Some understand this to mean that only one person does all the interpreting in a service, but it is more natural to understand it to mean that each glossolalic utterance must have only one person interpreting it. Otherwise there would be confusion. (2001, 242)

Each of the utterances should be followed immediately by interpretation. Each one should speak in turn, one at time, and uninterrupted by others. Someone should interpret each utterance. The speaker in tongues could be the interpreter of his or her own utterance. This point harmonizes well with this second view.

On practical grounds, it would appear this procedure would be more normal. Anyone who has spoken through an interpreter would favor this approach. It contributes much more to the attention of the audience and to clarity. One person would speak in tongues; then, immediately, someone would interpret.

Three, the debate cannot be decided on grammatical grounds. Based on grammar alone, we need not exclude either procedure, but the second approach is more practical and more likely to occur. The main point is not the procedure but the importance of balanced participation. This would place a limit on tongues with interpretation no matter which procedure was followed. There were other gifts to express. There should be not more than two or at the most three expressions of tongues with interpretation "at any given service."

The words "when you assemble" seem to suggest this limitation. Thus, Paul was limiting the tongues with interpretation

---

utterance" (2002, 133). Although holding that this approach is quite likely to be correct, Petts adds: "since we can't be sure, it must be left to the leadership of each local church to decide how best to understand the verse and to teach the people accordingly. In the final analysis, it will not matter whether one or two or three people are involved in interpreting, as long as everything is done in a fitting and orderly way (v. 40)" (2002, 133).

to two or at the most three at each assembly time. No doubt, Paul has in mind the normal service. It is unlikely that he would have held this same rule in an extended service. The rule might then have taken the form of "before the order of the service is changed."

Second, in verse 28, Paul says, "But if there is no interpreter (*diermēneutēs*), let him keep silent in the church; and let him speak to himself and to God." It is assumed that someone other than the speaker in tongues will interpret. Apparently, the speaker in tongues was to know whether or not an interpreter was present. This raises the question of how he or she would know. On this point, Bullock makes this comment:

> If you are a guest in a church and are unfamiliar with the congregants, then you can't know if an interpreter is present. So it is best to remain silent. But if you are in your home church, you are usually aware of those whom God may use to interpret tongues. (2009, 34)

Bullock recognizes that sometimes a person who might normally interpret does not do so. Given this circumstance, as Bullock suggests, there is a backup plan. The person who speaks in tongues (1 Cor. 14:13) should pray that he may interpret. If the speaker in tongues, or someone else, was not prepared to interpret, he was to keep silent and speak to himself and to God. This speaking might be "thinking within himself" (Calvin, Trans. Fraser, 1960, 301), but the prayer might be quietly vocalized as well.

Paul gives all these guidelines for the church in Corinth and the situation that existed. When similar situations exist, the guidelines are readily applied. When the situation is different, we have to build on the underlying principles such as the motivation of love and the edification of the church. When conditions exist that are not covered by Paul, the Holy Spirit will help us build on what he has said. As He leads, we will know what to do.

Prophecy

Paul turns now to present his guidelines for prophecy. Although he prefers prophecy as the main communication gift in the church, he lays down some guidelines for this gift as well. He writes:

²⁹And let two or three prophets speak, and let the others pass judgment. ³⁰But if a revelation is made to another who is seated, let the first keep silent. ³¹For you can all prophesy one by one, so that all may learn and all may be exhorted; ³²and the spirits of the prophets are subject to prophets;

First, verse 29 deals with the procedure for prophesying and the function of passing judgment. One, with regard to procedure, many believe that there should be only two or three prophets speak in any given service. The prophets should speak in turn, one by one. No doubt, many silently judged the prophetic messages even while the prophets were speaking. Concerning judgment that is spoken, this view allows for the passing of judgment to be prophecy-by-prophecy or after two or three prophetic words.

Another view is that only two or three should speak before others pass judgment. This view suggests that, after two or three have prophesied, time should be taken for judgment. This would be like the last approach above, but there would be no limit on the number of prophecies in a given service. Here, unlike in verse 27, Paul does not say "at the most," and verses 24 and 31 suggest that more, if not all, might prophesy.

Both of these views are grammatically possible, but the procedure is not Paul's main concern. His main point appears to be that there ought to be balanced participation. In a short service, there would not be time for more than two or three prophecies altogether. Even in an extended service, two or three prophecies should be the limit before the order of the service is changed. Later in the service, the prophets might speak again.

Two, the others are to pass judgment. Some believe that "the others" are others with the prophetic gift. Over against this, as Fee maintains, we see that "all" potentially can prophesy; moreover, in verse 24 all are involved in judging the unbeliever (1987, 694). As Palma explains:

Opinion is divided on the identity of 'the others' (v. 29). It may mean either the rest of the congregation or the other prophets. There is no indication that the weighing of prophecies was the prerogative of prophets. The contrary is the case when we observe the listing of spiritual gifts in 1 Corinthians 12:8-10 in which prophecy is given to one and distinguishing between spirits to another. (2001, 247-248)

In this verse, Paul uses the verb *diakrinetōsan* (διακρινέτωσαν); whereas, in 12:10, he uses the noun *diakriseis* (διακρίσεις). These cognate words have to do with passing judgment and distinguishing between spirits. Here, the verb primarily means to "weigh carefully" the content of the prophecies.[122] Grudem writes:

As a prophet was speaking, each member of the congregations would listen carefully, evaluating the prophecy in the light of the Scripture and the authoritative teaching which he or she already knew to be true. Soon there would be an opportunity to speak in the response, with the wise and mature no doubt making the most contribution. But no member of the body would have needed to feel useless (cf. 1 Cor. 12:22), for every member at least silently would weigh and evaluate what was said. (1988, 73-74)[123]

---

[122] According to Garland, "The verb διακρίνειν (*diakrinein*) has a wide range of meanings in Paul's writings (cf. 4:7; 6:5; 11:29, 31), but here it means to evaluate carefully" (2003, 662). Paul uses the noun διακρίσεις (*diakriseis*) in 12:10. There, I concluded that "the primary emphasis of 12:10 is on distinguishing between spirits, while the main emphasis on 14:29 is passing judgment on prophecies." However, the meaning in these verses should not be limited; the former can include the latter, and the latter can include the former."

[123] Concerning the basis for judgment, Garland writes: "Paul does not list any criteria for gauging what a prophet says, but we can infer some norms from his discussions in this letter. (1) Does what is said accord with the tradition of Jesus (7:10; 9:14; 11:23; 12:3; 15:3; cf. 2 Thess. 2:15-3:6) and with the preaching of Christ crucified (1 Cor. 1:18-25)? (2) Does it accord with the Scripture as it is properly interpreted through Christ (1:19, 31; 4:6)? (3) Does it accord with what their apostle has handed on to them and taught them (2:1-5; 7:25; 11:2; 15:3)? (4) Does it accord with sacrificial love for others (13:1-13; 8:1)? (5) Does it promote the community's good (14:3-5, 12, 17, 26; cf. 12:7)? (6) Does it not cause another Christian to stumble in the faith (8:7-13)? (7) Does it lead outsiders to come to faith by reproving, convicting, and convincing them that God is present in their midst (14:20-25)?" (2003, 664)

In churches today, sometimes one will hear prophetic utterances from members of the congregation. Quite often, the pastor will express approval of the prophetic word, but he rarely will make any negative comments. If he has any negative thoughts, he does not often express them. Probably many believers in our churches today silently weigh the content, but they seldom openly express judgments. Thus, it probably could be said that evaluation of prophecies is not often practiced in our churches.

Second, while a prophet is speaking, a "revelation" may come to another person. Although prophecy is a broader term than revelation, many prophecies are based on revelation. Here, Paul exhorts the first prophet to make way for the one who has just received a revelation. Those who prophesy must recognize the gifts of others. There is no reason to limit the content of the revelation that another person may receive. Such revelations could include those suggested by Harold Horton. He writes:

> Verse 30 may mean two things. I have already suggested it means that although many get the same revelation, only one, to obviate competition, must give it out. It also means no doubt that if a prophet is prophesying and another "judging" learns by the Spirit that the prophecy is not according to Scripture, the one prophesying must cease speaking at the moment he is challenged! (1962, 211)

Third, verse 31 tells us that all can prophesy one by one.[124] All can learn. All can be exhorted. Participation in the service brings benefit to all. It is not likely, however, that "all" prophesied in a given service. The meaning seems to be that, on some occasion, everyone can prophecy. Nevertheless, with a small crowd, participation by everyone in one service might be possible.

Fourth, there are several views concerning verse 32. One, some writers maintain that each prophet must be subject to other

---

[124]Writes Rea: "Paul evidently believed that every Spirit-baptized Christian potentially can have a manifestation of the gift of prophecy, as the Spirit wills, for he wrote, 'Now I wish that you all spoke in tongues, but even more that you would prophesy' (1 Cor. 14:5). Therefore, he ended his entire discussion of the spiritual gifts by exhorting, 'Desire earnestly to prophesy' (14:39)" (1998, 239).

prophets. This view is not likely because the emphasis of Paul is on each individual being responsible for himself. This view cannot be ruled out entirely, but it does not seem to express the main thought of Paul. Two, in contrast to this, others hold that each prophet is in control of his own spirit. Palma, who supports this view, states: "The prophet is able to control the impulse to prophesy if the proposed utterance will violate the regulations prescribed by Paul" (2001, 245). The prophets, in his view, are in control of their own spirits. This point is clearly true.

However, there are two more views that go further. Three, according to Palma, another view "is that 'spirits' equal spiritual gifts or manifestations. This would mean that the gift of prophecy is a possession of the prophet and is subject to his or her control" (2001, 245). Because the emphasis is on the prophet's control, we can agree with this. Four, closely related to this view is the one proposed by Fee. Fee states that "the phrase 'spirits of prophets' means 'the prophetic Spirit' by which each of them speaks through his or her own spirit" (1987, 136). Given the cooperation between the Holy Spirit and the prophet, these two approaches seem best to me.

God of Peace

At this point (verse 33), Paul writes a comment that could be the conclusion of what he has just said or the introduction to his next comments. He states, "For God is not a God of confusion but of peace, as in all the churches of the saints." All things must be done for the edification of the body. Confusion in the church will detract from edification. God is a God of peace and of order. Order and balanced participation contribute to edification.

Conclusion

Today, many of our services are designed for performance by Christian professionals. We may enlist a world renowned speaker and singers who have won special awards. We clap often to show appreciation. Sometimes, even our worship services are more performance than participation oriented. All of this, of course, can be inspired by the Spirit and heart-warming.

However, another type of service was held in Corinth. The service was marked by participation. Whether or not there was ever any applause, we can only speculate. We do know that, when the prophets spoke, others judged. What was said was a serious matter. The inspiration of the Spirit was expected. The Spirit moved the people to be a part of what was going on. Each one was expected, at some point, to participate. Apparently, there was considerable preparation of hearts before the service.

Whatever form our services take, we can encourage people to come with hearts prepared. If we as worshippers arrive at the place of assembly with faith, hearts prepared, and a sense of expectation, it would probably surprise us what the Lord would do. In many churches, the need is not to slow down participation but rather to encourage it within the Pauline guidelines.

CHAPTER FOURTEEN

WOMEN SPEAKING IN THE CHURCH

Introduction

In this chapter, we will continue studying Paul's regulations for worship services. Our focus will be on 1 Corinthians 14:33b-36. Much controversy arises over these verses because of the comments about women being silent in the churches. On the one hand, expositors defend the premise that men and women have complementary but different roles. On the other hand, others posit the egalitarian view that men and women should be equal in ministry; specifically, they should not be prevented from speaking in the church.

Scholars raise many cultural and theological issues. In recent decades, society has put much greater emphasis on the equality of women and men. Moreover, many churches have become more open to the ministries of women, including speaking roles. As a result, how we interpret and apply this passage is increasingly studied. Although the Word of God has not changed, our understandings of the message can be enriched over time. First Corinthians 14:33b-36 reads as follows:

> [33]for God is not *a God* of confusion but of peace, as in all the churches of the saints. [34]The women are to keep silent in the churches; for they are not permitted to speak, but are to subject themselves, just as the Law also says. [35]If they desire to learn anything, let them ask their own husbands at home; for it is improper for a woman to speak in church. [36]Was it from you that the word of God *first* went forth? Or has it come to you only?

Any study of this text inevitably involves related passages. What Paul says in 1 Corinthians 11:5 appears to contradict our text. He speaks about women praying and prophesying in what we assume are the meetings of the church. Another passage, 1 Timothy 2:11-12, seems to be in harmony with our text. Here, Paul says, "I do not allow a woman to teach or exercise authority over a man, but to remain quiet" (verse 12). These two passages, along with our text, put the controversy over women speaking in the church squarely into focus. My discussion below will deal primarily with 14:33b-36 as our text. I will give an exposition of the text and then present several viewpoints about its interpretation and application.

Exposition of the Text

My purpose here is to comment on the paragraph in 14:33b-36. All the views presented later will draw, to some extent, from this information. This paragraph deals with the issue of women being silent in the church. Even though verses 34-35 are at the heart of the subject, the discussion includes verses 33b and 36. Depending on one's viewpoint, either one of these verses or both are a part of the paragraph. So we will include both of them in our study.

Verse 33b-34a

In verse 33, Paul declares: "for God is not *a God* of confusion but of peace, as in all the churches of the saints." The phrase "as in all the churches of the saints" can refer to what Paul already has said or to what he is about to say. According to Lenski, this clause "is by most of the ancients, by Luther, and by our versions connected with the preceding sentence, but nearly all modern exegetes connect it with the following sentence" (1946, 614). Nevertheless, Lenski favors the position of the ancients.

When connected with what precedes, the phrase in verse 33b completes what Paul was saying, especially in verses 26-33a. Using this approach, what does Paul mean? In reply to this question, expositors often speak about conditions that exist in all the churches and that should exist in the church at Corinth. Calvin's comments on verse 33 are representative. He writes:

> The comparison does not refer merely to the first part of this verse, but to all he has outlined above. It is as though he said: "So far I have given you no directions, which are not followed in all the churches, and that is how those same churches are kept together in peace. Therefore you should be borrowing what other churches have found by experience make for their well-being, and are most valuable for preserving peace." (Trans. Fraser, 1960, 305-306)

When the phrase in 33b is connected with verse 34, it takes on a different meaning. Verse 33 then concludes with "for God is not a God of confusion but of peace." Therefore, 33b plus 34a together say, "As in all the churches of the saints, let the women keep silent in the churches or assemblies." Given this connection, asking women to be silent in the church at Corinth would be in harmony with the current practices of all the churches.

In both 33b and 34a, the author uses the Greek word *ekklēsiais* (ἐκκλησίαις). Depending on the context, it can mean either churches or assemblies (meetings) of the congregation. Garland, along with many others, says that the word "churches" in 33b refers to all the congregations, while in 34a it has to do with the "assemblies" in Corinth (2003, 670). Other scholars, such as Fee (1987, 706) contend that, in both cases, the word "churches" refers to all the congregations. Even though it refers to the churches, the "meetings" of the churches are included. In verse 35, the author uses the singular "church." Thus, the church in Corinth, with its meetings, is intended.

Assuming Paul was the author of verses 34-35, 33b could be connected with either 33a or 34a, but contemporary writers prefer the connection with 34a. If verses 34-35 express the views of the Corinthians, it is more likely that verse 33b connects with 33a. Nevertheless, 33b could be considered a part of the quotation. It appears to me that the best solution is to put a break after 33b.

Verses 34-35

When differences occur and issues become complex, the commentaries usually become much longer. A good example of this is the extended discussions of verses 34-35. Writers discuss these verses in many articles and books. My comments will have to be selective. The author of these verses writes:

> [34]The women (*gunaikes*, γυναῖκες) are to keep silent in the churches (*ekklēsiais*, ἐκκλησίαις); for they are not permitted to speak, but are to subject themselves, just as the Law also says. [35]If they desire to learn anything, let them ask their own husbands at home; for it is improper for a woman to speak in church (*ekklēsia*, ἐκκλήσια).

First, according to Thayer, the word *gunaikes* means *"a woman of any age, whether a virgin, or married, or a widow"* or *"a wife"* (1962, 128). In verse 34, the author does not specify which women; but in verse 35, the author narrows the meaning to wives. When the wives want to learn, they should "ask their husbands at home." Other women may not be excluded, but only married women are specified.

Second, the author says the women are to keep "silent." It is at this point that much debate occurs. What does it mean to keep silent? As some claim, does it mean silent in an absolute sense? Or, does it mean silent in a qualified way? If so, then the issue becomes what kind of speech is permitted or not permitted. The author names just one aspect of the required silence—the women should not ask questions in the public assembly. Beyond this, interpreters who would qualify the command must rely on data other than the text.

Third, in the NASB[95] version of verses 34-35, the author states, "they are not permitted to speak," "let them subject themselves," "if they desire to learn," and "let them ask their own husbands at home." The author does not address the women directly, but writes about them. No doubt, they indirectly received the message. By way of contrast, in verse 36, the author directly addresses his audience with the second person plural "you."

Fourth, the author says the women "are to subject themselves." This much is clear, but Fee states, "What is not clear is whether the women are to be subject to their own husbands or to the church as a whole in its worship. More likely it is the latter" (1987, 707). However, Garland holds to the former view. Concerning the women, he says, "Their submission is a token of their Christian love for their husbands" (2003, 672). Actually, this is a case where both points are true.

Fifth, the women are not permitted "to speak." This rule is given in both verses 34 and 35. In verse 35, the regulation clearly applies to speaking in the local assembly. Also, the word "speak" narrows the meaning of "silent" to vocal silence. What does the author mean by "speak?" The alternatives are absolute silence or some form of qualified silence. By qualified silence, expositors mean silence in some ways but not others. We will consider the "absolute silence" and "qualified silence" views below.

Sixth, the author declares that women are to be silent and subject themselves, "just as the Law also says."[125] The question is: Does "the Law" refer to secular law, the Old Testament, or Jewish tradition? Some scholars contend that the appeal is to secular law. However, most of them believe the author means the Old Testament even though there is no specific passage in the Old Testament that instructs women to be silent. Some of them maintain that either Genesis 3:16, Genesis 2:18-24, or both support what the author says. Both passages have to do with the roles of husbands and wives, but neither one says anything about women being silent. Others think that the author was referring to Jewish tradition.

Seventh, it is improper, or a shame, for a woman to speak. The author does not specify any particular group of women. The Greek word *aischron* (αἰσχρὸν) means "disgraceful" or "shameful" (Bauer 2000, 29). Garland says, "Shame, in this context, pertains to what society views as inappropriate behavior and is relative to a given culture" (2003, 668). With regard to this point, the debate continues over whether not speaking is absolute or qualified in some way.

Verse 36

Scholars differ greatly in their views about verse 36. The majority, but not all, holds that Paul wrote verse 36. Similarly, most contend that verse 36 is directly linked to verses 34-35, while others believe that the connection is with verse 37-38. My view is that Paul wrote verse 36 and that it directly connects with verses 34-35, but the message of verse 36 continues in verses 37-38.

First, with regard to verse 36, there is general agreement on one point. Very clearly, Paul gives a stinging rebuke to the Corinthians

---

[125]Janzen writes: "verse 34 appeals to the law without citing a text, another novel move for Paul. Historically, the appeal was connected with Genesis 3:16, but the male domination resulting from sin is scarcely normative. More recently, the unspecified law has been connected with the creation order mentioned earlier ([1 Cor.] 11:8). This is unlikely since the earlier passage made no mention of the law, did not directly quote Scripture, and undermined the attempt to draw enduring principles from that ordering with a 'nevertheless' statement ([1 Cor.] 11:11-12). Regardless, neither connection reveals a subjection that silences women" (2012, 62).

about their attitude. He asks two penetrating rhetorical questions: "Was it from you that the word of God *first* went forth? Or has it come to you only?" The correct answer to both is obviously "No!" The word of God did not originally go forth from Corinth; neither has it come only to the church in Corinth. The Corinthians thought the answer to these questions was "yes," or Paul would not have rebuked them.

Second, Paul uses the particle *ē* (ἤ) to introduce his two rhetorical questions. This particle can be translated "or," but also with the exclamation "what!" According to Bauer, this particle can be either a disjunctive or a comparative conjunction (2000, 277). When a comparative is intended, the word "than" (or "more than") is used. Because Paul opposes the attitude of the Corinthians, he is not using the particle in a comparative sense. Thus, most scholars agree that this conjunction, as used here, is disjunctive. As a disjunctive conjunction, says Bauer, the particle *ē* can refer to "opposites, which are mutually exclusive," or to "related and similar terms where one can take the place of the other or one supplements the other" (2000, 277). The particle does not require being "mutually exclusive," but it certainly can be used in that sense.

Third, the crucial question is: Given Paul's rebuke, what are the implications of the particle *ē* for verses 34-35? Janzen identifies two possibilities that deal with the attitude and resulting actions of the Corinthians. He writes:

> This particle does not necessarily contradict the preceding statement, but it does connect that statement to the following words. In this case, the rebuke is linked to the verses silencing women, rather than any previous discussion. Either Paul is rebuking those who do not accept his silencing of women, or he is rebuking the Corinthians whose attempt to silence women he just quoted. (2012, 61)

The first approach mentioned by Janzen can be identified as the reinforcement view, whereas the latter approach can be classified as the refutation view. Based on various sources, my understanding of these two views is as follows:

- The Refutation View.—According to this view, the Corinthians wrote their own rule about women being silent in the churches. Their attitude caused them to write the rule. The particle ē indicates that Paul was against their attitude and directly, as well as indirectly, against their rule.
- The Reinforcement View.—Advocates of this view assume that Paul wrote the rule. They explain how the particle ē reinforces the rule as follows: As with the refutation view, his questions show that Paul was against the attitude of the Corinthians. This indicates that their attitude was negative toward Paul's rule. Because Paul rebuked their attitude with his rhetorical questions, he indirectly reinforced his own rule.

The particle alone does not settle the issue. Janzen holds that both views are possible; but because of the context, he supports the refutation view. He believes, as one point of support, that "the surrounding encouragement for all to participate" in the services favors this view. The refutation view, I believe is the best approach.

Viewpoints

As a matter of convenience, I have organized the different viewpoints about 14:33b-36 under four headings dealing with verses 34-35. These views are: (1) that an interpolator inserted these verses into the text, (2) that Paul expressed his own view and that we should take his comments in their plain sense, (3) that Paul intended for us to qualify his comments in some way, and (4) that Paul is quoting the believers at Corinth. It is not my purpose to explicate every point of all the views, including the premises and rebuttals. However, I will present some of the critical points of the different views.

Under the interpolation view, verses 34-35 do not give guidance to Christian behavior. It may be important to understand them in a general sense, but not as guidance. Those who believe Paul was the original author of these verses maintain either that we should take them in an absolute sense or qualify their meaning in some way. Either way, there is a direct impact on our behavior. Advocates of the quotation view would find that the rebuttal of them is important in keeping the door open for women to speak in church.

Interpolation

One view is that an interpolator inserted verses 34-35 into our text, 14:33b-36. Just who the interpolator was is debated. He could have been someone who was opposed to Paul. Or, as Garland points out, some scholars "conclude that someone sharing the views expressed in 1 Timothy [2:11-12] added these words to ban women's participation in mixed assemblies" (2003, 675). Another variation of this view is that verses 33b and 36 were inserted as well (Carson 1991, 136-137). Most scholars who support the interpolation approach include only verses 34-35.

First, a representative of this view is Fee. Even though he favors the view that verses 34-35 are an interpolation, he comments on the meaning of all the verses. He says that verse 33b means that "what is true of God in terms of Christian worship is so 'in all the congregations of the saints'" (1987, 697). Without verses 34-35, verse 33b connects directly with verse 36. Fee paraphrases the result as follows: "'All the churches of the saints are intended to be orderly as we have just described, *or* did the word of God originate with you?'" (1987, 697). Moreover, Paul's rhetorical questions in verse 36 show that the church in Corinth is out of step with the other churches.

Second, in harmony with this position, Fee holds that, in verse 36, Paul is probably not referring to verses 34-35, but rather to verses 37-38 (1987, 710). Assuming this approach, then the issue is his disagreement with the Corinthians over who is spiritual. Given this, he was chiding them for thinking they were the exclusive receivers and custodians of the truth. Although this is possible, my position is that the use of the disjunctive conjunction $\bar{e}$ (or) points to the comments that precede verse 36.

Third, as Fee explains, arguments for this view have to do with the ancient transcripts and the content (intrinsic evidence) of the verses. Advocates note that, in some manuscripts, instead of verses 34-35 coming after verse 33, they have been placed after verse 40. This "displacement" shows, in their view, that the verses were not original. With regard to the intrinsic evidence, they say, among other things, that verses 34-35 contradict 11:5 where Paul speaks about a woman praying or prophesying.

Fourth, opponents of this view do not find the appearance of the text in two places or the seeming contradiction with 11:5 to be sufficient reasons to reject the authenticity of these verses. Both supporters (Fee 1987, 699) and opponents (Garland 2003, 675) indicate that verses 34-35 are found in all known manuscripts, either after verse 33 or following verse 40. Opponents believe that this fact strongly favors the authenticity of the verses. Without additional evidence to the contrary, I concur that the verses are authentic.

Absolute Silence

Under the "absolute silence" view of 14:33b-36, verses 34-35 express Paul's position and should be taken without qualification. This view sometimes holds that, when the women prayed and prophesied (11:5), they were not in the church.[126] Thus, there would be no contradiction between 11:5 and 14:34-35. The emphasis is on fully applying the rule that women should be silent in the church.

First, advocates may connect verse 33b with 33a or with 34a. When connected with 34a, the text says, "As in all the churches of the saints, women should remain silent in the churches." Scott changes the emphasis from existing conditions to conditions that should exist with this paraphrase: "I want all the women in Corinth to do what the women do in all the other churches" (1996, 1).

---

[126]Atkerson asserts: "It is a simple fact that nothing in 1 Corinthians 11a [11:5] (prayer and prophecy) specifically states that the setting is a church meeting. In contrast, 1 Corinthians 14 clearly does refer to a church meeting and teaches the silence of women. Letting the clear interpret the unclear, the logical conclusion is to understand the prayer and prophecy of 1 Corinthians 11a [11:5] to occur informally, outside the meeting, at a time when women can speak" (Part 1, n.d., 5-6). In contrast, Garland argues: "The parallelism with the statement about the men in 11:4 makes clear that Paul envisions both men and women praying and prophesying during the public gathering for worship . . . Were it only some private gathering among the family or among only women, their attire would not have been an issue" (2003, 518). I support the widely held view that women prayed and prophesied in the church.

Second, historically, many scholars have held this view. They contend that verses 34-35 apply without qualification to speaking in the public assembly. Women simply are not to speak. Moreover, women should not ask questions in the public assembly; rather they are to pose their questions to their husbands at home. In this regard, wives are to be in submission to their husbands. To keep silent really does mean being silent. Fee favors the interpolation view, but with regard to the "rule" that women should remain silent, he makes these comments:

> Despite protests to the contrary, the "rule" itself is expressed absolutely. That is, it is given without any form of qualification. Given the unqualified nature of the further prohibition that "the women" are not permitted to speak, it is very difficult to interpret this as meaning anything else than all forms of speaking out in public. (1987, 706)

Third, what is Paul rejecting with his rhetorical questions in verse 36? Many believe that Paul rebukes those who reject his regulations expressed in verses 34-35.

In Scott's view, the questions could belong with either verses 34-35 or verse 37, but he favors verses 33b-35. He states, "The first word in verse 36, 'or,' provides an immediate connection with what precedes, whereas there is a clear break between verse 36 and verse 37" (1996, 1). He says, "Paul simply preempts objections by reminding the Corinthians that they are a relatively young church" (1996, 3).

Fourth, although taking verses 34-35 at "face-value" may be attractive, there are drawbacks as well. In 14:26, Paul addresses his comments to the "brethren." However, the term "brethren" can refer inclusively to men and women. He writes: "When you assemble, each one has a psalm, has a teaching, has a revelation, has a tongue, has an interpretation." When this verse is combined with 11:5 where Paul speaks about women praying and prophesying, it is difficult to hold that the rule for women to "keep silent" is absolute. As a result, when some advocates of this view elaborate on what they mean, they tend to edge toward qualifying their remarks and becoming somewhat legalistic in terms of what being silent means.[127]

Fifth, discussions of verses 34-35 frequently refer to 1 Timothy 2:11-12. Here, Paul writes: "Let a woman quietly receive instruction with entire submissiveness. But I do not allow a woman to teach or exercise authority over a man, but to remain quiet." Scholars who hold either to the absolute silence or qualified silence views usually say that this passage is "parallel" to 14:34-35. However, supporters of the quotation view point out the differences between the two passages. Janzen, for example, argues that 14:34-35 and 1 Timothy 2:11-12 should not be read as meaning the same thing. He states, "While the latter exhorts women to learn in quietness, the former appears to be a far harsher command for women to be silent while in church" (2012, 58). There are, of course, various interpretations of 1 Timothy 2:11-12.

Qualified Silence

Under the most common approach to 14:33b-36, advocates hold that Paul teaches that women must be silent in the churches, but the meaning of "silent" has to be qualified. As Palma states, "The command for the women to keep silent in church is not absolute; it applies only under certain conditions" (2001, 250). Many different theories are proposed with regard to how the meaning of "silent" and other elements of the paragraph should be qualified.

Scholars who support qualified views include cultural, social, and contextual factors. Although these terms are not totally synonymous, they do overlap to a degree. All of them are concerned with how people view the actions of the believers. Using the term *culture* broadly, we can encompass all the other terms. Some

---

[127]Advocates of the absolute silence view are confronted with questions about how to apply this rule. Scott, for example, asks: "Would it be right for a minister to read a sermon or congregational prayer written out for him by a woman? Clearly not. Consider, then, whether it is right for him to lead the congregation in singing a song written out by a woman. As much as we may like the sentiments expressed by, say Fanny Crosby, her words should not be given authority in the worship of the church. To sing her hymns in public worship is to make her a teacher, a worship leader, and a prayer leader in the church assembly" (1996, 5). It is difficult for proponents of "absolute silence" to avoid issues about what is and what is not appropriate.

cultural factors are specific to one location, while others are cross-cultural.

When we consider how our text applies to us today, cultural considerations usually come to the front. The church at Corinth was influenced in varying degrees by Greek, Roman, and Jewish culture. In applying the text, we face the challenge of transposing the principles into our culture. On this point, Blomberg writes:

> If one of the cultural explanations for Paul's silencing women is accepted, then contemporary Christians will silence women in church only where comparable problems—lack of education, interfering chatter, or the promotion of false teaching—still exist. And they will impose silence on men who fall victim to one of these problems as well. (1994, 286)

Scholars make many different suggestions with regard to culture. Here I can only briefly describe three of the ideas: (1) disruptive speech, (2) husband and wife relationships, and (3) evaluation of prophecies. To some degree, scholars appeal to cultural factors in supporting each of these views.

First, some solutions soften the absolute tone of verses 34-35 by saying that the women were engaged in some form of disruptive speech. For example, one common idea is that men and women were separated in the meeting room.[128] The women would shout out their questions and disrupt the meeting. Another idea is that the women were largely uneducated and were interrupting the proceedings with questions which were better dealt with by their husbands in their homes. Whatever the case, Paul instructs them to be silent and ask their husbands the questions at home. These are only two of the many ways that speech can be disruptive.

Second, Garland contends that Paul was concerned about the relationships between husbands and wives. He bases this on what Paul says in verse 35: "And if they [the wives] desire to learn anything, let them ask their own husbands at home." He writes:

---

[128]Although many scholars propose this as a possibility, others seek to refute it. Kistemaker says the idea "has merit," but entertains other options as well (1993, 514). Atkerson says, "Absolutely nothing in the text of 1 Corinthians 14 suggests a physical separation between the men and the women" (Part 2, 2009, 4). The main lines of interpretation are not greatly affected by this issue.

I conclude that Paul's instructions are conditioned by the social realities of his age and a desire to prevent a serious breach in decorum. The negative effect that wives publicly interrupting or contradicting their husbands might have on outsiders (let alone the bruising it would cause to sensitive male egos) could not be far from his mind. (2003, 673)

Assuming Paul was adjusting to the culture of his day, what does that mean for today? On this point, Kistemaker writes: "To the point, no pastor wishes to be publicly criticized by his wife in a worship service; if she does, she undermines his ministry and is a disgrace to him. Paul wants the women to honor and respect their husbands in harmony with the Scriptures" (1993, 513). Presumably, what applies to pastors and their wives would apply to other husbands and wives as well.

Third, another view is that Paul teaches against women evaluating prophecies. Under this view, women can prophesy (11:5), but they cannot engage in the public evaluation of the prophecies. Carson puts the weight of his scholarship behind this view. He states:

Paul has been requiring that the church in Corinth carefully weigh the prophecies presented to it. Women, of course, may participate in such prophesyings: that was established in chapter 11. Paul's point here, however, is that they may *not* participate in the oral weighing of such prophecies. That is not permitted in the churches. In that connection, they are not allowed to speak—"as the Law says." (1987, 129)

Some commentators note a difference between evaluating and speaking. One may express an evaluation by speaking, but the evaluation itself is done either before the speaking or coincident with it. Greenbury asserts that "when Paul directs the Corinthians to judge prophecies (v. 29), he does not specify that this evaluation is to be expressed audibly" (2008, 726).[129] Similarly, Palma

---

[129]In addition, Greenbury says: another "concern I have with this interpretation is that the words 'if they want to learn anything' (v. 35) do not signify the authoritative weighing of prophecies. These words suggest that the women did not understand what was being said and that they were asking questions to learn, not that they were passing judgments on what they heard" (2008, 726).

maintains that "it is not clear precisely how prophecies were evaluated—whether an evaluation was made vocally or even whether it was done during a service" (2001, 250).

Fourth, assuming Paul is the author of verses 34-35, it makes sense that he meant "keep silent" in a qualified way. This avoids the problem of being in conflict with 11:5 and 14:26. However, it does raise the issue of how to qualify his rule. The only point Paul mentions is that women who want to learn should address their questions to their husbands at home. Beyond this, Paul does not specify what speaking should or should not be permitted.

Quoting the Corinthians

Scholars such as Odell-Scott (1983), Allison (1988), and Janzen (2012) advance the view that Paul quoted the Corinthians in verses 34-35 and then rejected what they said. This approach, they claim, solves the problem of the contradiction with 11:5 and keeps the door open for women to speak in church.

First, in support of this view, proponents point out that Paul was exchanging letters with Corinth and that he frequently used the method of dialogue. Although Paul does not explicitly say so, the supporters hold that this is one of those occasions. This is the underlying basic premise of this view. Janzen writes:

> First Corinthians is not Paul's first correspondence with the church at Corinth. He had written at least one earlier letter (1 Cor. 5:9) and received outside reports of their problems (1:11; 5:1; 11:18). After the Corinthians replied, Paul composed the first part of the conversation to be preserved, 1 Corinthians. His key concerns begin the letter, but he signals a different approach with the words, 'Now concerning the matters about which you wrote' (7:1). From then on, the expression 'Now concerning' continues to address topics from the Corinthian letter (7:25; 8:1; 12:1; 16:1; 16:12). The largest, "Now concerning spiritual gifts,' spans chapters 12 to 14. Within these chapters, Paul is likely to interact with what the Corinthians had written. (2012, 58)

Second, with regard to verse 33b, Janzen says, "Paul concludes his argument in verse 33 by declaring God's character and insisting that it be reflected in all churches that claim his name. Verse 34 begins a new statement" (2012, 57). Allison, another proponent, avers that an editor inserted verse 33b in order "to integrate the fragment smoothly into the preceding context" (1988, 48). Verse 33b, then, would be included in Paul's quotation of the Corinthian view. I favor the former approach; but either way, the two rhetorical questions in verse 36 represent Paul's strong rebuke of the opinion of the Corinthians.

Third, in my exposition of the text, I expressed my support for the refutation view of verses 34-35. A strong advocate of this view is Odell-Scott. Carson opposes the refutation view and counters with his reinforcement approach.[130] Odell-Scott contends for his position with these comments:

---

[130] Both Odell-Scott and Carson quote and interpret Thayer in support of their views. According to Thayer, the particle $\bar{e}$ (ἤ) can be used "before a sentence contrary to the one just preceding, to indicate that if one be denied or refuted the other must stand" (1962, 275). Odell-Scott and Carson interpret Thayer's comment as follows: Odell-Scott states:

> Funk points out that the particle $\bar{e}$ displays its sharpest disjunctive characteristics in interrogative sentences ([1983], 446). In such cases, the particle declares that if one phrase is the case then the other is not. Smyth points out that 'an $\bar{e}$ often introduces an argument ex contrario' [on the contrary] ([1963], 2861). Thayer made the same point when he asserted that an $\bar{e}$ may appear "before a sentence contrary to the one just preceding to indicate that if one be denies or refuted the other must stand" ([1962], 275). Interestingly, one of Thayer's examples of the $\bar{e}$ functioning in such a manner was 1 Cor 14:36! (1962, 90).

Carson does not cite Odell-Scott, but he does refer to Walter C. Kaiser, Jr. (*Christianity Today*, October 3, 1986, 124) who holds a similar refutation view. He believes that Kaiser has not accurately interpreted Thayer. So he gives his interpretation of Thayer. He begins by commenting on Matthew 20:15, which is listed by Thayer as an example of his definition.

In contrast to the refutation view, Carson holds, based on Thayer's comment, that the disjunctive particle in 14:36 has the force of reinforcing the rule that Paul wrote in 14:34-35. With his rhetorical questions, Paul rebukes the Corinthians for opposing his rule about women being silent in the church. This has the impact of reinforcing the rule. He holds that the construction is a form of argument that reinforces the preceding clause. Carson cites Matthew 20:15 as an example, making these comments:

> There, the first part finds the landowner saying to the grumbling workers, 'Don't I have the right to do what I want with my own money?' As Jesus proceeds, He certainly does *not* want to overturn the principle

222

The particle which introduces the interrogative sentence of 14:36 indicates that the rhetorical questions to follow will serve to refute the sentences which preceded it. It is my contention that the ē which introduces 1 Corinthians 14:36 declares that vv. 33b-35 are to be emphatically refuted by the two-fold rhetorical query of v. 36. . . . The silencing of women in church is to be questioned, refuted and overcome by the two-fold negative rhetorical query of v. 36.

First Corinthians 14:33b-36 is not the only passage in 1 Corinthians where Paul employs the particle ē to introduce a rhetorical query which serves to deny or refute the passages preceding it. 1 Cor. 11:20-22 is structurally identical.

> [20]When you meet together, it is not the Lord's supper that you eat. [21]For in eating, each one goes ahead with his own meal, and one is hungry and another is drunk. [22]What! Do you not have houses to eat and drink in? Or do you despise the church of God and humiliate those who have nothing? What shall I say to you? Shall I commend you in this? No I will not.

---

articulated by this rhetorical question; *of course* the landowner has that right. But since the workers have not accepted this principle, Jesus introduces a 'sentence contrary to [this one]' to force the workers to see the preposterous nature of their criticism. . . . In other words, if the workers 'deny or refute' the first clause (which both the landowner and Jesus affirm), then at least they had better face up to the second." (1991, 140-141)

In other words, Jesus rebuked the attitude of the workers who opposed the actions of the landowner. By this opposition, they would be deemed envious. Jesus was directly rebuking their attitude; indirectly, one could say that the landowner's right to do what he wanted was reinforced. By analogy, in 14:36, Paul rebuked the attitude of the Corinthians toward a rule that he wrote. Indirectly, this reinforced his rule.

As I stated earlier, the refutation and reinforcement views are both possible. The supporting evidence for either view is not limited to Thayer's one statement. He makes other comments as well. In addition, evidence is found in other grammatical sources and in the context. In my opinion, the evidence favors the refutation view.

The state of affairs at Corinth is represented in vv. 20-21. These verses are followed by the particle ē which introduces a rhetorical line of query whose purpose is to refute vv. 20-21 and to admonish those who humiliate the poor with their insensitive consumption. There has been no debate that I can find regarding the grammatical structure of 11:20-22. The particle ē serves its dramatic function without incident or confusion. (1983, 91)

Fourth, in verse 36 the word "only" in the second question is a translation of the Greek masculine plural adjective *monous* (μόνους). Because it is masculine and plural, some scholars argue that Paul was addressing men only. Others think the masculine plural was used in an inclusive way to apply to both men and women. Even if men were specifically addressed, the women would hear about the rule. Either view is possible grammatically. As I understand the verse, the men were the primary audience, but the women were not excluded.

Fifth, advocates of the quotation view hold that it was the Corinthians, not Paul, who cited the Law. Odell-Scott argues that the opponents of Paul were the Judaizers, the legalists (1983, 92). However, Janzen says they may have been "merely church leaders who used any possible source of authority to bolster their case," and "they insisted the Law agreed with them without going to the trouble of showing where" (2012, 62). The quotation approach allows for either position.

Sixth, an argument against the quotation view is that Paul does not explicitly say that he is quoting the Corinthians. However, other views include positions that Paul does not explicitly state. For example, Paul does not specifically say that women were not to evaluate prophecies, but many hold to this view. So the lack of an explicit statement does not in itself refute the quotation view. Moreover, if we assume that the rhetorical questions in verse 36 refer to the attitude of the Corinthians and what they said, then Paul implies that he is quoting them.

Seventh, proponents contend that this approach overcomes the contradiction between 14:34-35 and what Paul has written elsewhere. In 11:5, Paul writes about women publicly praying and prophesying. When Paul discusses the gifts of the Spirit, he does not limit their exercise to men. In 14:26, "each one" surely includes both men and women. The body of Christ includes men and women.

Conclusion

Few Scriptures have attracted more controversy than 14:33b-36. This is because the author says that women should "keep silent in the church." As we interpret these verses, many cultural issues become involved, including current as well as past culture. Also, verses 34-35 seem to both contradict and harmonize with what Paul says elsewhere. I have presented solutions to these problems under these headings: (1) interpolation, (2) absolute silence, (3) qualified silence, and (4) quotation of the Corinthians. My conclusions are as follows:

- One, with regard to the interpolation view, without more evidence, it would be difficult to support this view. Therefore, I accept these verses as an authentic part of the text.
- Two, the absolute silence view does not solve the problem of being in conflict with what Paul says elsewhere. Moreover, in practice, the churches generally accept some qualifications. In effect, advocates of this view really hold to the qualified silence view.
- Three, the qualified silence approach is widely accepted, but it has the difficulty of identifying what should or should not be permitted. As silence is often defined, it is very limited in scope. Given that, there is little difference between this view and the quotation approach.
- Four, the best approach is that the Corinthians stated their position in verses 34-35. Paul rebuked them in verse 36 for their attitude. Their attitude was an underlying factor in producing their position. Thus, Paul rejected the rule as well.

No matter which of these views one holds, it is important not to minimize the importance of culture. Our task is to preach the gospel and establish the church in all nations and cultures. Within these cultures we must proclaim the truth and exercise our spiritual gifts. Without compromising the gospel, we sometimes have to make cultural adjustments in our ministries. We can make these adjustments with confidence that the Spirit will lead us. The Holy Spirit helps us avoid unnecessary clashes with culture. He directs, empowers, and makes relevant all of our ministries.

In Paul's terms, "What is the outcome then?" Our worship services in church today often focus on people being spectators rather than participants. The early church services provided opportunities for all members of the body of Christ, both male and female, to participate. This participation includes the vocal gifts as well as other ministries. Today, as in the early church, the church leaders have the responsibility of making sure everything is done properly and in order. When this is done, the result will be a united sense of community and worship that will honor and glorify God.

CHAPTER FIFTEEN

THE OUTCOME

Introduction

In 1 Corinthians 12-14, Paul deals with spiritual gifts as they should be exercised by spiritual people in spiritual churches. He includes his comments about love in the middle of his teaching about the gifts. The great motivation for desiring and exercising spiritual gifts is love. It is love that will lead believers to act in the interest of the full body of Christ. Paul sets forth some regulations that people should follow in exercising the gifts. He strongly stresses that speech should be intelligible. When speakers are understood, the body can be edified. The overarching principle is that spiritual gifts in the assembly should be used properly and in an orderly manner. Now, in verses 37-40, Paul makes his concluding remarks. He writes:

> [37]If anyone thinks he is a prophet or spiritual, let him recognize that the things which I write to you are the Lord's commandment. [38]But if anyone does not recognize *this*, he is not recognized. [39]Therefore, my brethren, desire earnestly to prophesy, and do not forbid to speak in tongues. [40]But all things must be done properly and in an orderly manner.

The Lord's Commandment

Verses 37-38 continue the chord struck by Paul in verse 36. As many believe, I understand that verse 36 connects directly with verses 34-35, but this does not preclude a transition to verses 37-38 as well. In verses 34-35, Paul asks two rhetorical questions: "[Or] was it from you that the word of God first went forth? Or has it come to you only?" With regard to what follows, Taylor affirms that:

> The rhetorical questions combine with 14:37-38 for a direct confrontation between Paul and those who deem themselves to be a "prophet" or a "spiritual person." This reference to the "spiritual person" (14:37) recalls the opening of Paul's

discussion of 12:1-3 and confirms that this has been the primary issue all along. (2014, 362)

First, Paul says, "If anyone thinks he is a prophet or spiritual, let him recognize that the things which I write to you are the Lord's commandment" (14:37). With direct speech and apostolic authority, Paul challenges the arrogance of the believers.

One, twice before in this epistle, Paul uses the same "if anyone thinks" approach to confront the Corinthians.[131] In 3:18, he says, "If any man among you thinks that he is wise in this age, he must become foolish, so that he may become wise." Then, in 8:2-3, he says, "If anyone supposes that he knows anything, he has not yet known as he ought to know; but if anyone loves God, he is known by Him." Obviously, the people placed a high value on wisdom and knowledge. The Corinthians must not only know the true wisdom and knowledge, but also have the right attitude.

Two, in 14:37, Paul mentions anyone who *thinks* he is a prophet. It is interesting that he lists this first. The role of a prophet and the gift of prophecy were highly valued. Paul does not minimize this role in any way. Indeed, he urges the Corinthians to eagerly desire "especially that you may prophesy" (14:1). The problem was that some thought they were prophets and had the authority of a prophet, when they were not accepting the apostolic authority of Paul. They did not recognize that what he said was the Lord's commandment.

Three, Paul rebukes anyone who thinks he is spiritual, but really is not. There are many factors that cause people to think they are "spiritual."[132] The question is: What specific factors does Paul

---

[131]With regard to the three occurrences, Fee says, "Each occurs in one of the three major sections of the letter (chaps. 1-4; 8-10; 12-14); and the argument in each case indicates that by this formula Paul is zeroing in on the Corinthians' perspective as to their own spirituality. They do indeed think of themselves as 'the wise' (3:18) and as 'having knowledge' (8:2), probably in both cases because they also think of themselves as being *pneumatikoi*" (1987, 711).

[132]Fee writes: "As argued throughout the commentary, this is the central issue. There seems to be no other good reason for Paul to have spoken to them in this way if they did not consider themselves to be 'spiritual,' the primary evidence of which was the gift of tongues. They were sure that they themselves were Spirit people; they were less sure of the apostle" (1987,

228

have in mind? There are many reasons why people take pride in their spirituality. Some are proud because they pray a lot; others are proud because they give a lot; and still others are proud because they are unduly humble!

We know that the Corinthians (14:12) were eager to have spiritual gifts (*pneumatōn*, πνευμάτων). Some of the believers thought they were "spiritual" because they exercised spiritual gifts. The Greek word *pneumatōn* is a noun meaning "spirits;" but translators usually treat it as an adjective and supply the noun "gifts." This term could apply to any of the spiritual gifts. The context of 14:1-40 deals with tongues, interpretation of tongues, and prophecy. Given this, we can assume that Paul rebukes anyone who thinks they are spiritual because they exercise any one of these gifts. Perhaps some of the believers who sought wisdom and knowledge also exercised the gifts of "word of wisdom" and "word of knowledge" (12:8).

Four, Paul says (verse 37): "let him recognize (*epiginōsketō*, ἐπιγινωσκέτω) that the things which I write to you are the Lord's commandment." According to Thayer, this verb means to "know well" (1962, 11). With regard to this verse, he says that some say the term means "acknowledge" (1962, 11). Paul uses the imperative form of the verb. The emphasis is not just on knowledge itself, but acceptance of the truth of what Paul is saying. The spiritual person should acknowledge and obey the Lord's commands. Moreover, Paul makes the point that, as an apostle, what he writes is from the Lord. He has the apostolic authority to write the Lord's commandment. We cannot be spiritual without a proper relationship with the Lord and the body of Christ.

Second, in verse 38 Paul writes: "But if anyone does not recognize (*agnoei*, ἀγνοεῖ) *this*, he is not recognized (*agnoeitai*, ἀγνοεῖται)."[133] The second clause in this verse has just one word in

---

711). The context is clear that the Corinthians highly valued tongues, but it probably would be more accurate to say that they thought the "vocal gifts" were the "primary evidences" of spirituality. Paul has just mentioned anyone who thinks he is a prophet.

[133] According to Thayer, the verb *agnoei* (present indicative) can be translated "to be ignorant" or "not to know" (1962, 8). The NIV translation is "acknowledge."

Greek, so other words have to be supplied. The Greek verb that Paul uses is *agnoeō* (ἀγνοέω), but scholars differ over whether he uses the present indicative (*agnoeitai*) or the present imperative (*agnoeitō*, ἀγνοείτω).[134] Some maintain that he uses the future tense. The differences are based on mixed textual evidence and are evident in translations. Kistemaker gives the following explanation:

> For this text, translations usually provide a marginal note in which they show an alternative reading for the second half of verse 38. To illustrate, the New American Standard Bible gives the text as "he is not recognized" (*agnoeitai*) and the note as "let him be ignorant" (*agnoeitō*). By contrast, the New King James Version has the text as "let him be ignorant" and the note as "he is not recognized." The one reading is the indicative (NASB[95]) and the other, the imperative (NKJV). And last, some translations have the future tense in the text itself: "he himself will be ignored" (e.g., NIV). (1993, 517)

According to Thiselton, the majority of current scholars support the present indicative passive verb (2000, 1163). The passive voice calls for an agent which, in this context, would either be Paul, the Corinthians believers, or God. Barrett holds that the disapproving agent is Paul (1971, 334), while Lenski names the Corinthians (1946, 622). The majority view is reflected by Bauer who gives this translation, "if anyone disregards (it), he is disregarded (by God)" (2000, 13). Although Paul and others may disapprove, it is ultimately God who does not recognize or acknowledge those who do not submit to Paul's teaching.

Another variable is the nature and severity of the judgment against one who thinks he is a prophet or spiritual but does not

---

[134]Thiselton indicates that some manuscripts have the present indicative passive verb *agnoeitai* while others have the present imperative active *agnoeitō*. He says: "Many modern VSS and some textual specialists are divided. Thus Metzger, NIV, and NJB favor the passive indicative, Zuntz, NRSV (but not RSV), REB, ASV, and KJV/AV favor the imperative. However, the overwhelming majority of modern commentators support the reading of the indicative" (2000, 1162-1163).

acknowledge and accept the commandment of the Lord.[135] It may be, as Lenski contends, that "if he fails to see the divine character of Paul's words, the proof is conclusive (evidential proof) that this man is no prophet, that he really has no spiritual gift" (1946, 621). Going further, some exegetes believe that being disregarded by God means not being a Christian. Paul does not explicitly address the issue.

Final Exhortation

In verse 26, Paul asks the question, "What is the outcome then, brethren?" The emphasis of the question is on what we should do as a result of his teaching. Now, as we consider verses 39-40, we ask his question again. In these verses, Paul answers the question with a call to action. These two verses highlight the main points he has in mind in 14:1-40.

First, Paul begins verse 39 with: "Therefore, my brethren." He uses this same term in 14:6, 20, and 26. Scholars normally say that this designation includes the sisters as well as the brothers. Paul, for example, includes women in 11:5. Beyond this, it is inconceivable that the spiritual gifts in chapters 12-14 would only be for men. In 14:26, Paul says, "When you assemble, each one has a psalm, has a teaching, has a revelation, has a tongue, has an interpretation." The phrase "each one" should not be limited to men only.

Second, the first clause, "desire earnestly (*zēloute*, ζηλοῦτε) to prophesy," repeats what Paul says in 14:1. The form of the verb that Paul uses can be translated as an imperative or an indicative. Here, as in 14:1, Paul speaks in the imperative mood. An outcome of Paul's teaching is that the Corinthian believers should eagerly desire to prophesy. His teaching on love in chapter 13 puts in place the proper motivation for this desire. We should desire the gift of prophecy to meet the needs of the people. In 14:3, Paul says, "But one who prophesies speaks to men for edification and exhortation and consolation."

---

[135]Barrett argues that "Paul means that he does not recognize the man in question as inspired in his opinion, not that he does not recognize him as a Christian. There is nothing here to suggest excommunication, nor is it necessary to suppose . . . that the man *is not recognized*, known, by God" (1971, 334).

Third, the second clause of verse 39 says, "and do not forbid (*mē kōluete*, μὴ κωλύετε) to speak in tongues."[136] Paul uses the present imperative form of the verb. He does not say in this verse whether he means in private or in public. Neither does he say whether he means with or without interpretation. However, we know from the context that he encourages tongues with interpretation in public and tongues spoken privately whether interpreted or not.

The remaining question has to do with speaking in tongues in public without interpretation. Although Paul says that tongues should be interpreted, he does not forbid all speaking in tongues without interpretation. One reason, no doubt, is that the one who speaks in tongues may not know whether or not his utterance will be interpreted. In such a case, Paul exhorts the speaker to pray that he may interpret. If tongues could be uttered only when the speaker knows that either he or someone else will interpret, then there probably would be few utterances in tongues.

In 14:40, Paul says, "But all things must be done properly (*ginesthō*, γινέσθω) and in an orderly manner." Once again, Paul uses a present imperative to express his regulation. The phrase, "properly and in an orderly manner," expresses the general principle. In verses 26-33, Paul has discussed some of the elements of an orderly service, but it was not possible to include them all. This means that pastors have the responsibility of interpreting what these words mean in many different situations. They must be led of the Spirit in guiding the order of the meetings.

Conclusion

Paul has covered many topics in 1 Corinthians 12-14. In 14:37-40, he focuses on the major points that he wants to emphasize. Thus, 14:37-40 is an action statement for his entire discussion in chapters 12-14. As my conclusion, I will add a summary statement of the themes addressed by Paul.

---

[136]Kistemaker holds that *mē kōluete* "actually means that Paul is saying: 'you are presently forbidding people to speak in tongues, but now that you have received my regulations, do not discourage people from using the gift of tongue-speaking" (1993, 518).

Throughout these chapters, Paul teaches about spiritual things or matters. These spiritual matters include spiritual persons, spiritual gifts, and spiritual churches. As Paul makes plain in 14:37, some of the believers in the church at Corinth thought they were spiritual because of their exercise of spiritual gifts. Paul uses the occasion to teach them that, unless they are motivated by love and exercise the gifts for the edification of the church, they are not spiritual. Speaking more broadly, they must obey the Lord's commandment, not only with regard to the gifts, but in all things.

Concerning spiritual gifts, Paul starts with his teaching on spiritual gifts in 12:1 by saying, "Now concerning spiritual *gifts*, brethren, I do not want you to be ignorant." In chapter 12, he starts with a broad discussion of the gifts and the body of Christ and concludes the chapter with the admonition to "earnestly desire" spiritual gifts. Then, he gives us, in chapter 13, his powerful treatment of love. His teaching applies broadly to all of our lives. With regard to the gifts, we are to seek them through love. In the fourteenth chapter, Paul narrows the discussion primarily to tongues, interpretation of tongues, and prophecy. He tells us to earnestly desire to prophesy and not to forbid tongues. Then he exhorts us to do all things properly and in an orderly manner.

Spiritual churches consist of spiritual people who live and act in spiritual ways. Paul is especially concerned about the services in the church. He is concerned about the impact of what happens on the outsiders who visit the church. And, for the sake of the edification of the body, he is concerned that there be an orderly approach. He insists that speech be intelligible. Any utterance in tongues should be interpreted. Paul sees no conflict between order and the powerful presence and work of the Spirit. The Spirit must be allowed to work.

The gifts of the Spirit are not confined to the church service. Persons such as apostles, prophets, and teachers do many things outside the walls of the church. Gifts such as helps and administrations are in evidence in all kinds of settings. The gift of evangelism is best seen as the evangelist presents the gospel and persuades people to believe in Christ. As servants of God, we need the empowerment of the Spirit wherever we serve. As we serve, we exalt the name of the Lord Jesus. Therefore, let us pray that our relationship with the Triune God will always be strong.

Sources

Allison, R. W. 1988. "Let Women Be Silent in the Churches (1 Cor. 14:33b-36): What Did Paul Really Say and What Did It Mean?" *Journal for the Study of the New Testament* 32:27-60.

Arrington, French. 2003. *Encountering the Holy Spirit: Paths of Christian Growth and Service.* Cleveland: Pathway Press.

Atkerson, Steve. 2009. "Correctly Interpreting 1 Corinthians 14:33b-35 (Part 1)" New Testament Reformation Fellowship.

_____. 2009. "Correctly Interpreting 1 Corinthians 14:33b-35 (Part 2)" New Testament Reformation Fellowship.

Bagster, Samuel. n.d. *The Analytical Greek Lexicon.* London: Samuel Bagster and Sons Limited.

Baker, John. 1967. *Baptized in One Spirit.* Plainfield: Logos Books.

Balfour, Glenn. 2009. "Spiritual Gifts: 'To Use or not to Use—That is the Question.'" In *Contemporary Issues in Pneumatology.* ed. James E. Richardson. Springfield: Global University.

Barrett, C. K. 1971. *A Commentary on the First Epistle to the Corinthians.* 2. ed. London: Adam and Charles Black.

Bauer, Walter. 2000. *A Greek–English Lexicon of the New Testament and Other Early Christian Literature.* Third edition (BDAG). Chicago: University of Chicago Press.

Beasley-Murray, G. R. 1962. *Baptism in the New Testament.* Grand Rapids: William B. Eerdmans Publishing Company.

Berding, Kenneth. 2006. *What Are Spiritual gifts: Rethinking the Conventional View.* Grand Rapids: Kregel Publications.

Blomberg, Craig L. 1994. *1 Corinthians: The NIV Application Commentary.* Grand Rapids: Zondervan.

Boyd, Frank M. 1970. *The Spirit Works Today.* Springfield: Gospel Publishing House.

234

Brandt, R. L. 1981. *Charismatics: Are We Missing Something?* Plainfield: Logos International.

Bruce, F. F. 1984. *The Epistles to the Colossians, to Philemon, and to the Ephesians: New International Commentary on the New Testament.* Grand Rapids: William B. Eerdmans Publishing Company.

Brumback, Carl. 1947. *"What Meaneth This?" A Pentecostal Answer to a Pentecostal Question.* Springfield: Gospel Publishing House.

Bullock, Warren D. 2009. *When the Spirit Speaks.* Springfield: Gospel Publishing House.

Carson, D. A. 1987. *Showing the Spirit: A Theological Exposition of 1 Corinthians 12-14.* Grand Rapids: Baker Academic.

_____. 1991. "Silent in the Churches": On the Role of Women in 1 Corinthians 14:33b-36, 133-147. Chapter 6 in *Recovering Biblical Manhood and Womanhood.* Ed. John Piper and Wayne Grudem. Wheaton: Crossway Books.

Carter, Howard. 1976. *Questions and Answers on Spiritual Gifts.* Tulsa: Harrison House, Inc.

Chafin, Kenneth L. 1985. *1, 2 Corinthians: The Communicator's Commentary.* Gen. Ed., Lloyd J. Ogilvie. Waco: Word Books, Publisher.

Christenson, Laurence. 1968. *Speaking in Tongues.* Minnesota: Bethany Fellowship Publishers.

Chrysostom, St. John. 1889. NPNF, XII. Ed. Philip Schaff. *Homilies of St. John Chrysostom on the First Epistle of St. Paul the Apostle to the Corinthians.* New York: The Christian Literature Company.

Drummond, Henry. n.d. *The Greatest Thing in the World.* London and Glasgow: Collins.

Dunn, James D. G. 1970. *Baptism in the Holy Spirit.* London: SCM Press Ltd.

_____. 1975. *Jesus and the Spirit.* London: SCM Press Ltd.

Erdman, Charles R. 1983. *The First Epistle of Paul to the Corinthians*. Grand Rapids: Baker Book House.

Ervin, Howard M. 1968. *These Are Not Drunken As Ye Suppose*. Plainfield: Logos International.

Fee, Gordon D. 1987. *The First Epistle to the Corinthians*. Grand Rapids: William B. Eerdmans Publishing Company.

_____. 1994. *God's Empowering Presence*. Peabody, MA: Hendrickson Publishers.

_____. 1996. *Paul, the Spirit, and the People of God*. Grand Rapids: Baker Academic.

Flattery, George M. 2009a. A Biblical Theology of the Holy Spirit: Old Testament, Vol. 1. Springfield: Global University.

_____. 2009b. A Biblical Theology of the Holy Spirit: Luke-Acts, Vol. 2. Springfield: Global University.

_____. 2009c. A Biblical Theology of the Holy Spirit: John-Paul, Vol . 3. Springfield: Global University.

_____. 1968. *Teaching for Christian Maturity*. Springfield: Gospel Publishing House.

_____. 2012. *The Holy Spirit in Your Life: A Systematic Approach to a Vibrant Relationship*. Springfield: Network211.

_____. 2014. "Speaking in Tongues: Its Essence, Purposes, and Use." Springfield: Unpublished Article.

Flynn, Leslie B. 1985. *19 Gifts of the Spirit*. Wheaton: Victor Books.

Fraser, John W., Trans. Eds., David W. Torrance, and Thomas F. Torrance. 1960. *Calvin's New Testament Commentaries: The First Epistle of Paul to the Corinthians*. Grand Rapids: William B. Eerdmans Publishing Company.

Funk, Robert W. 1961. *A Greek Grammar of the New Testament and Other Early Christian Literature*. Chicago: The University of Chicago Press.

Gangel, Kenneth O. 1985. *Unwrap Your Spiritual Gifts*. Wheaton: Victor Books.

236

Garland, David E. 2003. *1 Corinthians. Baker Exegetical Commentary on the New Testament*. Eds. Robert W. Yarbrough and Robert H. Stein. Grand Rapids: Baker Academic.

Gee, Donald. 1980. *Concerning Spiritual Gifts*. Springfield: Radiant Books.

Greenbury, James 2008. "1 Corinthians 14:34-35: Evaluation of Prophecy Revisited." *Journal of Evangelical Theological Society* 51:4 (December) 721-31.

Grosheide, F. W. 1953. *First Epistle to the Corinthians: New International Commentary on the New Testament*. Grand Rapids: William B. Eerdmans Publisher

Grudem, Wayne A. 1982. *The Gift of Prophecy in 1 Corinthians*. Washington, DC: University Press of America.

_____. 1988. *The Gift of Prophecy in the New Testament and Today*. Westchester: Crossway Books.

Horton, Harold. 1962. *The Gifts of the Spirit*. London: Assemblies of God Publishing House.

Horton, Stanley M. 1999. *I and II Corinthians*. Springfield: Logion Press.

_____. 1976. *What the Bible Says About the Holy Spirit*. Springfield: Gospel Publishing House.

Hubbard, David Allan 1985. *Unwrapping Your Spiritual Gifts*. Waco: Word Books.

Hummel, Charles E. 1979. *Fire in the Fireplace: Contemporary Charismatic Renewal*. Downers Grove: InterVarsity Press.

Jamieson, Robert, A. R. Faussett, and David Brown. 1871. *Commentary Critical and Explanatory of the Whole Bible*.

Janzen, Marshall. June 12, 2012. "Orderly Participation or Silenced Women." A Theological Treatment Paper for the Evangelical Free Church of Canada. (55-70)

Johanson, B. C. 1979. "Tongues, A Sign for Unbelievers?: A Structural and Exegetical Study of I Corinthians XIV.20-25." *New Testament Studies* 25, pages 180-293.

Keener, Craig. S. 2005. General Editor. Ben Witherington. *1-2 Corinthians: The New Cambridge Bible Commentary.* Cambridge: Cambridge University Press.

_____ 2001. *Gift & Giver: The Holy Spirit for Today.* Grand Rapids: Baker Academic.

_____ 2011. *Miracles: The Credibility of the New Testament Accounts*, Vol. 1. Grand Rapids: Baker Academic.

Kistemaker, Simon J. 1993. *Exposition of the First Epistle to the Corinthians: New Testament Commentary.* Grand Rapids: Baker Academic.

Ladd, George Eldon. 1974. *A Theology of the New Testament.* Grand Rapids: William B. Eerdmans Publishing Company.

Lenski, R. C. H. 1946. *St. Paul's First and Second Epistle to the Corinthians.* Columbus: Wartburg Press.

Lim, David. 1991. *Spiritual Gifts: A Fresh Look.* Springfield: Gospel Publishing House.

MacGorman, J. W. 1974. *The Gifts of the Spirit.* Nashville: Broadman Press.

Menzies, Robert P. 2013. *Pentecost: This Story Is Our Story.* Springfield: Gospel Publishing House.

_____. 2014. "Tongues as a Sign: Reconciling Luke and Paul." Unpublished Article, 1-21.

Miller, Denzil R. 2005. *Empowered for Global Mission.* Springfield, Life Publishers International.

_____. 2008. *In Step with the Spirit: Studies in the Spirit-Filled Walk.* Springfield: AIA Publications.

_____. n.d. *The Kingdom and the Power.* Springfield: AIA Publications.

Montague, George T. 1976. *The Holy Spirit: Growth of a Christian Tradition.* New York: Paulist Press.

Morris, Leon. 1958. *The First Epistle of Paul to the Corinthians. Tyndale New Testament Commentaries.* Grand Rapids: William B. Eerdmans Publishing Company.

238

Mounce, William D. 1993. *Basics of Biblical Greek*. 2. ed. Grand Rapids: Zondervan.

Muhlen, Heribert. 1978. *A Charismatic Theology: Initiation in the Spirit*. London: Burns & Oates.

Odell-Scott, David W. 1983. "Let the Women Speak in Church: An Egalitarian Interpretation of 1 Cor 14:33b-36." *Biblical Theology Bulletin* 13:90-93.

Palma, Anthony D. 2001. *The Holy Spirit: A Pentecostal Perspective*. Springfield: Gospel Publishing House.

Petts, David. 2002. *Body Builders: Gifts to Make God's People Grow*. Mattersey: Mattersey Hall.

Rea, John. 1998. *Charisma's Bible Handbook on the Holy Spirit*. Lake May: Creation House.

Ridderbos, Herman. 1975. *Paul: An Outline of His Theology*. Trans. John Richard DeWitt. Grand Rapids: William B. Eerdmans Publishing Company.

Riggs, Ralph M. 1949. *The Spirit Himself*. Springfield: the Gospel Publishing House.

Robertson, A. T. 1931. *Word Pictures in the New Testament*. 6 Vols. Nashville: Broadman Press.

_____. 1934. *A Grammar of the Greek New Testament in the Light of Historical Research*. Nashville: Broadman Press.

Robertson, Archibald and Plummer, A. 1914. *A Critical and Exegetical Commentary on the First Epistle of St Paul to the Corinthians*. Edinburgh: T&T Clark.

Schatzmann, Siegfried S. 1987. *A Pauline Theology of Charismata*. Peabody: Hendrickson Publishers.

Schep, John A. 1972. *Baptism in the Spirit*. Plainfield: Logos International.

Scott, James W. 1996. "May Women Speak in Church?" *New Horizons:* The Orthodox Presbyterian Church.

Smyth, H. W. 1963. *Greek Grammar*. Cambridge: Harvard University Press.

Stott, John R. W. 1964. *The Baptism and Fullness of the Holy Spirit.* Downers Grove, Inter-Varsity Press.

Sullivan, Francis A. 1982. *Charisms and Charismatic Renewal.* Ann Arbor: Servant Books.

Talbert, C. H. 1987. *Reading Corinthians: A Literary and Theological Commentary on 1 and 2 Corinthians.* New York: Crossroad.

Taylor, Mark. 2014. General Editor: E. Ray Clendenen. *1 Corinthians: The New American Commentary,* vol. 28. Nashville: B&H Publishing Group.

Thayer, Joseph Henry. 1962. *Greek-English Lexicon of the New Testament.* Grand Rapids: Zondervan.

Thiselton, Anthony C. 2000. *The First Epistle to the Corinthians: A Commentary on the Greek Text: NIGTC.* Grand Rapids: William B. Eerdmans Publishing Company

Torrey, R. A. 1927. *The Holy Spirit.* Westwood: Fleming H. Revell Company.

Turner, Max. 1996. *The Holy Spirit and Spiritual Gifts.* Peabody, MA: Hendrickson Publishers.

Unger, Merrill F. 1974. *The Baptism & Gifts of the Holy Spirit.* Chicago: Moody Press.

Verbrugge, Verlyn. 2008. "1 Corinthians." Pages 239-414 in *Galatians-Romans. Expositor's Bible Commentary.* Edited by Tremper Longman and David E. Garland. Rev. ed. Grand Rapids: Zondervan.

Wallace, Daniel B. 1996. *Greek Grammar beyond the Basics.* Grand Rapids: Zondervan.

Winter, B. W. 2001. *After Paul Left Corinth: The Influence of Secular Ethics and Social Change.* Grand Rapids: William B. Eerdmans Publishing Company.

Wood, George O. with Randy Hurst. 2009. *Living in the Spirit.* Springfield: Gospel Publishing House.

240

Wood, Leon J. 1976. *The Holy Spirit in the Old Testament.* Grand Rapids: Zondervan Publishing House.

Young, Edward J. 1969. *The Book of Isaiah*, Vol. II. Grand Rapids: William B. Eerdmans Publishing Company.

Zodhiates, Spiro, ed. 2008. *Hebrew-Greek Key Word Study Bible.* Chattanooga: AMG Publishers.

Scripture Index

GENESIS
2:18-24—211
3:16—211

NUMBERS
11:29—139

JUDGES
3:27—154

2 SAMUEL
20:1—154

PSALMS
32:2—111
68:18—23

PROVERBS
16:9—41

ISAIAH
28:11—178
28:11-12—174, 175, 176, 178, 179,
 180, 181, 184, 185, 187
28:12—179
45:14—188

JEREMIAH
4:19—154
6:1—154
6:17—154
51:27—154

EZEKIEL
33:3-6—154

HOSEA
5:8—154

JOEL
2:1—154

ZECHARIAH
8:17—111

MATTHEW
3:11—74

10:2-4—90
10:20—41
20:15—221
20:25-27—89
25:15—35, 51, 52

MARK
1:8—74
1:32-34—47
4:35-41—52
5:1-10—52
5:2-16—56
5:42—9
6:34-44—52
16:18—47

LUKE
3:16—74
6:49—116
7:11-17—52
8:40-42—52
8:49-56—52
10:21—40
11:13—75
12:11-12—41

JOHN
3:16—127

ACTS
1:5—74, 79
1:24-25—90
2:4—79, 80, 92, 96
2:11—142
2:17-18—28, 92
2:46—192
4:8-12—41
5:1-5—43
5:1-9—57
5:42—192
7:54-60—12
10:44-48—186
11:16—74, 79
11:27—92

242

13:1—92, 93
13:6-12—57
13:33—195
14:4—90
14:14—90
15:28—41
16:16-18—57
17:2—193
18:1-17—xi
18:2—192
18:2-18—192
18:4—193
18:8—6
18:11—xii
19:1-6—186
19:1-7—80
19:8-22—xii
20:20—192
20:31—xii
20:35—141
27:11—95

ROMANS
1:11—20
4:6-11—112
4:8—112
4:22-25—112
5:1-5—124
5:2-3—107
5:5—102
5:15-16—20
6:17—153
6:23—20
8:9—78
8:24—126
8:26-27—138, 139
8:26—134
8:32—56
9:30-31—131
10:12—76
10:17—187
11:29—20
12:3—22, 45, 85
12:4-8—84
12:6—20, 34, 46, 53, 54, 55, 82, 83,
    91, 196
12:6-8—21, 82, 83, 84

12:7—42, 60, 93, 153
12:8—94, 95, 107
12:13-14—131
14:19—131
15:13—127
15:19—52
16:3-5—193
16:7—90, 153
16:23—193

1 CORINTHIANS
1-4—227
1:4-7—20
1:7—20, 34
1:11—xiii, 220
1:11-12—2
1:17-2:16—40
1:18-25—203
1:19—178, 203
1:23—12
1:31—178, 203
2:1—134
2:1-4—40
2:1-5—203
2:6—120
2:7—134
2:9—178
2:10—40
2:15—103
3:2—77
3:5—35
3:6-8—77
3:9—26, 136
3:18—227
3:19—178
4:3—203
4:5—109
4:6—203
4:7—29, 203
4:8—109
4:12—131
5:1—xiii, 2, 220
5:9—xiii, 220
6:1—2
6:5—203
6:9-11—7
6:11—73

6:15—66
7:1—xiii, 2, 175, 220
7:7—20
7:10—203
7:25—xiii, 2, 175, 203, 220
8-10—227
8:1—xiii, 2, 175, 203, 220
8:1-10:22—7
8:2—227
8:2-3—227
8:4—xiii, 2, 175
8:7—9
8:7-13—203
9:9—178
9:14—203
10:2—73
10:2-4—90
10:7—178
10:19-20—8
11—219
11:2—203
11:2-16—87
11:3—87
11:4—215
11:5—4, 207, 215, 216, 219, 220,
 223, 230
11:7-12—87
11:8—211
11:11-12—211
11:17-22—2
11:18—xiii, 2, 220
11:20-21—223
11:20-22—222, 223
11:23—203
11:29—203
11:31—203
12—21, 74, 96, 102, 129, 144, 232
12-14—v, vi, xiv, 1, 3, 4, 21, 22, 26,
 27, 33, 53, 58, 59, 80, 129, 139,
 144, 161, 190, 220, 226, 227, 230,
 231, 232
12:1—v, xiii, xiv, 2, 4, 5, 10, 11, 22,
 132, 175, 220, 232
12:1-3—1, 14, 33, 65, 182, 227
12:1-27—82
12:1-31—64

12:2—5, 6. 7, 8, 9, 10, 11
12:3—4, 8, 9, 10, 11, 14, 15, 23, 73,
 203
12:4—19, 20, 22, 25, 29
12:4-6—vii, 17, 25, 26, 27, 29, 31,
 33, 65
12:4-11—17, 18, 78
12:5—23, 25, 29
12:6—24, 27, 29, 30, 50, 55, 62, 85
12:6-15—66
12:7—17, 19, 27, 34, 35, 38, 42, 58,
 62, 85, 134, 193, 203
12:7-9—49
12:7-10—38
12:7-11—17, 33, 44, 48, 49, 50, 61,
 62, 65, 69
12:8—34, 37, 38, 39, 42, 50, 55,
 105, 107, 118, 150, 228
12:8-10—vii, 5, 21, 47, 60, 80, 82,
 83, 89, 202
12:9—20, 44, 73, 105
12:9-10—44, 87
12:10—24, 44, 49, 50, 51, 54, 55,
 56, 57, 58, 60, 91,105, 118, 135,
 161, 198, 203
12:10-11—49
12:11—18, 19, 22. 23, 34, 35, 36,
 38, 58, 61, 62, 85, 134, 193
12:12—66, 69
12:12-13—64, 66,
12:12-27—ix, 34, 37, 64, 65, 70, 81
12:13—64, 66, 70, 71, 72, 73, 74,
 75, 76, 77, 78, 79, 81
12:14—66
12:14-19—66, 67
12:15-16—67
12:15-17—67
12:17—67
12:18—23, 35, 67, 85, 89
12:19—67
12:15-16—67
12:20-26—66, 68
12:15-16—67
12:21—68
12:22—68, 139, 203
12:23-24—68, 87

12:24—23
12:24-25—85, 89
12:27—66, 69, 86
12:28—viii, 20, 23, 30, 42, 46, 51, 53, 54, 58, 69, 84, 85, 86, 88, 89, 91, 92, 95, 97, 130, 196
12:28-29—51, 93
12:28-30—21, 83, 84, 89
12:28-31—21, 69, 82, 86, 99
12:29—51, 54, 91, 92
12:29-30—69, 84, 87, 89, 95, 141
12:30—20, 46, 58, 60, 87, 89, 95, 161
12:31—3, 20, 22, 25, 69, 83, 85, 87, 96, 97, 98, 99, 102, 109, 114, 115, 128, 130, 131, 132, 140, 196
13—4, 101, 102, 129, 144, 172, 190, 230, 232
13:1—58, 59, 103, 104, 105,
13:1-2—84
13:1-3—97, 102, 103, 104, 114
13:1-4—115
13:1-7—101
13:1-12—125
13:1-13—101, 102, 177, 203, 204
13:2—42, 45, 54, 105, 106, 125
13:3—106, 107
13:4—109, 111, 113
13:4-7—108, 113, 115, 116
13:5—110
13:6—112
13:7—112, 113, 125
13:8—42, 58, 115, 116, 118, 120, 125
13:8-9—84
13:8-11—118
13:8-12—42, 114, 115, 116, 118, 124, 127
13:8-13—101, 114, 115, 118, 127
13:9—54, 119, 120
13:10—118, 120
13:11—118, 121
13:12—120, 121, 122, 123
13:13—viii, 102, 114, 115, 124, 125, 126, 127, 128

14—25, 59, 98, 102, 105, 106, 118, 129, 130, 139, 143, 151, 172, 190, 215, 218
14:1—3, 22, 25, 35, 54, 98, 99, 102, 109, 114, 128, 130, 131, 132, 139, 141, 143, 227, 230
14:1-5—130, 143, 144, 159
14:1-40—228, 230
14:2—58, 60, 105, 146, 161
14:3—54, 92, 135, 148, 151, 188, 230
14:3-5—203
14:4—54, 58, 61, 130, 137, 161, 163, 182, 197
14:5—54, 58, 60, 92, 98, 108, 130, 138, 139, 141, 144, 145, 147, 148, 151, 157, 158, 160, 161, 182, 200, 204
14:6—4, 42, 54, 58, 60, 93, 103, 106, 132, 133, 141, 142, 143, 144, 145, 146, 148, 149, 153, 191, 197, 230
14:6-12—143, 144, 145, 157, 158, 159, 160
14:7-8—155
14:7-9—154
14:9—155
14:10—156
14:10-11—156
14:10-12—156
14:11—156
14:12—56, 97, 130, 131, 136, 156, 157, 161, 203, 228
14:13—25, 58, 59, 60, 140, 144, 148, 158, 160, 161, 165, 166, 201
14:13-16—59
14:13-18—158
14:13-19—159, 160, 172
14:14—58, 134, 138, 161, 162, 163
14:14-15—135, 146
14:14-17—144
14:14-19—160
14:15—25, 164, 166, 167, 170, 171, 191, 195, 196
14:15-16—161, 171
14:16—165, 169, 170, 171

14:16-17—166, 169, 170
14:17—169, 170, 203
14:18—58, 139, 140, 165, 182
14:18-19—140, 171
14:19—58, 130, 171
14:20—4, 120, 174, 175, 176, 178, 191, 230
14:20-25—173, 175, 182, 186, 188, 203
14:21—174, 175, 176, 178, 179, 180
14:21-22—174, 175, 178, 179, 180, 181, 184, 188
14:21-25—176
14:22—54, 58, 174, 175, 176, 178, 179, 180, 181, 182, 183, 184, 185, 186, 187, 188
14:22-25—181
14:23—58, 130, 175, 181, 183, 184, 185, 186, 188, 189, 198
14:23-24—170, 183
14:23-25—13, 174, 175, 176, 178, 188, 189
14:24—54, 151, 167, 186, 187, 188, 202
14:24-25—36, 37, 92, 136, 186, 187, 189
14:25—186, 187, 188
14:26—4, 35, 58, 60, 84, 93, 147, 153, 161, 165, 166, 191, 195, 196, 203, 216, 220, 224, 230
14:26-32—136
14:26-33—190, 191, 208, 231
14:26-40—198
14:27—58, 60, 183, 200
14:27-28—133, 199, 200
14:28—54, 60, 94, 130, 139, 146, 147, 161, 201
14:29—25, 54, 55, 56, 57, 60, 202, 203, 219
14:29-32—202
14:30—197, 204
14:31—28, 54, 92, 151, 152, 202, 204
14:32—10, 26, 54, 56, 91, 204
14:33—130, 205, 208, 209, 214, 215, 221

14:33-34—208
14:33-35—216, 222
14:33-36—207, 208, 213, 214, 215, 217, 222, 224
14:34—130, 178, 209, 210, 211, 215, 220
14:34-35—4, 208, 209, 210, 211, 212, 213, 214, 215, 216, 217, 218, 220, 221, 23, 226
14:35—130, 209, 210, 218, 219
14:36—208, 210, 211, 214, 216, 221, 222, 223, 224, 226
14:37—3, 5, 54, 91, 132, 216, 226, 227, 228, 232
14:37-38—26, 211, 214, 226
14:37-40—226, 231
14:38—5, 228, 229
14:39—4, 25, 26, 54, 58, 98, 131, 141, 191, 204, 230, 231
14:39-40—143, 230
14:40—200, 214, 215, 231
15:3—203
15:9—131
15:12—xiii, 2
15:36-37—122
15:45—178
15:51—134
16:1—xiii, 2, 175, 220
16:4—12
16:7—xiii
16:8—xii
16:12—xiii, 2, 175, 220
16:19—193

2 CORINTHIANS
1:10-11—20
1:11—20
1:14—107
4:9—131
5:7—126
5:11—131
5:19—112
5:22-23—35
6:1—26
6:12—131
8:23—90

246

GALATIANS
1:19—90
3:28—76
4:6—75
4:8-9—9
4:16—180
5:5-6—124
5:22—102
5:22-23—35
6:1—3

EPHESIANS
2:19-20—92
3:5—92
4:3—79
4:4—79
4:4-6—25
4:7—22, 23, 35, 83
4:7-11—23
4:8—21, 23, 82, 83, 84,197
4:8-11—84
4:11—21, 22, 23, 35, 53, 54, 60, 82, 83, 84, 85, 88, 91, 92, 93, 197
4:12-13—91
4:13—120
5:18—172, 182
5:18-19—59, 167, 168
5:19-20—195
6:11—134

PHILIPPIANS
1:19—79
2:1—136
2:25—90
3:6—131
3:12—131
3:14—131
3:15—120

COLOSSIANS
1:4-5—124
1:28—26, 120
1:28-29—26
1:29—27
2:2—106
3:16—59, 168, 172, 182, 195
4:12—120

1 THESSALONIANS
1:3—124
1:9—9
2:6—90
4:8—79
5:8—124
5:15—131
5:20-21—56
5:23—56

2 THESSALONIANS
2:15-3:6—203

1 TIMOTHY
2:11-12—207, 214, 217
2:12—208
4:14—20
6:11—131

2 TIMOTHY
1:6—5, 20, 21, 23, 189
2:22—131
3:12—131

HEBREWS
3:1—90
6:10-12—124
10:22-24—124

JAMES
1:17—30, 93
2:23—112
5:14—47

1 PETER
1:3-8—124
1:21-22—124
4:8—113
4:10—20, 35
4:10-11—84

1 JOHN
4:1—56
4:8—126, 127

REVELATION
5:9-14—195
18:17—95
18:22—154

GREEK INDEX BY TEXTUAL FORM

TEXTUAL FORM	LEXICAL FORM	PAGES
A, α		
ἀγάπη, (agapē)	ἀγάπη, (agapē)	101, 104
ἀδελφοι, (adelphoi)	ἀδελφος, (adelphos)	2, 4
ἀγνοει, (agnoei)	ἀγνοέω, (agnoeō)	5, 228
ἀγνοεῖν, (agnoein)	ἀγνοέω, (agnoeō)	2, 4
ἀγνοεῖται, (agnoeitai)	ἀγνοέω, (agnoeō)	228, 229
ἀγνοείτω, (agnoeitō)	ἀγνοέω, (agnoeō)	229
ἀγνοέω, (agnoeō)	ἀγνοέω, (agnoeō)	4, 229
αἰνίγματι, (ainigmati)	αἴνιγμα, (ainigma)	122
αἰσχρὸν, (aischron)	αἰσχρός, (aischros)	211
ἄκαρπός, (akarpos)	ἄκαρπος, (akarpos)	162
ἄλλῳ, (allō)	ἄλλος, (allos)	37, 42, 44, 46, 49, 50, 53, 55
ἀνὰ, (ana)	ἀνὰ, (ana)	199
ἀνάθεμα, (anathema)	ἀνάθεμα, (anathema)	11, 12
ἀντιλήμψεις, (antilēmpseis)	ἀντίλημψίς, (antilēmpsis)	30, 94
ἀπαγόμενοι, (apagomenoi)	ἀπάγω, (apagō)	7, 8
ἄπιστοι, (apistoi)	ἄπιστος, (apistos)	183
ἄπιστος, (apistos)	ἄπιστος, (apistos)	186
ἀποκαλύψει, (apokalupsei)	ἀποκάλυψις, (apokalupsis)	149
ἀποκάλυψιν, (apokalupsin)	ἀποκάλυψις, (apokalupsis)	197
ἀποστολος, (apostolos)	ἀποστολος, (apostolos)	89, 90
ἄρτι, (arti)	ἄρτι, (arti)	122
ἀσχήμονα, (aschēmona)	ἀσχήμων, (aschēmōn)	68
ἀσχημονεῖ, (aschēmonei)	ἀσχημονέω, (aschēmoneō)	110
αὐλὸς, (aulos)	αὐλός, (aulos)	154
αὐτο, (auto)	αὐτός, (autos)	42
ἄφωνα, (aphōna)	ἄφωνος, (aphōnos)	7
ἄφωνον, (aphōnon)	ἄφωνος, (aphōnos)	156
B, β		
βάρβαρος, (barbaros)	βάρβαρος, (barbaros)	156
Γ, γ		
γὰρ, (gar)	γὰρ, (gar)	37, 120
γένη, (genē)	γένος, (genos)	57
γινεσθω, (ginesthō)	γίνομαι, (ginomai)	198, 231
γινώσκομεν, (ginōskomen)	γινώσκω, (ginōskō)	119
γινώσκω, (ginōskō)	γινώσκω, (ginōskō)	123

248

γλῶσσαι, (glōssai)	γλῶσσα, (glōssa)	118
γλῶσσαν, (glōssan)	γλῶσσα, (glōssa)	197
γλώσσῃ, (glōssē)	γλῶσσα, (glōssa)	132, 137, 160, 161, 194
γλώσσης, (glōssēs)	γλῶσσα, (glōssa)	155
γλωσσῶν, (glōssōn)	γλῶσσα, (glōssa)	57
γνώσει, (gnōsei)	γνῶσις, (gnōsis)	150
γνώσεως, (gnōseōs)	γνῶσις, (gnōsis)	37, 42
γνῶσις, (gnōsis)	γνῶσις, (gnōsis)	42, 118
γυναῖκες, (gunaikes)	γυνή, (gunē)	209, 210

Δ, δ

δὲ, (de)	δὲ, (de)	18, 85, 96, 97, 124, 130, 139, 187
διὰ, (dia)	διὰ, (dia)	37, 38, 39
διαιρέσεις, (diaireseis)	διαίρεσις, (diairesis)	18, 23, 24
διαιροῦν, (diairoun)	διαιρέω, (diaireō)	18, 61, 62
διακονιῶν, (diakoniōn)	διακονία, (diakonia)	23, 28
διακρίνειν, (diakrinein)	διακρίνω, (diakrinō)	203
διακρινέτωσαν, (diakrinetōsan)	διακρίνω, (diakrinō)	55, 203
διακρίνω, (diakrinō)	διακρίνω, (diakrinō)	55
διακρίσεις, (diakriseis)	διάκρισις, (diakrisis)	55, 203
διακρίσις, (diakrisis)	διάκρισις, (diakrisis)	56
διδασκαλίᾳ, (didaskalia)	διδασκαλία, (didaskalia)	196
διδασκάλους, (didaskalous)	διδάσκολος, (didaskolos)	196
διδάσκων, (didaskōn)	διδάσκολος, (didaskolos)	84, 153, 196
διδαχῇ, (didachē)	διδαχῇ, (didachē)	152, 196
διδαχή, (didachē)	διδαχή, (didachē)	196
διδαχήν, (didachēn)	διδαχῇ, (didachē)	196
δίδοται, (didotai)	δίδωμι, (didōmi)	34, 36, 37, 38, 39
διερμηνευετής, (diermēneuetēs)	διερμηνεύω, (diermēneuō)	199, 201
διερμηνευέτω, (diermēneuetō)	διερμηνεύω, (diermēneuō)	199
διερμηνεύῃ, (diermēneuē)	διερμηνεύω, (diermēneuō)	141, 142
διερμηνεύω, (diermēneuō)	διερμηνεύω, (diermēneuō)	139
διο, (dio)	διο, (dio)	10, 160
διώκετε, (diōkete)	διώκω, (diōkō)	130, 131
διώκω, (diōkō)	διώκω, (diōkō)	131
δόματα, (domata)	δόμα, (domata)	21, 23, 82, 83, 84, 196, 197
δωρεᾶς, (dōreas)	δωρεά, (dōrea)	83
δύναμαι, (dunamai)	δύναμαι, (dunamai)	53
δύναμει, (dunamei)	δύναμις, (dunamis)	52

δυνάμεων, (dunameōn)	δύναμις, (dunamis)	50, 51
δύναμιν, (dunamin)	δύναμις, (dunamis)	53, 156
δύναμις, (dunamis)	δύναμις, (dunamis)	51, 52, 156
δωρεᾶς, (dōreas)	δωρεά, (dōrea)	23

Ε, ε

ἐάν, (ean)	εἰ, (ei)	183, 184
ἐάν δὲ, (ean de)	εἰ δε, (ei de)	187
ἐάν μὴ, (ean mē)	εἰ μὴ, (ei mē)	145, 146
ἑαυτῆς, (heautēs)	ἑαυτοῦ, (heautou)	110
ἐβαπτίσθημεν, (ebaptisthēmen)	βαπτίζω, (baptizō)	70, 79
ἔδωκεν, (edōken)	δίδωμι, (didōmi)	23
ἔθετο, (etheto)	τίθημι, (tithēmi)	85, 89
ἔθνη, (ethnē)	ἔθνος, (ethnos)	5, 6, 7
εἰ μὴ, (ei mē)	εἰ μὴ, (ei mē)	141
εἴδωλα, (eidōla)	εἴδωλον, (eidōlon)	7
εἰς, (eis)	εἰς, (eis)	70, 72, 74, 76, 181
εἷς, (heis)	εἷς, (heis)	199
εἰσιν, (eisin)	ειμι, (eimi)	181, 186
εἴτε, (eite)	εἴτε, (eite)	193, 194
ἐκ, (ek)	ἐκ, (ek)	119, 120
ἕκαστος, (hekastos)	ἕκαστος, (hekastos)	193
ἑκάστῳ, (hekastō)	ἕκαστος, (hekastos)	34
ἐκκλησία, (ekklēsia)	ἐκκλησία, (ekklēsia)	209
ἐκκλησίαις, (ekklēsiais)	ἐκκλησία, (ekklēsia)	209
ἐκκλησίαν, (ekklēsian)	ἐκκλησία, (ekklēsia)	137, 138
ἔκστασις, (ekstasis)	ἔκστασις, (ekstasis)	9
ἐκτὸς, (ektos)	ἐκτός, (ektos)	141
ἔλθῃ, (elthē)	ἔρχομαι, (erchomai)	120
ἐλπίζει, (elpizei)	ἐλπίζω, (elpizō)	113
ἐν, (en)	ἐν, (en)	38, 44, 46, 70, 72, 73, 74, 75, 122, 145, 149, 169, 196
ἐνέργειαν, (energeian)	ἐνέργεια, (energeia)	27
ἐνεργεῖ, (energei)	ἐνεργέω, (energeō)	61
ἐνεργέω, (energeō)	ἐνεργέω, (energeō)	24
ἐνεργήματα, (energēmata)	ἐνέργημα, (energēma)	50
ἐνεργημάτων, (energēmatōn)	ἐνέργημα, (energēma)	24, 27, 28, 51
ἐνεργουμένην, (energoumenēn)	ἐνεργέω, (energeō)	26
ἐνεργῶν, (energōn)	ἐνεργέω, (energeō)	24, 51
ἔπειτα, (epeita)	ἔπειτα, (epeita)	86
ἐπιγίνωσκέτω, (epiginōsketō)	ἐπιγινώσκω, (epiginōskō)	228

ἐπιγνώσομαι, (epignōsomai) | ἐπιγινώσκω, (epiginōskō) | 123
ἐπιγνώσθην, (epignōsthēn) | ἐπιγινώσκω, (epiginōskō) | 123
ἐποτίσθημεν, (epotisthēmen) | ποτίζω, (potizō) | 70, 77, 79
ἑρμηνεία, (hermēneia) | ἑρμηνεία, (hermēneia) | 59, 60, 198
ἑρμηνείαν, (hermēneian) | ἑρμηνεία, (hermēneia) | 198
ἑρμηνεύω, (hermēneuō) | ἑρμηνεύω, (hermēneuō) | 139
ἐστιν, (estin) | ειμι, (eimi) | 191
ἑτέρῳ, (heterō) | ἕτερος, (heteros) | 44, 46, 50, 57
εὐλογέω, (eulogeō) | εὐλογέω, (eulogeō) | 169
εὐλογῇς, (eulogēis) | εὐλογέω, (eulogeō) | 169
εὐλογία, (eulogia) | εὐλογία, (eulogia) | 169
εὐσχήμονα, (euschēmona) | εὐσχήμων, (euschēmōn) | 68
εὐχαριστεῖς, (eucharisteis) | εὐχαριστέω, (eucharisteō) | 169
εὐχαριστίᾳ, (eucharistia) | εὐχαριστία, (eucharistia) | 169
ἔχει, (echei) | ἔχω, (echō) | 194

Z, ζ

ζηλοῖ, (zēloi) | ζῆλος, (zēlos) | 109
ζηλοῦτε, (zēloute) | ζηλόω, (zēloō) | 97, 130, 131
ζητεῖ, (zētei) | ζητέω, (zēteō) | 110
ζητέω, (zēteō) | ζητέω, (zēteō) | 110

H, η

ἤ, (ē) | ἤ, (ē) | 212, 213, 221
ἤγεσθε, (ēgesthe) | ἄγω, (agō) | 7, 8
ἦτε, (ēte) | εἰμὶ, (eimi) | 7
ἠχῶν, (ēchōn) | ἠχέω, (ēcheō) | 105

I, ι

ἰαμάτων, (iamatōn) | ἴαμα, (iama) | 46
ἰδίᾳ, (idia) | ἴδιος, (idios) | 61, 62
ἰδιῶται, (idiōtai) | ἰδιώτης, (idiōtēs) | 169, 183
ἰδιώτης, (idiōtēs) | ἰδιώτης, (idiōtēs) | 169, 170, 186
ἰδιώτου, (idiōtou) | ἰδιώτης, (idiōtēs) | 169

K, κ

κακίᾳ, (kakia) | κακός, (kakos) | 176, 177
κακόν, (kakon) | κακός, (kakos) | 111
καλύπτει, (kaluptei) | καλύπτω, (kaluptō) | 113
κατα, (kata) | κατα, (kata) | 37, 38, 42
καταργέω, (katargeō) | καταργέω, (katargeō) | 118
καταργηθήσεται, (katargēthēsetai) | καταργέω, (katargeō) | 118, 120
καταργηθήσονται, (katargēthēsontai) | καταργέω, (katargeō) | 118
κατήργηκα, (katērgēka) | καταργέω, (katargeō) | 121
καυθήσομαι, (kauthēsomai) | καίω, (kaiō) | 107
καυθήσωμαι, (kauthēsōmai) | καίω, (kaiō) | 107

καυχήσωμαι, (kauchēsōmai)   καυχαομαι, (kauchaomai)   107
κιθάρα, (kithara)   κιθάρα, (kithara)   154
κοπιῶ, (kopiō)   κοπιάω, (kopiaō)   27
κυβερνήσεις, (kubernēseis)   κυβέρνησις, (kubernēsis)   95
κυβερνήσις, (kubernēsis)   κυβέρνησις, (kubernēsis)   95
κυβερνήτης, (kubernētēs)   κυβερνήτης, (kubernētēs)   95
κύμβαλον, (kumbalon)   κύμβαλον, (kumbalon)   104, 105
κωλύετε, (kōluete)   κωλύω, (kōluō)   231

Λ, λ

λαλῶν, (lalōn)   λαλέω, (laleō)   132, 137
λογίζεσθαι, (logizesthai)   λογίζομαι, (logizomai)   111
λογίζεται, (logizetai)   λογίζομαι, (logizomai)   111
λόγος, (logos)   λόγος, (logos)   37, 38, 39, 40, 42

Μ, μ

μακροθυμεῖ, (makrothumei)   μακρόθυμος, (makrothumos)   109, 111, 113
μᾶλλον, (mallon)   μᾶλλον, (mallon)   130, 139, 140
μέγας, (megas)   μέγας, (megas)   126
μεγίστος, (megistos)   μεγίστος, (megistos)   126
μείζονα, (meizona)   μέγας, (megas)   98
μείζων, (meizōn)   μέγας, (megas)   98, 126
μὲν, (men)   μὲν, (men)   85, 96
μένει, (menei)   μένω, (menō)   124, 125
μέρος, (meros)   μέρος, (meros)   199
μέρους, (merous)   μέρος, (meros)   119, 120
μὴ, (mē)   μὴ, (mē)   231
μόνους, (monous)   μόνος, (monos)   223
μου, (mou)   ἐγώ, (egō)   161
μυστήρια, (mustēria)   μυστήριον, (mustērion)   134

Ν, ν

νηπιάζετε, (nēpiazete)   νηπιάζω, (nēpiazō)   176, 177
νοΐ, (noi)   νοῦς, (nous)   164
νοῦς, (nous)   νοῦς, (nous)   161
νυνι, (nuni)   νυνι, (nuni)   124, 125

Ο, ο

ὅ, (ho)   ὅ, (ho)   40, 84, 196
οἰκοδομέω, (oikodomeō)   οἰκοδομέω, (oikodomeō)   135
οἰκοδομην, (oikodomēn)   οἰκοδομέω, (oikodomeō)   135, 198
ὅταν, (hotan)   ὅταν, (hotan)   192
ὅτε, (hote)   ὅτε, (hote)   7
ὅτι, (hoti)   ὅτι, (hoti)   7
οὖν, (oun)   οὖν, (oun)   183, 184, 191

οὖς, (hous)   ὅς, (hos)   85

Π, π

παιδία, (paidia)	παιδίον, (paidion)	176, 177
πάντα, (panta)	πᾶς, (pas)	113
παράκλησιν, (paraklēsin)	παράκλησις, (paraklēsis)	136
παραμυθίαν, (paramuthian)	παραμυθία, (paramuthia)	136
παροξύνεται, (paroxunetai)	παροξύνω, (paroxunō)	111
παύσονται, (pausontai)	παύομαι, (pauomai)	118
περὶ δε, (peri de)	περὶ δε, (peri de)	xiii, 2, 175
περπερεύεται, (perpereuetai)	περπερεύομαι, (perpereuomai)	110,
πίπτει, (piptei)	πίπτω, (piptō)	115, 116
πιστεύει, (pisteuei)	πιστεύω, (pisteuō)	113
πνεῦμα, (pneuma)	πνεῦμα, (pneuma)	161
πνεύματι, (pneumati)	πνεῦμα, (pneuma)	134, 164, 169
πνευματικά, (pneumatika)	πνευματικός, (pneumatikos)	3, 22, 130, 132,
πνευματικός, (pneumatikos)	πνευματικός, (pneumatikos)	3, 103, 132
πνευματικῶν, (pneumatikōn)	πνευματικός, (pneumatikos)	2, 3, 22, 132
πνευμάτων, (pneumatōn)	πνεῦμα, (pneuma)	55, 56, 97, 156, 157, 228
ποτίζω, (potizō)	ποτίζω, (potizō)	77
προϊστάμενος, (proistamenos)	προΐστημι, (proistēmi)	94, 95
προΐστημι, (proistēmi)	προΐστημι, (proistēmi)	95
πρὸς, (pros)	πρὸς, (pros)	7
προφῆται, (prophētai)	προφήτης, (prophētēs)	91
προφήταις, (prophētais)	προφήτης, (prophētēs)	91
προφήτας, (prophētas)	προφήτης, (prophētēs)	91
προφητεία, (prophēteia)	προφητεία, (prophēteia)	150
προφητεῖαι, (prophēteiai)	προφητεία, (prophēteia)	118
προφητείαν, (prophēteian)	προφητεία, (prophēteia)	91
προφητεύομεν, (prophēteuomen)	προφητέω, (prophēteō)	119
προφητεύων, (prophēteuōn)	προφητέω, (prophēteō)	137
προφήτης, (prophētēs)	προφήτης, (prophētēs)	91, 92
προφήτων, (prophētōn)	προφήτης, (prophētēs)	91

Σ, σ

σάλπιγξ, (salpinx)	σάλπιγξ, (salpinx)	154
σημεῖον, (sēmeion)	σημεῖον, (sēmeion)	181
σοφίας, (sophias)	σοφία, (sophia)	37, 39
στέγει, (stegei)	στέγω, (stegō)	112, 113
στέγω, (stegō)	στέγω, (stegō)	112
συμφέρον, (sumpheron)	συμφέρω, (sumpherō)	34, 36
συνεκέρασεν, (sunekerasen)	συγκεράννυμι, (sunkerannumi)	89
συνέρχησθε, (sunerchēsthe)	συνέρχομαι, (sunerchomai)	192

συνεργοί, (sunergoi)	συνεργός, (sunergos)	26
συγχαίρει, (sunchairei)	συγχαίρω, (sunchairō)	112

T, τ

τὰ, (ta)	ὁ, (ho)	7, 110, 132
τέλειοι, (teleioi)	τέλειος, (teleios)	176, 177
τέλειον, (teleion)	τέλειος, (teleios)	120
τελειόω, (teleioō)	τελειόω, (teleioō)	120`
τῇ, (tē)	ὁ, (ho)	196
τί, (ti)	τίς, (tis)	191
τίθημι, (tithēmi)	τίθημι, (tithēmi)	85
τόπον, (topon)	τόπος, (topos)	169, 170
τότε, (tote)	τότε, (tote)	122
τῷ, (tō)	ὁ, (ho)	164

Υ, υ

ὑπερβολὴν, (huperbolēn)	ὑπερβολή, (huperbolē)	99
ὑπομένει, (hupomenei)	ὑπομένω, (hupomenō)	113

Φ, φ

φανέρωσις, (phanerōsis)	φανέρωσις, (phanerōsis)	34, 35
φυσιοῦται, (phusioutai)	φυσιόω, (phusioō)	110
φωνῆς, (phōnēs)	φωνῆς, (phōnēs)	156
φωνῶν, (phōnōn)	φωνῆς, (phōnēs)	156

Χ, χ

χαίρει, (chairei)	χαίρω, (chairō)	112
χαλκὸς, (chalkos)	χαλκὸς, (chalkos)	104, 105
χαρίζομαι, (charizomai)	χαρίζομαι, (charizomai)	20
χάριν, (charin)	χάρις, (charis)	83
χάρις, (charis)	χάρις, (charis)	20, 21, 23, 83
χάρισμα, (charisma)	χάρισμα, (charisma)	20, 21, 34, 45
χαρίσματα, (charismata)	χάρισμα, (charisma)	3, 21, 22, 28, 29, 36, 46, 47, 82, 83, 84, 88, 98, 130, 197
χαρισμάτων, (charismatōn)	χάρισμα, (charisma)	19
Χριστὸς, (Christos)	Χριστὸς, (christos)	109
χρηστεύεται, (chrēsteuetai)	χρηστεύομαι, (chrēsteuomai)	109

Ψ, ψ

ψάλλω, (psallō)	ψάλλω, (psallō)	164, 195
ψαλμὸν, (psalmon)	ψαλμός, (psalmos)	195
ψαλμός, (psalmos)	ψαλμός, (psalmos)	195
ψαλῶ, (psalō)	ψάλλω, (psallō)	164, 196
ψωμίσω, (psōmisō)	ψωμίζω, (psōmizō)	106

254

Ω, ω

ᾧ, (hō)	ὅς, (hos)	37
ὡς ἄν, (hōs an)	ὡς ἄν, (hōs an)	7
ὥστε, (hōste)	ὥστε, (hōste)	179, 180

GREEK INDEX BY LEXICAL FORM

LEXICAL FORM	*TEXTUAL FORM*	*PAGES*
Α, α		
ἀγάπη, (agapē)	ἀγάπη, (agapē)	101, 104
ἀδελφος, (adelphos)	ἀδελφοι, (adelphoi)	2, 4
ἀγνοέω, (agnoeō)	ἀγνοει, (agnoei)	5, 228
	ἀγνοεῖν, (agnoein)	2, 4
	ἀγνοεῖται, (agnoeitai)	228, 229
	ἀγνοεῖτω, (agnoeitō)	229
	ἀγνοέω, (agnoeō)	4, 229
ἄγω, (agō)	ἤγεσθε, (ēgesthe)	7, 8
αἴνιγμα, (ainigma)	αἰνίγματι, (ainigmati)	122
αἰσχρός, (aischros)	αἰσχρὸν, (aischron)	211
ἄκαρπος, (akarpos)	ἄκαρπός, (akarpos)	162
ἄλλος, (allos)	ἄλλῳ, (allō)	37, 42, 44, 46, 49, 50, 53, 55
ἀνὰ, (ana)	ἀνὰ, (ana)	199
ἀνάθεμα, (anathema)	ἀνάθεμα, (anathema)	11, 12
ἀντίλημψίς, (antilēmpsis)	ἀντιλήμψείς, (antilēmpseis)	30, 94
ἀπάγω, (apagō)	ἀπαγόμενοι, (apagomenoi)	7, 8
ἄπιστος, (apistos)	ἄπιστοι, (apistoi)	183
	ἄπιστος, (apistos)	186
ἀποκάλυψις, (apokalupsis)	ἀποκαλύψει, (apokalupsei)	149
	ἀποκάλυψιν, (apokalupsin)	197
ἀποστολος, (apostolos)	ἀποστολος, (apostolos)	89, 90
ἄρτι, (arti)	ἄρτι, (arti)	122
ἀσχήμων, (aschēmōn)	ἀσχήμονα, (aschēmona)	68
ἀσχημονέω, (aschēmoneō)	ἀσχημονεῖ, (aschēmonei)	110
αὐλός, (aulos)	αὐλὸς, (aulos)	154
αὐτός, (autos)	αὐτο, (auto)	42
ἄφωνος, (aphōnos)	ἄφωνα, (aphōna)	7
	ἄφωνον, (aphōnon)	156
Β, β		
βαπτίζω, (baptizō)	ἐβαπτίσθημεν, (ebaptisthēmen)	70, 72, 79
βάρβαρος, (barbaros)	βάρβαρος, (barbaros)	156
Γ, γ		
γὰρ, (gar)	γὰρ, (gar)	37, 120
γένος, (genos)	γένη, (genē)	57
γίνομαι, (ginomai)	γινεσθω, (ginesthō)	198, 231

γινώσκω, (ginōskō) | γινώσκομεν, (ginōskomen) | 119
| γινώσκω, (ginōskō) | 123
γλῶσσα, (glōssa) | γλῶσσαι, (glōssai) | 118
| γλώσσαν, (glōssan) | 197
| γλώσσῃ, (glōssē) | 132, 137, 160, 161, 194
| γλώσσης, (glōssēs) | 155
| γλωσσῶν, (glōssōn) | 57
γνῶσις, (gnōsis) | γνώσει, (gnōsei) | 150
| γνώσεως, (gnōseōs) | 37, 42
| γνῶσις, (gnōsis) | 42, 118
γυνή, (gunē) | γυναῖκες, (gunaikes) | 209, 210

Δ, δ

δὲ, (de) | δὲ, (de) | 18, 85, 96, 97, 124, 130, 139, 187
διὰ, (dia) | διὰ, (dia) | 37, 38, 39
διαίρεσις, (diairesis) | διαιρέσεις, (diaireseis) | 18, 23, 24
διαιρέω, (diaireō) | διαιροῦν, (diairoun) | 18, 61, 62
διακονία, (diakonia) | διακονιῶν, (diakoniōn) | 23, 28
διακρίνω, (diakrinō) | διακρίνειν, (diakrinein) | 203
| διακρινέτωσαν, (diakrinetōsan) | 55, 203
| διακρίνω, (diakrinō) | 55
διακρίσις, (diakrisis) | διακρίσεις, (diakriseis) | 55, 203
| διακρίσις, (diakrisis) | 56
διδασκαλία, (didaskalia) | διδασκαλίᾳ, (didaskalia) | 196
διδάσκολος, (didaskolos) | διδασκάλους, (didaskalous) | 196
| διδάσκων, (didaskōn) | 84, 153, 196
διδαχῇ, (didachē) | διδαχῇ, (didachē) | 152, 196
| διδαχή, (didachē) | 196
| διδαχήν, (didachēn) | 196
δίδωμι, (didōmi) | δίδοται, (didotai) | 34, 36, 37, 38, 39
| ἔδωκεν, (edōken) | 23
διερμηνεύω, (diermēneuō) | διερμηνευετής, (diermēneuetēs) | 199, 201
| διερμηνευέτω, (diermēneuetō) | 199
| διερμηνεύῃ, (diermēneuē) | 141, 142
| διερμηνεύω, (diermēneuō) | 139
διο, (dio) | διο, (dio) | 10, 160
διώκω, (diōkō) | διώκετε, (diōkete) | 130, 131
| διώκω, (diōkō) | 131
δόμα, (domata) | δόματα, (domata) | 21, 23, 82, 83, 84, 196, 197
δύναμαι, (dunamai) | δύναμαι, (dunamai) | 53

δύναμις, (dunamis)	δύναμει, (dunamei)	52
	δυνάμεων, (dunameōn)	50, 51
	δύναμιν, (dunamin)	53, 156
	δύναμις, (dunamis)	51, 52, 156
δωρεά, (dōrea)	δωρεᾶς, (dōreas)	23, 83

Ε, ε

ἑαυτοῦ, (heautou)	ἑαυτῆς, (heautēs)	110
ἐγώ, (egō)	μου, (mou)	161
ἔθνος, (ethnos)	ἔθνη, (ethnē)	5, 6, 7
εἰ, (ei)	ἐάν, (ean)	183, 184
εἰ δε, (ei de)	ἐάν δὲ, (ean de)	187
εἰ μὴ, (ei mē)	ἐάν μὴ, (ean mē)	145, 146
	εἰ μὴ, (ei mē)	141
εἴδωλον, (eidōlon)	εἴδωλα, (eidōla)	7
ειμι, (eimi)	εἰσιν, (eisin)	181, 186
	ἐστιν, (estin)	191
	ἦτε, (ēte)	7
εἰς, (eis)	εἰς, (eis)	70, 72, 74, 76, 181
εἷς, (heis)	εἷς, (heis)	199
εἴτε, (eite)	εἴτε, (eite)	193, 194
ἐκ, (ek)	ἐκ, (ek)	119, 120
ἔκάστος, (hekastos)	ἔκάστος, (hekastos)	193
	ἔκάστῳ, (hekastō)	34
ἐκκλησία, (ekklēsia)	ἐκκλησία, (ekklēsia)	209
	ἐκκλησίαις, (ekklēsiais)	209
	ἐκκλησίαν, (ekklēsian)	137, 138
ἔκστασις, (ekstasis)	ἔκστασις, (ekstasis)	9
ἐκτός, (ektos)	ἐκτὸς, (ektos)	141
ἐλπίζω, (elpizō)	ἐλπίζει, (elpizei)	113
ἐν, (en)	ἐν, (en)	38, 44, 46, 70, 72, 73, 74, 75, 122, 145, 149, 169, 196
ἐνέργεια, (energeia)	ἐνέργειαν, (energeian)	27
ἐνεργέω, (energeō)	ἐνεργεῖ, (energei)	61
	ἐνεργέω, (energeō)	24
	ἐνεργουμένην, (energoumenēn)	26
	ἐνεργῶν, (energōn)	24, 51
ἐνέργημα, (energēma)	ἐνεργημάτα, (energēmata)	50
	ἐνεργημάτων, (energēmatōn)	24, 27, 28, 51
ἔπειτα, (epeita)	ἔπειτα, (epeita)	86

258

ἐπιγινώσκω, (epiginōskō)   ἐπιγίνωσκέτω, (epiginōsketō)   228
    ἐπιγνώσομαι, (epignōsomai)   123
    ἐπιγνώσθην, (epignōsthēn)   123
ἑρμηνεία, (hermēneia)   ἑρμηνεία, (hermēneia)   59, 60, 198
    ἑρμηνείαν, (hermēneian)   198
ἑρμηνεύω, (hermēneuō)   ἑρμηνεύω, (hermēneuō)   139
ἔρχομαι, (erchomai)   ἔλθῃ, (elthē)   120
ἕτερος, (heteros)   ἑτέρῳ, (heterō)   44, 46, 50, 57
εὐλογέω, (eulogeō)   εὐλογέω, (eulogeō)   169
    εὐλογῇς, (eulogēis)   169
εὐλογία, (eulogia)   εὐλογία, (eulogia)   169
εὐσχήμων, (euschēmōn)   εὐσχήμονα, (euschēmona)   68
εὐχαριστέω, (eucharisteō)   εὐχαριστεῖς, (eucharisteis)   169
εὐχαριστία, (eucharistia)   εὐχαριστίᾳ, (eucharistia)   169
ἔχω, (echō)   ἔχει, (echei)   194

Z, ζ
ζῆλος, (zēlos)   ζηλοῖ, (zēloi)   109
ζηλόω, (zēloō)   ζηλοῦτε, (zēloute)   97, 130, 131
ζητέω, (zēteō)   ζητεῖ, (zētei)   110
    ζητέω, (zēteō)   110

H, η
ἤ, (ē)   ἤ, (ē)   212, 213, 221
ἠχέω, (ēcheō)   ἠχῶν, (ēchōn)   105

I, ι
ἴαμα, (iama)   ἰαμάτων, (iamatōn)   46
ἴδιος, (idios)   ἰδίᾳ, (idia)   61, 62
ἰδιώτης, (idiōtēs)   ἰδιῶται, (idiōtai)   169, 183
    ἰδιώτης, (idiōtēs)   169, 170, 186
    ἰδιώτου, (idiōtou)   169

K, κ
καίω, (kaiō)   καυθήσομαι, (kauthēsomai)   107
    καυθήσωμαι, (kauthēsōmai)   107
κακός, (kakos)   κακίᾳ, (kakia)   176, 177
    κακόν, (kakon)   111
καλύπτω, (kaluptō)   καλύπτει, (kaluptei)   113
κατα, (kata)   κατα, (kata)   37, 38, 42
καταργέω, (katargeō)   καταργέω, (katargeō)   118
    καταργηθήσεται, (katargēthēsetai)   118, 120
    καταργηθήσονται, (katargēthēsontai)   118
    κατήργηκα, (katērgēka)   121
καυχαομαι, (kauchaomai)   καυχήσωμαι, (kauchēsōmai)   107
κιθάρα, (kithara)   κιθάρα, (kithara)   154

κοπιάω, (kopiaō)   κοπιῶ, (kopiō)   27

κυβέρνησις, (kubernēsis)   κυβερνήσεις, (kubernēseis)   95

κυβερνήσις, (kubernēsis)   95

κυβερνήτης, (kubernētēs)   95

κύμβαλον, (kumbalon)   κύμβαλον, (kumbalon)   104, 105

κωλύω, (kōluō)   κωλύετε, (kōluete)   231

Λ, λ

λαλέω, (laleō)   λαλῶν, (lalōn)   132, 137

λογίζομαι, (logizomai)   λογίζεσθαι, (logizesthai)   111

λογίζεται, (logizetai)   111

λόγος, (logos)   λόγος, (logos)   37, 38, 39, 40, 42

Μ, μ

μακρόθυμος, (makrothumos)   μακροθυμεῖ, (makrothumei)   109, 111, 113

μᾶλλον, (mallon)   μᾶλλον, (mallon)   130, 139, 140

μέγας, (megas)   μέγας, (megas)   126

μείζονα, (meizona)   98

μείζων, (meizōn)   98, 126

μεγίστος, (megistos)   μεγίστος, (megistos)   126

μὲν, (men)   μὲν, (men)   85, 96

μένω, (menō)   μένει, (menei)   124, 125

μέρος, (meros)   μέρος, (meros)   199

μέρους, (merous)   119, 120

μή, (mē)   μή, (mē)   231

μόνος, (monos)   μόνους, (monous)   223

μυστήριον, (mustērion)   μυστήρια, (mustēria)   134

Ν, ν

νηπιάζω, (nēpiazō)   νηπιάζετε, (nēpiazete)   176, 177

νοῦς, (nous)   νοΐ, (noi)   164

νοῦς, (nous)   161

νυνι, (nuni)   νυνι, (nuni)   124, 125

Ο, ο

ὅ, (ho)   ὅ, (ho)   40, 84, 196

τὰ, (ta)   7, 110, 132

τῇ, (tē)   196

τῷ, (tō)   164

οἰκοδομέω, (oikodomeō)   οἰκοδομέω, (oikodomeō)   135

οἰκοδομην, (oikodomēn)   135, 198

ὅς, (hos)   οὓς, (hous)   85

ᾧ, (hō)   37

ὅταν, (hotan)   ὅταν, (hotan)   192

ὅτε, (hote)   ὅτε, (hote)   7

ὅτι, (hoti)   ὅτι, (hoti)   7

οὖν, (oun)	οὖν, (oun)	183, 184, 191

Π, π

παιδίον, (paidion)	παιδία, (paidia)	176, 177
πᾶς, (pas)	πάντα, (panta)	113
παράκλησις, (paraklēsis)	παράκλησιν, (paraklēsin)	136
παραμυθία, (paramuthia)	παραμυθίαν, (paramuthian)	136
παροξύνω, (paroxunō)	παροξύνεται, (paroxunetai)	111
παύομαι, (pauomai)	παύσονται, (pausontai)	118
περὶ δε, (peri de)	περὶ δε, (peri de)	xiii, 2, 175
περπερεύομαι, (perpereuomai)	περπερεύεται, (perpereuetai)	110,
πίπτω, (piptō)	πίπτει, (piptei)	115, 116
πιστεύω, (pisteuō)	πιστεύει, (pisteuei)	113
πνεῦμα, (pneuma)	πνεῦμα, (pneuma)	161
	πνεύματι, (pneumati)	134, 164, 169
	πνευμάτων, (pneumatōn)	55, 56, 97, 156, 157, 228
πνευματικός, (pneumatikos)	πνευματικά, (pneumatika)	3, 22, 130, 132,
	πνευματικός, (pneumatikos)	3, 103, 132
	πνευματικῶν, (pneumatikōn)	2, 3, 22, 132
ποτίζω, (potizō)	ἐποτίσθημεν, (epotisthēmen)	70, 77, 79
	ποτίζω, (potizō)	77
προΐστημι, (proistēmi)	προϊστάμενος, (proistamenos)	94, 95
	προΐστημι, (proistēmi)	95
πρὸς, (pros)	πρὸς, (pros)	7
προφητεία, (prophēteia)	προφητείᾳ, (prophēteia)	150
	προφητεῖαι, (prophēteiai)	118
	προφητείαν, (prophēteian)	91
προφητέω, (prophēteō)	προφητεύομεν, (prophēteuomen)	119
	προφητεύων, (prophēteuōn)	137
προφήτης, (prophētēs)	προφῆται, (prophētai)	91
	προφήταις, (prophētais)	91
	προφήτας, (prophētas)	91
	προφήτης, (prophētēs)	91, 92
	προφήτων, (prophētōn)	91

Σ, σ

σάλπιγξ, (salpinx)	σάλπιγξ, (salpinx)	154
σημεῖον, (sēmeion)	σημεῖον, (sēmeion)	181
σοφία, (sophia)	σοφίας, (sophias)	37, 39
στέγω, (stegō)	στέγει, (stegei)	112, 113
	στέγω, (stegō)	112
συγκεράννυμι, (sunkerannumi)	συνεκέρασεν, (sunekerasen)	89
συμφέρω, (sumpherō)	συμφέρον, (sumpheron)	34, 36

συνέρχομαι, (sunerchomai)   συνέρχησθε, (sunerchēsthe)   192
συνεργός, (sunergos)   συνεργοί, (sunergoi)   26
συγχαίρω, (sunchairō)   συγχαίρει, (sunchairei)   112

T, τ

τέλειος, (teleios)   τέλειοι, (teleioi)   176, 177
 τέλειον, (teleion)   120
τελειόω, (teleioō)   τελειόω, (teleioō)   120`
τίθημι, (tithēmi)   ἔθετο, (etheto)   85, 89
 τίθημι, (tithēmi)   85
τίς, (tis)   τί, (ti)   191
τόπος, (topos)   τόπον, (topon)   169, 170
τότε, (tote)   τότε, (tote)   122

Υ, υ

ὑπερβολή, (huperbolē)   ὑπερβολὴν, (huperbolēn)   99
ὑπομένω, (hupomenō)   ὑπομένει, (hupomenei)   113

Φ, φ

φανέρωσις, (phanerōsis)   φανέρωσις, (phanerōsis)   34, 35
φυσιόω, (phusioō)   φυσιοῦται, (phusioutai)   110
φωνῆς, (phōnēs)   φωνῆς, (phōnēs)   156
 φωνῶν, (phōnōn)   156

X, χ

χαίρω, (chairō)   χαίρει, (chairei)   112
χαλκὸς, (chalkos)   χαλκὸς, (chalkos)   104, 105
χαρίζομαι, (charizomai)   χαρίζομαι, (charizomai)   20
χάρις, (charis)   χάριν, (charin)   83
 χάρις, (charis)   20, 21, 23, 83
χάρισμα, (charisma)   χάρισμα, (charisma)   20, 21, 34, 45
 χαρίσματα, (charismata)   3, 21, 22, 28, 29, 36,
  46, 47, 82, 83, 84, 88,
  98, 130, 197
 χαρισμάτων, (charismatōn)   19
χρηστεύομαι, (chrēsteuomai)   χρηστεύεται, (chrēsteuetai)   109
Χριστὸς, (christos)   Χριστὸς, (Christos)   109

Ψ, ψ

ψάλλω, (psallō)   ψάλλω, (psallō)   164, 195
 ψαλῶ, (psalō)   164, 196
ψαλμός, (psalmos)   ψαλμὸν, (psalmon)   195
 ψαλμός, (psalmos)   195
ψωμίζω, (psōmizō)   ψωμίσω, (psōmisō)   106

Ω, ω

ὡς ἄν, (hōs an)   ὡς ἄν, (hōs an)   7
ὥστε, (hōste)   ὥστε, (hōste)   179, 180

TRANSLITERATED GREEK INDEX BY TEXTUAL FORM

TEXTUAL FORM	LEXICAL FORM	PAGES
A		
adelphoi, (ἀδελφοι)	(adelphos, ἀδελφος)	2, 4
agapē, (ἀγάπη)	(agapē, ἀγάπη)	101, 104
agnoei, (ἀγνοει)	(agnoeō, ἀγνοέω)	5, 228
agnoein, (ἀγνοεῖν)	(agnoeō, ἀγνοέω)	2, 4
agnoeitai, (ἀγνοεῖται)	(agnoeō, ἀγνοέω)	228, 229
agnoeitō, (ἀγνοεῖτω)	(agnoeō, ἀγνοέω)	229
agnoeō, (ἀγνοέω)	(agnoeō, ἀγνοέω)	4, 229
ainigmati, (αἰνίγματι)	(ainigma, αἴνιγμα)	122
aischron, (αἰσχρὸν)	(aischros, αἰσχρός)	211
akarpos, (ἄκαρπός)	(akarpos, ἄκαρπος)	162
allō, (ἄλλῳ)	(allos, ἄλλος)	37, 42, 44, 46, 49, 50, 53, 55
ana, (ἀνὰ)	(ana, ἀνὰ)	199
anathema, (ἀνάθεμα)	(anathema, ἀνάθεμα)	11, 12
antilēmpseis, (ἀντιλήμψεις)	(antilēmpsis, ἀντίλημψίς)	30, 94
apagomenoi, (ἀπαγόμενοι)	(apagō, ἀπάγω)	7, 8
aphōna, (ἄφωνα)	(aphōnos, ἄφωνος)	7
aphōnon, (ἄφωνον)	(aphōnos, ἄφωνος)	156
apistoi, (ἄπιστοι)	(apistos, ἄπιστος)	183
apistos, (ἄπιστος)	(apistos, ἄπιστος)	186
apokalupsei, (ἀποκαλύψει)	(apokalupsis, ἀποκάλυψις)	149
apokalupsin, (ἀποκάλυψιν)	(apokalupsis, ἀποκάλυψις)	197
apostolos, (ἀποστολος)	(apostolos, ἀποστολος)	89, 90
arti, (ἄρτι)	(arti, ἄρτι)	122
aschēmona, (ἀσχήμονα)	(aschēmōn, ἀσχήμων)	68
aschēmonei, (ἀσχημονεῖ)	(aschēmoneō, ἀσχημονέω)	110
aulos, (αὐλὸς)	(aulos, αὐλός)	154
auto, (αὐτο)	(autos, αὐτός)	42
B		
barbaros, (βάρβαρος)	(barbaros, βάρβαρος)	156
C		
chairei, (χαίρει)	(chairō, χαίρω)	112
chalkos, (χαλκὸς)	(chalkos, χαλκὸς)	104, 105
charin, (χάριν)	(charis, χάρις)	83
charis, (χάρις)	(charis, χάρις)	20, 21, 23, 83
charisma, (χάρισμα)	(charisma, χάρισμα)	20, 21, 34, 45

charismata, (χαρίσματα)   (charisma, χάρισμα)   3, 21, 22, 28, 29, 36, 46, 47, 82, 83, 84, 88, 98, 130, 197

charismatōn, (χαρισμάτων)   (charisma, χάρισμα)   19
charizomai, (χαρίζομαι)   (charizomai, χαρίζομαι)   20
chrēsteuetai, (χρηστεύεται)   (chrēsteuomai, χρηστεύομαι)   109
Christos, (Χριστὸς)   (Christos, Χριστὸς)   109

D

de, (δὲ)   (de, δὲ)   18, 85, 96, 97, 124, 130, 139, 187

dia, (διὰ)   (dia, διὰ)   37, 38, 39
diaireseis, (διαιρέσεις)   (diairesis, διαίρεσις)   18, 23, 24
diairoun, (διαιροῦν)   (diaireō, διαιρέω)   18, 61, 62
diakoniōn, (διακονιῶν)   (diakonia, διακονία)   23, 28
diakrinein, (διακρίνειν)   (diakrinō, διακρίνω)   203
diakrinetōsan, (διακρινέτωσαν)   (diakrinō, διακρίνω)   55, 203
diakrinō, (διακρίνω)   (diakrinō, διακρίνω)   55
diakriseis, (διακρίσεις)   (diakrisis, διακρίσις)   55, 203
diakrisis, (διακρίσις)   (diakrisis, διακρίσις)   56
didaskalia, (διδασκαλία)   (didaskalia, διδασκαλία)   196
didaskalous, (διδασκάλους)   (didaskolos, διδάσκολος)   196
didaskōn, (διδάσκων)   (didaskolos, διδάσκολος)   84, 153, 196
didachē, (διδαχῇ)   (didachē, διδαχῇ)   152, 196
didachēn, (διδαχήγ)   (didachē, διδαχῇ)   196
didotai, (δίδοται)   (didōmi, δίδωμι)   34, 36, 37, 38, 39

diermēneuē, (διερμηνεύῃ)   (diermēneuō, διερμηνεύω)   141, 142
diermēneuetēs, (διερμηνευετής)   (diermēneuō, διερμηνεύω)   199, 201
diermēneuetō, (διερμηνευέτω)   (diermēneuō, διερμηνεύω)   199
diermēneuō, (διερμηνεύω)   (diermēneuō, διερμηνεύω)   139
dio, (διο)   (dio, διο)   10, 160
diōkete, (διώκετε)   (diōkō, διώκω)   130, 131
diōkō, (διώκω)   (diōkō, διώκω)   131
domata, (δόματα)   (domata, δόμα)   21, 23, 82, 83, 84, 196, 197

dōreas, (δωρεᾶς)   (dōrea, δωρεά)   23, 83
dunamai, (δύναμαι)   (dunamai, δύναμαι)   53
dunamei, (δύναμει)   (dunamis, δύναμις)   52
dunameōn, (δυνάμεων)   (dunamis, δύναμις)   50, 51
dunamin, (δύναμιν)   (dunamis, δύναμις)   53, 156
dunamis, (δύναμις)   (dunamis, δύναμις)   51, 52, 156

264

E

ē, (ἤ)	(ē, ἤ)	212, 213, 221
ean, (ἐὰν)	(ei, εἰ)	183, 184
ean de, (ἐάν δὲ)	(ei de, εἰ δε)	187
ean mē, (ἐάν μὴ)	(ei mē, εἰ μὴ)	145, 146
ebaptisthēmen,, (ἐβαπτίσθημεν)	(baptizō, βαπτίζω)	70, 79
echei, (ἔχει)	(echō, ἔχω)	194
ēchōn, (ἠχῶν)	(ēcheō, ἠχέω)	105
edōken, (ἔδωκεν)	(didōmi, δίδωμι)	23
ēgesthe, (ἤγεσθε)	(agō, ἄγω)	7, 8
ei mē, (εἰ μὴ)	(ei mē, εἰ μὴ)	141
eidōla, (εἴδωλα)	(eidōlon, εἴδωλον)	7.
eis, (εἰς)	(eis, εἰς)	70, 72, 74, 76, 181
eisin, (εἰσιν)	(eimi, ειμι)	181, 186
eite, (εἴτε)	(eite, εἴτε)	193, 194
ek, (ἐκ)	(ek, ἐκ)	119, 120
ekklēsia, (ἐκκλησία)	(ekklēsia, ἐκκλησία)	209
ekklēsiais, (ἐκκλησίαις)	(ekklēsia, ἐκκλησία)	209
ekklēsian, (ἐκκλησίαν)	(ekklēsia, ἐκκλησία)	137, 138
ekstasis, (ἔκστασις)	(ekstasis, ἔκστασις)	9
ektos, (ἐκτὸς)	(ektos, ἐκτός)	141
elpizei, (ἐλπίζει)	(elpizō, ἐλπίζω)	113
elthē, (ἔλθῃ)	(erchomai, ἔρχομαι)	120
en, (ἐν)	(en, ἐν)	38, 44, 46, 70, 72, 73, 74, 75, 122, 145, 149, 169, 196
energei, (ἐνεργεῖ)	(energeō, ἐνεργέω)	61
energeian, (ἐνέργειαν)	(energeia, ἐνέργεια)	27
energēmata, (ἐνεργημάτα)	(energēma, ἐνέργημα)	50
energēmatōn, (ἐνεργημάτων)	(energēma, ἐνέργημα)	24, 27, 28, 51
energeō, (ἐνεργέω)	(energeō, ἐνεργέω)	24
energōn, (ἐνεργῶν)	(energeō, ἐνεργέω)	24, 51
energoumenēn, (ἐνεργουμένην)	(energeō, ἐνεργέω)	26
epeita, (ἔπειτα)	(epeita, ἔπειτα)	86
epiginōsketō, (ἐπιγίνωσκέτω)	(epiginōskō, ἐπιγινώσκω)	228
epignōsomai, (ἐπιγνώσομαι)	(epiginōskō, ἐπιγινώσκω)	123
epignōsthēn, (ἐπιγνώσθην)	(epiginōskō, ἐπιγινώσκω)	123
epotisthēmen, (ἐποτίσθημεν)	(potizō, ποτίζω)	70, 77, 79
estin, (ἐστιν)	(eimi, ειμι)	191
ēte, (ἦτε)	(eimi, εἰμὶ)	7
etheto, (ἔθετο)	(tithēmi, τίθημι)	85, 89

ethnē, (ἔθνη) | (ethnos, ἔθνος) | 5, 6, 7
eucharisteis, (εὐχαριστεῖς) | (eucharisteō, εὐχαριστέω) | 169
eucharistia, (εὐχαριστία) | (eucharistia, εὐχαριστία) | 169
eulogēis, (εὐλογῇς) | (eulogeō, εὐλογέω) | 169
eulogeō, (εὐλογέω) | (eulogeō, εὐλογέω) | 169
eulogia, (εὐλογία) | (eulogia, εὐλογία) | 169
euschēmona, (εὐσχήμονα) | (euschēmōn, εὐσχήμων) | 68

G

gar, (γὰρ) | (gar, γὰρ) | 37, 120
genē, (γένη) | (genos, γένος) | 57
ginesthō, (γινεσθω) | (ginomai, γίνομαι) | 198, 231
ginōskō, (γινώσκω) | (ginōskō, γινώσκω) | 123
ginōskomen, (γινώσκομεν) | (ginōskō, γινώσκω) | 119
glōssai, (γλώσσαι) | (glōssa, γλῶσσα) | 118
glōssan, (γλώσσαν) | (glōssa, γλῶσσα) | 197
glōssē, (γλώσσῃ) | (glōssa, γλῶσσα) | 132, 137, 160, 161, 194
glōssēs, (γλώσσης) | (glōssa, γλῶσσα) | 155
glōssōn, (γλωσσῶν) | (glōssa, γλῶσσα) | 57
gnōsei, (γνώσει) | (gnōsis, γνῶσις) | 150
gnōseōs, (γνώσεως) | (gnōsis, γνῶσις) | 37, 42
gnōsis, (γνώσις) | (gnōsis, γνῶσις) | 42, 118
gunaikes, (γυναῖκες) | (gunē, γυνή) | 209, 210

H

heautēs, (ἑαυτῆς) | (heautou, ἑαυτοῦ) | 110
heis, (εἷς) | (heis, εἷς) | 199
hekastō, (ἑκάστῳ) | (hekastos, ἑκάστος) | 34
hekastos, (ἑκάστος) | (hekastos, ἑκάστος) | 193
hermēneia, (ἑρμηνεία) | (hermēneia, ἑρμηνεία) | 59, 60, 198
hermēneian, (ἑρμηνείαν) | (hermēneia, ἑρμηνεία) | 198
hermēneuō, (ἑρμηνεύω) | (hermēneuō, ἑρμηνεύω) | 139
heterō, (ἑτέρῳ) | (heteros, ἑτέρος) | 44, 46, 50, 57
ho, (ὅ) | (ho, ὅ) | 40, 84, 196
hō, (ᾧ) | (hos, ὅς) | 37
hōs an, (ὡς ἄν) | (hōs an, ὡς ἄν) | 7
hōste, (ὥστε) | (hōste, ὥστε) | 179, 180
hotan, (ὅταν) | (hotan, ὅταν) | 192
hote, (ὅτε) | (hote, ὅτε) | 7
hoti, (ὅτι) | (hoti, ὅτι) | 7
hous, (οὓς) | (hos, ὅς) | 85
huperbolēn, (ὑπερβολὴν) | (huperbolē, ὑπερβολή) | 99
hupomenei, (ὑπομένει) | (hupomenō, ὑπομένω) | 113

266

I

iamatōn, (ἰαμάτων)	(iama, ἴαμα)	46
idia, (ἰδίᾳ)	(idios, ἴδιος)	61, 62
idiōtai, (ἰδιῶται)	(idiōtēs, ἰδιώτης)	169, 183
idiōtēs, (ἰδιώτης)	(idiōtēs, ἰδιώτης)	169, 170, 186
idiōtou, (ἰδιώτου)	(idiōtēs, ἰδιώτης)	169

K

kakia, (κακίᾳ)	(kakos, κακός)	176, 177
kakon, (κακόν)	(kakos, κακός)	111
kaluptei, (καλύπτει)	(kaluptō, καλύπτω)	113
kata, (κατα)	(kata, κατα)	37, 38, 42
katargeō, (καταργέω)	(katargeō, καταργέω)	118
katargēthēsetai, (καταργηθήσεται)	(katargeō, καταργέω)	118, 120
katargēthēsontai, (καταργηθήσονται)	(katargeō, καταργέω)	118
katērgēka, (κατήργηκα)	(katargeō, καταργέω)	121
kauchēsōmai, (καυχήσωμαι)	(kauchaomai, καυχαομαι)	107
kauthēsomai, (καυθήσομαι)	(kaiō, καίω)	107
kauthēsōmai, (καυθήσωμαι)	(kaiō, καίω)	107
kithara, (κιθάρα)	(kithara, κιθάρα)	154
kōluete, (κωλύετε)	(kōluō, κωλύω)	231
kopiō, (κοπιῶ)	(kopiaō, κοπιάω)	27
kubernēseis, (κυβερνήσεις)	(kubernēsis, κυβέρνησις)	95
kubernēsis, (κυβερνήσις)	(kubernēsis, κυβέρνησις)	95
kubernētēs, (κυβερνήτης)	(kubernētēs, κυβερνήτης)	95
kumbalon, (κύμβαλον)	(kumbalon, κύμβαλον)	104, 105

L

lalōn, (λαλῶν)	(laleō, λαλέω)	132, 137
logizesthai, (λογίζεσθαι)	(logizomai, λογίζομαι)	111
logizetai, (λογίζεταί)	(logizomai, λογίζομαι)	111
logos, (λόγος)	(logos, λόγος)	37, 38, 39, 40, 42

M

makrothumei, (μακροθυμεῖ)	(makrothumos, μακρόθυμος)	109, 111, 113
mallon, (μᾶλλον)	(mallon, μᾶλλον)	130, 139, 140
mē, (μή)	(mē, μή)	231
megas, (μέγας)	(megas, μέγας)	126
megistos, (μέγιστος)	(megistos, μεγίστος)	126
meizōn, (μείζων)	(megas, μέγας)	98, 126
meizona, (μείζονα)	(megas, μέγας)	98
men, (μὲν)	(men, μὲν)	85, 96
menei, (μένει)	(menō, μένω)	124, 125
meros, (μέρος)	(meros, μέρος)	199

merous, (μέρους)	(meros, μέρος)	119, 120
monous, (μόνους)	(monos, μόνος)	223
mou, (μου)	(egō, ἐγώ)	161
mustēria, (μυστήρια)	(mustērion, μυστήριον)	134

N

nēpiazete, (νηπιάζετε)	(nēpiazō, νηπιάζω)	176, 177
noi, (νοΐ)	(nous, νοῦς)	164
nous, (νοῦς)	(nous, νοῦς)	161
nuni, (νυνι)	(nuni, νυνι)	124, 125

O

oikodomēn, (οἰκοδομην)	(oikodomeō, οἰκοδομέω)	135, 198
oikodomeō, (οἰκοδομέω)	(oikodomeō, οἰκοδομέω)	135
oun, (οὖν)	(oun, οὖν)	183, 184, 191

P

paidia, (παιδία)	(paidion, παιδίον)	176, 177
panta, (πάντα)	(pas, πᾶς)	113
paraklēsin, (παράκλησιν)	(paraklēsis, παράκλησις)	136
paramuthian, (παραμυθίαν)	(paramuthia, παραμυθία)	136
paroxunetai, (παροξύνεται)	(paroxunō, παροξύνω)	111
pausontai, (παύσονται)	(pauomai, παύομαι)	118
peri de, (περὶ δε)	(peri de, περὶ δε)	xiii, 2, 175
perpereuetai, (περπερεύεται)	(perpereuomai, περπερεύομαι)	110,
phanerōsis, (φανέρωσις)	(phanerōsis, φανέρωσις)	34, 35
phōnēs, (φωνῆς)	(phōnēs, φωνῆς)	156
phōnōn, (φωνῶν)	(phōnēs, φωνῆς)	156
phusioutai, (φυσιοῦται)	(phusioō, φυσιόω)	110
piptei, (πίπτει)	(piptō, πίπτω)	115, 116
pisteuei, (πιστεύει)	(pisteuō, πιστεύω)	113
pneuma, (πνεῦμα)	(pneuma, πνεῦμα)	161
pneumati, (πνεύματι)	(pneuma, πνεῦμα)	134, 164, 169
pneumatika, (πνευματικά)	(pneumatikos, πνευματικός)	3, 22, 130, 132,
pneumatikōn, (πνευματικῶν)	(pneumatikos, πνευματικός)	2, 3, 22, 132
pneumatikos, (πνευματικός)	(pneumatikos, πνευματικός)	3, 103, 132
pneumatōn, (πνευμάτων)	(pneuma, πνεῦμα)	55, 56, 97, 156, 157, 228
potizō, (ποτίζω)	(potizō, ποτίζω)	77
proistamenos, (προϊστάμενος)	(proistēmi, προΐστημι)	94, 95
proistēmi, (προΐστημι)	(proistēmi, προΐστημι)	95
prophētai, (προφήται)	(prophētēs, προφήτης)	91
prophētais, (προφήταις)	(prophētēs, προφήτης)	91
prophētas, (προφήτας)	(prophētēs, προφήτης)	91
prophēteia, (προφητείᾳ)	(prophēteia, προφητεία)	150

268

prophēteiai, (προφητεῖαι)	(prophēteia, προφητεία)	118
prophēteian, (προφητείαν)	(prophēteia, προφητεία)	91
prophētēs, (προφήτης)	(prophētēs, προφήτης)	91, 92
prophēteuomen, (προφητεύομεν)	(prophēteō, προφητέω)	119
prophēteuōn, (προφητεύων)	(prophēteō, προφητέω)	137
prophētōn, (προφήτων)	(prophētēs, προφήτης)	91
pros, (πρὸς)	(pros, πρὸς)	7
psallō, (ψάλλω)	(psallō, ψάλλω)	164, 195
psalmon, (ψαλμὸν)	(psalmos, ψαλμός)	195
psalmos, (ψαλμός)	(psalmos, ψαλμός)	195
psalō, (ψαλῶ)	(psallō, ψάλλω)	164, 196
psōmisō, (ywmivsw)	(psōmizō, ψωμίζω)	106

S

sophias, (σοφίας)	(sophia, σοφία)	37, 39
stegei, (στέγει)	(stegō, στέγω)	112, 113
stegō, (στέγω)	(stegō, στέγω)	112
sumpheron, (συμφέρον)	(sumpherō, συμφέρω)	34, 36
sunchairei, (συγχαίρει)	(sunchairō, συγχαίρω)	112
sunekerasen, (συνεκέρασεν)	(sunkerannumi, συγκεράννυμι)	89
sunerchēsthe, (συνέρχησθε)	(sunerchomai, συνέρχομαι)	192
sunergoi, (συνεργοί)	(sunergos, συνεργός)	26

T

ta, (τὰ)	(ho, ὅ)	7, 110, 132
teleioi, (τέλειοι)	(teleios, τέλειος)	176, 177
teleion, (τέλειον)	(teleios, τέλειος)	120
teleioō, (τελειόω)	(teleioō, τελειόω)	120
tē, (τῇ)	(ho, ὅ)	196
ti, (τί)	(tis, τίς)	191
tithēmi, (τίθημι)	(tithēmi, τίθημι)	85
tō, (τῷ)	(ho, ὅ)	164
topon, (τόπον)	(topos, τόπος)	169, 170
tote, (τότε)	(tote, τότε)	122

Z

zēloi, (ζηλοῖ)	(zēlos, ζῆλος)	109
zēloute, (ζηλοῦτε)	(zēloō, ζηλόω)	97, 130, 131
zētei, (ζητεῖ)	(zēteō, ζητέω)	110
zēteō, (ζητέω)	(zēteō, ζητέω)	110

TRANSLITERATED GREEK INDEX BY LEXICAL FORM

LEXICAL FORM	TEXTUAL FORM	PAGES
A		
adelphos, (ἀδελφος)	adelphoi, (ἀδελφοι)	2, 4
agapē, (ἀγάπη)	agapē, (ἀγάπη)	101, 104
agnoeō, (ἀγνοέω)	agnoei, (ἀγνοει)	5, 228
	agnoein, (ἀγνοεῖν)	2, 4
	agnoeitai, (ἀγνοεῖται)	228, 229
	agnoeitō, (ἀγνοεῖτω)	229
	agnoeō, (ἀγνοέω)	4, 229
agō, (ἄγω)	ēgesthe, (ἤγεσθε)	7, 8
ainigma, (αἴνιγμα)	ainigmati, (αἰνίγματι)	122
aischros, (αἰσχρός)	aischron, (αἰσχρὸν)	211
akarpos, (ἄκαρπος)	akarpos, (ἄκαρπός)	162
allos, (ἄλλος)	allō, (ἄλλῳ)	37, 42, 44, 46, 49, 50, 53, 55
ana, (ἀνὰ)	ana, (ἀνὰ)	199
anathema, (ἀνάθεμα)	anathema, (ἀνάθεμα)	11, 12
antilēmpsis, (ἀντίλημψίς)	antilēmpseis, (ἀντιλήμψείς)	30, 94
apagō, (ἀπάγω)	apagomenoi, (ἀπαγόμενοι)	7, 8
aphōnos, (ἄφωνος)	aphōna, (ἄφωνα)	7
	aphōnon, (ἄφωνον)	156
apistos, (ἄπιστος)	apistoi, (ἄπιστοι)	183
	apistos, (ἄπιστος)	186
apokalupsis, (ἀποκάλυψις)	apokalupsei, (ἀποκάλυψει)	149
	apokalupsin, (ἀποκάλυψιν)	197
apostolos, (ἀποστολος)	apostolos, (ἀποστολος)	89, 90
arti, (ἄρτι)	arti, (ἄρτι)	122
aschēmōn, (ἀσχήμων)	aschēmona, (ἀσχήμονα)	68
aschēmoneō, (ἀσχημονέω)	aschēmonei, (ἀσχημονεῖ)	110
aulos, (αὐλός)	aulos, (αὐλὸς)	154
autos, (αὐτός)	auto, (αὐτο)	42
B		
baptizō, (βαπτίζω)	baptizō, (βαπτίζω)	72
	ebaptisthēmen, (ἐβαπτίσθημεν)	70, 79
barbaros, (βάρβαρος)	barbaros, (βάρβαρος)	156
C		
chairō, (χαίρω)	chairei, (χαίρει)	112
chalkos, (χαλκὸς)	chalkos, (χαλκὸς)	104, 105

270

charis, (χάρις)	charin, (χάριν)	83
	charis, (χάρις)	20, 21, 23, 83
charisma, (χάρισμα)	charisma, (χάρισμα)	20, 21, 34, 45
	charismata, (χαρίσματα)	3, 21, 22, 28, 29, 36, 46, 47, 82, 83, 84, 88, 98, 130, 197
	charismatōn, (χαρισμάτων)	19
charizomai, (χαρίζομαι)	charizomai, (χαρίζομαι)	20
chrēsteuomai, (χρηστεύομαι)	chrēsteuetai, (χρηστεύεται)	109
Christos, (Χριστὸς)	Christos, (Χριστὸς)	109

D

de, (δὲ)	de, (δὲ)	18, 85, 96, 97, 124, 130, 139, 187
dia, (διὰ)	dia, (διὰ)	37, 38, 39
diaireō, (διαιρέω)	diairoun, (διαιροῦν)	18, 61, 62
diairesis, (διαίρεσις)	diaireseis, (διαιρέσεις)	18, 23, 24
diakonia, (διακονία)	diakoniōn, (διακονιῶν)	23, 28
diakrinō, (διακρίνω)	diakrinein, (διακρίνειν)	203
	diakrinetōsan, (διακρινέτωσαν)	55, 203
	diakrinō, (διακρίνω)	55
diakrisis, (διακρίσις)	diakriseis, (διακρίσεις)	55, 203
	diakrisis, (διακρίσις)	56
didaskalia, (διδασκαλία)	didaskalia, (διδασκαλίᾳ)	196
didaskalos, (διδάσκαλος)	didaskalous, (διδασκάλους)	196
	didaskōn, (διδάσκων)	84, 153, 196
didachē, (διδαχῇ)	didachē, (διδαχῇ)	152, 196
	didachēn, (διδαχήγ)	196
didōmi, (δίδωμι)	didotai, (δίδοται)	34, 36, 37, 38, 39
	edōken, (ἔδωκεν)	23
diermēneuō, (διερμηνεύω)	diermēneuē, (διερμηνεύη)	141, 142
	diermēneuetēs, (διερμηνευετής)	199, 201
	diermēneuetō, (διερμηνευέτω)	199
	diermēneuō, (διερμηνεύω)	139
dio, (διο)	dio, (διο)	10, 160
diōkō, (διώκω)	diōkete, (διώκετε)	130, 131
	diōkō, (διώκω)	131
domata, (δόμα)	domata, (δόματα)	21, 23, 82, 83, 84, 196, 197
dōrea, (δωρεά)	dōreas, (δωρεᾶς)	23, 83
dunamai, (δύναμαι)	dunamai, (δύναμαι)	53

dunamis, (δύναμις)   dunamei, (δύναμει)   52
                           dunameōn, (δυνάμεων)   50, 51
                           dunamin, (δύναμιν)   53, 156
                           dunamis, (δύναμις)   51, 52, 156

E

ē, (ἤ)   ē, (ἤ)   212, 213, 221
ei, (εἰ)   ean, (ἐὰν)   183, 184
ei de, (εἰ δε)   ean de, (ἐάν δὲ)   187
ei mē, (εἰ μὴ)   ean mē, (ἐάν μὴ)   145, 146
                           ei mē, (εἰ μὴ)   141
ēcheō, (ἠχέω)   ēchōn, (ἠχῶν)   105
echō, (ἐχω)   echei, (ἔχει)   194
egō, (ἐγώ)   mou, (μου)   161
eidōlon, (εἴδωλον)   eidōla, (εἴδωλα)   7
eimi, (ειμι)   eisin, (εἰσιν)   181, 186
                           estin, (ἐστιν)   191
                           ēte, (ἦτε)   7
eis, (εἰς)   eis, (εἰς)   70, 72, 74, 76,
                                                           181
eite, (εἴτε)   eite, (εἴτε)   193, 194
ek, (ἐκ)   ek, (ἐκ)   119, 120
ekklēsia, (ἐκκλησία)   ekklēsia, (ἐκκλησία)   209
                           ekklēsiais, (ἐκκλησίαις)   209
                           ekklēsian, (ἐκκλησίαν)   137, 138
ekstasis, (ἔκστασις)   ekstasis, (ἔκστασις)   9
ektos, (ἐκτός)   ektos, (ἐκτὸς)   141
elpizō, (ἐλπίζω)   elpizei, (ἐλπίζει)   113
en, (ἐν)   en, (ἐν)   38, 44, 46, 70,
                                                           72, 73, 74, 75,
                                                           122, 145, 149,
                                                           169, 196
energeia, (ἐνέργεια)   energeian, (ἐνέργειαν)   27
energēma, (ἐνέργημα)   energēmata, (ἐνεργηγμάτα)   50
                           energēmatōn, (ἐνεργημάτων)   24, 27, 28, 51
energeō, (ἐνεργέω)   energei, (ἐνεργεῖ)   61
                           energeō, (ἐνεργέω)   24
                           energōn, (ἐνεργῶν)   24, 51
                           energoumenēn, (ἐνεργουμένην)   26
epeita, (ἔπειτα)   epeita, (ἔπειτα)   86
epiginōskō, (ἐπιγινώσκω)   epiginōsketō, (ἐπιγίνωσκέτω)   228
                           epignōsomai, (ἐπιγνώσομαι)   123
                           epignōsthēn, (ἐπιγνώσθην)   123
erchomai, (ἔρχομαι)   elthē, (ἔλθῃ)   120

ethnos, (ἔθνος)	ethnē, (ἔθνη)	5, 6, 7
eucharisteō, (εὐχαριστέω)	eucharisteis, (εὐχαριστεῖς)	169
eucharistia, (εὐχαριστία)	eucharistia, (εὐχαριστίᾳ)	169
eulogeō, (εὐλογέω)	eulogēis, (εὐλογῇς)	169
	eulogeō, (εὐλογέω)	169
eulogia, (εὐλογία)	eulogia, (εὐλογία)	169
euschēmōn, (εὐσχήμων)	euschēmona, (εὐσχήμονα)	68

G

gar, (γὰρ)	gar, (γὰρ)	37, 120
genos, (γένος)	genē, (γένη)	57
ginomai, (γίνομαι)	ginesthō, (γινεσθω)	198, 231
ginōskō, (γινώσκω)	ginōskō, (γινώσκω)	123
	ginōskomen, (γινώσκομεν)	119
glōssa, (γλῶσσα)	glōssai, (γλώσσαι)	118
	glōssan, (γλώσσαν)	197
	glōssē, (γλώσσῃ)	132, 137, 160, 161, 194
	glōssēs, (γλώσσης)	155
	glōssōn, (γλωσσῶν)	57
gnōsis, (γνῶσις)	gnōsei, (γνώσει)	150
	gnōseōs, (γνώσεως)	37, 42
	gnōsis, (γνώσις)	42, 118
gunē, (γυνή)	gunaikes, (γυναῖκες)	209, 210

H

heautou, (ἑαυτοῦ)	heautēs, (ἑαυτῆς)	110
heis, (εἷς)	heis, (εἷς)	199
hekastos, (ἕκαστος)	hekastō, (ἑκάστῳ)	34
	hekastos, (ἕκαστος)	193
hermēneia, (ἑρμηνεία)	hermēneia, (ἑρμηνεία)	59, 60, 198
	hermēneian, (ἑρμηνείαν)	198
hermēneuō, (ἑρμηνεύω)	hermēneuō, (ἑρμηνεύω)	139
heteros, (ἑτέρος)	heterō, (ἑτέρῳ)	44, 46, 50, 57
ho, (ὁ)	ho, (ὁ)	40, 84, 196
	ta, (τὰ)	7, 110, 132
	tē, (τῇ)	196
	tō, (τῷ)	164
hos, (ὅς)	hō, (ᾧ)	37
	hous, (οὺς)	85
hōs an , (ὡς ἄν)	hōs an , [ὡς ἄν)	7
hōste, (ὥστε)	hōste, (ὥστε)	179, 180
hotan, (ὅταν)	hotan, (ὅταν)	192
hote, (ὅτε)	hote, (ὅτε)	7

hoti, (ὅτι) hoti, (ὅτι) 7
huperbolē, (ὑπερβολή) huperbolēn, (ὑπερβολὴν) 99
hupomenō, (ὑπομένω) hupomenei, (ὑπομένει) 113

I

iama, (ἴαμα) iamatōn, (ἰαμάτων) 46
idios, (ἴδιος) idia, (ἰδίᾳ) 61, 62
idiōtēs, (ἰδιώτης) idiōtai, (ἰδιῶται) 169, 183
　idiōtēs, (ἰδιώτης) 169, 170, 186
　idiōtou, (ἰδιώτου) 169

K

kaiō, (καίω) kauthēsomai, (καυθήσομαι) 107
　kauthēsōmai, (καυθήσωμαι) 107
kakos, (κακός) kakia, (κακία) 176, 177
　kakon, (κακόν) 111
kaluptō, (καλύπτω) kaluptei, (καλύπτει) 113
kata, (κατα) kata, (κατα) 37, 38, 42
katargeō, (καταργέω) katargeō, (καταργέω) 118
　katargēthēsetai, (καταργηθήσεται) 118, 120
　katargēthēsontai, (καταργηθήσονται) 118
　katērgēka, (κατήργηκα) 121
kauchaomai, (καυχαομαι) kauchēsōmai, (καυχήσωμαι) 107
kithara, (κιθάρα) kithara, (κιθάρα) 154
kōluō, (κωλύω) kōluete, (κωλύετε) 231
kopiaō, (κοπιάω) kopiō, (κοπιῶ) 27
kubernēsis, (κυβέρνησις) kubernēseis, (κυβερνήσεις) 95
　kubernēsis, (κυβερνήσις) 95
　kubernētēs, (κυβερνήτης) 95
kumbalon, (κύμβαλον) kumbalon, (κύμβαλον) 104, 105

L

laleō, (λαλέω) lalōn, (λαλῶν) 132, 137
logizomai, (λογίζομαι) logizesthai, (λογίζεσθαι) 111
　logizetai, (λογίζεται) 111
logos, (λόγος) logos, (λόγος) 37, 38, 39, 40, 42

M

makrothumos, (μακρόθυμος) makrothumei, (μακροθυμεῖ) 109, 111, 113
mallon, (μᾶλλον) mallon, (μᾶλλον) 130, 139, 140
mē, (μὴ) mē, (μὴ) 231
megas, (μέγας) megas, (μέγας) 126
　meizōn, (μείζων) 98, 126
　meizona, (μείζονα) 98
megistos, (μεγίστος) megistos, (μεγίστος) 126

men, (μὲν)   men, (μὲν)   85, 96
menō, (μὲνω)   menei, (μένει)   124, 125
meros, (μέρος)   meros, (μέρος)   199
     merous, (μέρους)   119, 120
monos, (μόνος)   monous, (μόνους)   223
mustērion, (μυστήριον)   mustēria, (μυστήρια)   134

N
nēpiazō, (νηπιάζω)   nēpiazete, (νηπιάζετε)   176, 177
nous, (νοῦς)   noi, (νοί)   164
     nous, (νοῦς)   161
nuni, (νυνι)   nuni, (νυνι)   124, 125

O
oikodomeō, (οἰκοδομέω)   oikodomēn, (οἰκοδομην)   135, 198
     oikodomeō, (οἰκοδομέω)   135
oun, (οὖν)   oun, (οὖν)   183, 184, 191

P
paidion, (παιδίον)   paidia, (παιδία)   176, 177
pas, (πᾶς)   panta, (πάντα)   113
paraklēsis, (παράκλησις)   paraklēsin, (παράκλησιν)   136
paramuthia, (παραμυθία)   paramuthian, (παραμυθίαν)   136
paroxunō, (παροξύνω)   paroxunetai, (παροξύνεται)   111
pauomai, (παυόμαι)   pausontai, (παύσονται)   118
peri de, (περὶ δε)   peri de, (περὶ δε)   xiii, 2, 175
perpereuomai, (περπερεύομαι)   perpereuetai, (περπερεύεται)   110,
phanerōsis, (φανέρωσις)   phanerōsis, (φανέρωσις)   34, 35
phōnēs, (φωνῆς)   phōnēs, (φωνῆς)   156
     phōnōn, (φωνῶν)   156
phusioō, (φυσιόω)   phusioutai, (φυσιοῦται)   110
piptō, (πίπτω)   piptei, (πίπτει)   115, 116
pisteuō, (πιστεύω)   pisteuei, (πιστεύει)   113
pneuma, (πνεῦμα)   pneuma, (πνεῦμα)   161
     pneumati, (πνεύματι)   134, 164, 169
     pneumatōn, (πνευμάτων)   55, 56, 97, 156, 157, 228
pneumatikos, (πνευματικός)   pneumatika, (πνευματικά)   3, 22, 130, 132,
     pneumatikōn, (πνευματικῶν)   2, 3, 22, 132
     pneumatikos, (πνευματικός)   3, 103, 132
potizō, (ποτίζω)   epotisthēmen, (ἐποτίσθημεν)   70, 77, 79
     potizō, (ποτίζω)   77
proistēmi, (προΐστημι)   proistamenos, (προϊστάμενος)   94, 95
     proistēmi, (προΐστημι)   95

prophēteia, (προφητεία)	prophēteia, (προφητείᾳ)	150
	prophēteiai, (προφητεῖαι)	118
	prophēteian, (προφητείαν)	91
prophēteō, (προφητέω)	prophēteuomen, (προφητεύομεν)	119
	prophēteuōn, (προφητεύων)	137
prophētēs, (προφήτης)	prophētai, (προφήται)	91
	prophētais, (προφήταις)	91
	prophētas, (προφήτας)	91
	prophētēs, (προφήτης)	91, 92
	prophētōn, (προφήτων)	91
pros, (πρὸς)	pros, (πρὸς)	7
psallō, (ψάλλω)	psallō, (ψάλλω)	164, 195
	psalō, (ψαλῶ)	164, 196
psalmos, (ψαλμός)	psalmon, (ψαλμὸν)	195
	psalmos, (ψαλμός)	195
psōmizō, (ψωμίζω)	psōmisō, (ψωμίσω)	106

S

sophia, (σοφία)	sophias, (σοφίας)	37, 39
stegō, (στέγω)	stegei, (στέγει)	112, 113
	stegō, (στέγω)	112
sumpherō, (συμφέρω)	sumpheron, (συμφέρον)	34, 36
sunchairō, (συγχαίρω)	sunchairei, (συγχαίρει)	112
sunerchomai, (συνέρχομαι)	sunerchēsthe, (συνέρχησθε)	192
sunergos, (συνεργός)	sunergoi, (συνεργοί)	26
sunkerannumi, (συγκεράννυμι)	sunekerasen, (συνεκέρασεν)	89

T

teleios, (τέλειος)	teleioi, (τέλειοι)	176, 177
	teleion, (τέλειον)	120
teleioō, (τελειόω)	teleioō, (τελειόω)	120
tis, (τίς)	ti, (τί)	191
tithēmi, (τίθημι)	etheto, (ἔθετο)	85, 89
	tithēmi, (τίθημι)	85
topos, (τόπος)	topon, (τόπον)	169, 170
tote, (τότε)	tote, (τότε)	122

Z

zēloō, (ζηλόω)	zēloute, (ζηλοῦτε)	97, 130, 131
zēlos, (ζῆλος)	zēloi, (ζηλοῖ)	109
zēteō, (ζητέω)	zētei, (ζητεῖ)	110
	zēteō, (ζητέω)	110

14388023R00174

Printed in Great Britain
by Amazon.co.uk, Ltd.,
Marston Gate.